D0203557

JAZZ VISIONS

Popular Music History

Series Editor: Alyn Shipton, journalist, broadcaster and
former lecturer in music at Oxford Brookes University

This new series publishes books that challenge established orthodoxies in
popular music studies, examine the formation and dissolution of canons,
interrogate histories of genres, focus on previously neglected forms, or
engage in archaeologies of popular music.

Recently published:

Handful of Keys:
Conversations with Thirty Jazz Pianists
Alyn Shipton

The Last Miles:
The Music of Miles Davis, 1980–1991
George Cole

Chasin' the Bird
The Life and Legacy of Charlie Parker
Brian Priestley

Forthcoming in the series:

Lester Young:
His Life and Music
Dave Gelly

JAZZ VISIONS

REFLECTIONS ON LENNIE TRISTANO AND HIS LEGACY

PETER IND

LONDON

Published by

UK: Equinox Publishing Ltd
Unit 6, The Village,
101 Amies St.,
London, SW11 2JW

US: DBBC,
28 Main Street,
Oakville, CT 06779

www.equinoxpub.com

British Library Cataloguing-in-Publication Data
A catalogue record for this book is available from the British Library

Library of Congress Cataloging-in-Publication Data
Ind, Peter.
  Jazz visions : Lennie Tristano and his legacy / Peter Ind.
     p. cm. -- (Popular music history)
  Includes index.
  ISBN 1-84553-045-4 (hb)
  1. Tristano, Lennie--Criticism and interpretation. 2. Jazz--History
and criticism. I. Title. II. Series.
  ML417.T8I63 2005
  786.2'165'092--dc22

                          2005021560

ISBN 1 84553 045 4 (hardback)

Typeset by CA Typesetting, www.sheffieldtypesetting.com
Printed and bound in Great Britain by Antony Rowe, Chippenham, Wiltshire

contents

preface

I would like to make it clear from the beginning that this book is not intended as an objective account of a man's life but, rather, an attempt to portray Lennie Tristano as I knew him and as I heard his music. Now, half a century later, the world is a very different place. It must be extremely difficult for today's student of jazz music to identify the various stages of his musical creativity, so I have tried to illuminate not just his music in isolation, but in the context of life as it was in the fifties and sixties, paying particular attention to crucial political events that were taking place in the fifties, some of which have been ignored or apparently forgotten.

I find it ironic that in our present culture, recognition is seldom accorded for genuine effort and achievement; those most recognized are not always the most creative. I knew Lennie Tristano as a supreme example of a great creative musician, who never received the recognition he deserved. How can it be that, in such a sophisticated society as ours, with its ubiquitous media and instantaneous communications, such a person and his achievements remain known only to a few? Gradually I began to come to the conclusion that such sidelining of people of great merit is not restricted to the creative arts, but also obtains in other areas of achievement, especially in the realm of the sciences.

I hope that many people will enjoy this book, not only people who remember the New York jazz scene as it was in those days, but also those who are curious about Lennie Tristano and his place in the evolution of jazz since the late forties. Because different people may be interested in particular aspects, I have organized the book so that readers can dip into specific chapters for what they might seek. Those more interested in what was happening and what New York was like in the late forties through to the fifties will be more interested in Part I, Chapters 1–7. I have included in this section, in Chapter 6, a short summary of some of the lives of musicians associated with Lennie at the time. I have grouped together the more technical aspects of improvisation, in which musicians will be interested, in Part II. Chapters 8–10 focus on a discussion of jazz improvisation and Lennie's contribution in terms of playing, teaching and his understanding of the music. Part III focuses on a reconsideration first of all of Lennie's legacy (Chapters 11 and 12), the jazz scene as I see it (Chapter 13) and a final chapter (Chapter 14), which summarizes all the discussion. So, if you want a quick guide to the book, it is there.

This final chapter deals with the legacy of Lennie and lays to rest some of the misunderstandings that have arisen, particularly regarding Lennie's influence and work. It has been great to pull together all of these memories, to go back and talk to various people and look through old articles etc. We have had a really good time putting this book together and I want to thank Sue Jones for all her support and encouragement, especially her editing skills, which substantially helped to shape this book.

I would also like to thank Charles Alexander of *Jazzwise*, who commissioned bassist and author Alyn Shipton to interview me on behalf of *Jazzwise*. This led to Alyn's interest in the book and his introducing me to Janet Joyce of Equinox. Thanks also to Ira Gitler who reminded me of details of several events all those years ago and who has always been an encouragement. To Marian McPartland, who knew Lennie when he first arrived in New York and for her encouragement also. To Peter Rubie, a long-time friend who has been of great help as my agent. To guitarist Billy Bauer, who knew Lennie longer than most of us, and to whom I am very grateful for his reminiscences; to Lennie's daughter Carol and her partner Lennie Popkin, who helped fill me in about Lennie's later years. To John Chilton, for his encouragement and his correction about the myth of Bessie Smith's tragic death. Also to saxophonist Peter Cook for his enthusiasm and encouragement for this project. To all our friends in Barbados, Susan Bain, Adrian Clarke and pianist Ebby who were so supportive during the years I was trying to bring the book to fruition. To Rufus and Doris Reid also, for their friendship and support and especially Rufus's reflections on the jazz scene. To our friends in Auvers-sur-Oise, Sylvie, Tierry and family for their introducing me to the world of jazz in France, and to bassist Herve Czak who arranged concerts in Auvers and in Paris; to the Maire of Pierrelaye, who is so supportive of jazz and ensures the continuance of live concerts there that are enjoyed by both young and old. Lastly especial thanks to Chris Parker for his scholarly comments; which have added that extra touch of professionalism to the book. I hope you enjoy it, but most of all I hope it makes you want to know more about jazz.

Peter Ind
May 2005

Part I

Lennie: The Man and His Music

1 my early contact with jazz – the sounds of lennie tristano and of charlie parker (bird)

Lennie Tristano is one of those jazz musicians people either admire greatly, as one of the seminal influences in jazz, or have never heard of! How crazy is that?

When I was running the Bass Clef jazz club in London in the eighties and nineties, I can guarantee that at least 50 percent of the punters looked blank when I mentioned Lennie's name. They would say they had never heard of him, as though I was somehow making it up that this man was important. When you write, therefore, about someone like that, it is tempting to be apologetic. I was when I first started writing this book. Why should this be? His recordings are available. His reputation is established among jazz musicians. His influence is recognized by those who write about jazz history. But because his name is not up there in commercial lights, few people accept that he is anyone of importance.

Yet Lennie Tristano had a tremendous influence on a wide range of jazz musicians and on the shape and direction of jazz during that vibrant period of creativity in the late forties and early fifties. He certainly had an influence on my playing and how I viewed jazz.

Over the years I have often been asked, "What was Lennie like?" and I began writing this book as a response. Initially my concern was to talk about the Lennie I knew in those years, to provide a very personal account, mainly because the man (and musician) I knew was so different from the impression conveyed by many of the articles I read. And I can talk in detail about him, what he said, how he played and how he influenced others. But the more I thought about him and looked back at recordings and videos, the more it seemed to me that people need to listen to his music to understand Lennie. No matter how much I write, people cannot experience what he was like through my writing. But they can still listen to him (and I have suggested a selection of his recordings that people could start with, at the end of the book). And maybe this is the problem: Lennie was always a musician, always concerned to explore the potential of music and stretch its boundaries. To really understand Lennie you have to put in some hard work: understand the craft of jazz improvisation. Few people are interested in that; they are more interested in the quick fix, the easy pen portrait, the funny anecdotes and the intimate personal details. There is so much more to Lennie, and I hope this account will interest people enough to go and listen to his various recordings and make a decision for themselves, not be swayed by those setters of fashion who superficially decide what is "in" or what is "out."

Lennie was a remarkable man and I consider myself lucky to have known and played with him in New York in the forties and fifties. Looking back, there was nothing in my own background to suggest that I would go in the direction of jazz or make that decisive move to New York. In fact, for me personally, the early years of jazz remain a mystery. Dimly, as a child, I remember hearing Lester Young and Billie Holiday, but I realized this only many years later, when I listened to those recordings of the thirties and knew that I had heard them before. As a child there was little music to listen to apart from what was played on the radio. During time away from school, fighting asthma attacks, I would listen to classical music on the radio, but there was little jazz. At eight years of age I started learning the violin, and later joined the school orchestra. The violin always felt somewhat alien to me. It had belonged to my mother and though I treasured it (I still have it), I somehow sensed that I would move on to other instruments. Occasionally I went to concerts given by the RAF brass band, which was stationed locally. I found that music depressing, but could not describe why. But I locked into the dance music of the day, such as "I'm Beginning to See the Light," learning to play it on the piano, and by the middle of World War II found work in the dance halls. I suppose in some peculiar way this paralleled the way jazz musicians had learned their craft in the early days of jazz. Here at last was music played with rhythm. I had been kidded about my response to this rhythm as a child, as if it was my little joke and one day I would grow out of it, but this could not stop my enjoyment.

I had been moved by what I heard, but could not always make sense of it. When the Allied forces went into Germany (in late 1944/early 1945), in England we tuned the radio to AFN, the American Forces Network. Broadcast from Munich, in what was then occupied Germany, it brought us sounds we had never heard before: dance bands led by the likes of Glenn Miller, Woody Herman, Artie Shaw and Charlie Barnet. I also vividly remember recordings of Lester Young. With my head virtually inside the loudspeakers, trying to soak up these revolutionary sounds and make sense out of them, the music became addictive even before I knew the meaning of the word. It was a time of incredible austerity in Britain, of so-called light entertainment and simple comedies, of respectability and rationing. This was a country coming to terms with its loss of worldwide power and influence, but which had not yet come to terms with the social changes that would affect it, partly resulting from the expectation that there would be more equality of opportunities: "a home fit for heroes" as the politicians promised. Looking back to those early post-war years, you can recognize the start of social shifts: the emergence of the *nouveaux riches*, the muted haughtiness of the former landed gentry and the beginning of a change, as a consequence of which Britain would become more of a critical observer of world events and less of a powerful actor.

By then in my late teens, I only dimly sensed these changes. My ambition was to discover the new music and somehow become a participator. As with many musicians, my early musical interests had been mixed. My family had acquired an extremely old piano, a straight strung wooden-framed upright with a fretted front, candlesticks, and mottled brown ivories. I used to experiment as a child and began to find simple harmonies, which I memorized by the patterns and marks on the faded keys. My parents, who were both amateur musicians, had planned that my sister, Marjorie, should learn the piano and I the violin. As it turned out, she never really became committed to this and after taking a piano lesson from my father, Marjorie would soon leave the piano stool, and I would promptly sit down and learn to play the pieces she had been given. The piano fascinated me more than the violin. The enjoyment of learning to harmonize and also learning the popular tunes of the day kept me at the keyboard for hours at a time. Gradually, I became competent enough to begin to play at dances. So it was as a piano player that I started my career. My musical abilities developed in a very haphazard manner. I wanted to be able to create exciting sounds, without really understanding what I was listening to. It reminds me of the way many present-day fans relate to the music. They are attracted to it, often without any inkling of its underlying structure and of how musicians conceptualize the way they create their music.

But despite the technical facility I had gained, there was no guidance available for the musical path I wanted to follow. At the tender age of fourteen I played my first gigs. These were in the vicinity of my hometown (Uxbridge) in west London. I had not yet learned about jazz, but formed a dance band with friends, others at my school who seemed to have a flair for music. There was the violinist John Hare, a very talented musician who subsequently turned to engineering as his profession, but was still playing in classical orchestras when I met him again at a gig in 2002 (sadly he died just a year later). Another member of the band, Colin Lewry, also went into another profession, in his case computing, but he has always played piano and I heard him sitting in recently at Kettners, a jazz restaurant in London's Soho.

To me it seemed natural to form a band in those days; people far more readily made their own music then because there was not much else available. In the twenties, my father had set up his own radio station (imagine that nowadays). Having built his own transmitter, he broadcast his violinist brother's local orchestra regularly on a Tuesday evening in the Gerrard's Cross area where he lived. This was in the days before licencing was required and before the BBC established itself; the London radio station then was 2LO, broadcast from a small cinema in the Strand and transmitted from a former furniture warehouse.

What I enjoyed playing most at local dances were the hit songs of those days, music that had a swing to it, tunes such as "Chattanooga Choo Choo," "I Don't Want to Set the World on Fire," "Whispering Grass," and "In the Mood." There were also the songs of the twenties and thirties: "Margie", "My Blue Heaven," "Somebody Stole My Gal." The harmonic structures of many of these were later taken by jazz musicians and used as vehicles for jazz improvisation, but in our dance hall bands we played them as regular dance music. In the rather straitlaced, middle-class environment of the time, however, our efforts were looked on askance, as if they were racy or somehow uncultured. Nevertheless, the gigs kept coming in.

Playing at local dances became the chief source of income for me. These were war years and I played the piano regularly from 1942 to 1945, when I was in my mid-teens. As the majority of professional musicians were serving in the armed forces, only those too old or too young for military service were available to form bands and play at these dances. They were wild times. Even though the music lacked sophistication, our enthusiasm overcame our musical and technical shortcomings (or so we believed). As the preparation for D-Day (June 6, 1944) drew near there were many American and Canadian servicemen around, and dances were held every night of the week.

By the time I was sixteen I was earning more money than my father was. This somewhat upset the family equilibrium. Paradoxically, the asthma that had plagued me during my childhood now seemed in recession, despite my working days and nights; during these times I had managed to hold down some kind of day-job employment as well. I had numerous day jobs in these later war years, and for a while I worked on a farm, following the doctor's recommendation that I take outdoor employment. I also worked for a while in the building trade, then as a trainee clerk in a London law office, all the time playing gigs at night. That was the life of a musician in London at the time – there was plenty of work.

But there were times when I was not doing a day job. This upset my father, who wanted me to get a "proper job." He was continually urging me to find a career. "Musicians always argue," he would say. "Why don't you study building or architecture?" (Building was his own chosen profession.) And indeed for a while I took a part-time evening course in building construction in what was then the Regent Street Polytechnic in central London (this was to stand me in good stead later in life). But the evening courses conflicted with playing music, so music won out!

Even though I played piano at dances at this time, I loved the sound of the bass, especially the pizzicato sound (when the instrument is plucked). I also felt that I lacked sufficient technique on the piano. So I learned to play the bass gradually and by osmosis from others. Not knowing how to develop further, I enrolled at the Trinity College of Music in London as a part-time student in 1944/5 and in 1945/6, studying classical harmony and piano. This was helpful, but did not entirely fulfill my musical needs. I was attending just twice a week, paying for the lessons myself – which were expensive – and I had contact only with the person who taught me: Douglas Mews, who later became a Dean of the Faculty. He was teaching me classical harmony, but like virtually all teaching in those days, it did not give me what I was looking for in what I later came to understand was jazz harmony. When I played some of the chordal harmonies that I had picked up he was fascinated, but seemed unable to relate what I was doing to what he was teaching me. I liked him as a teacher, but was somewhat in awe of him, and eventually I quit studying, partly because I felt I was not a good enough student and partly because I could not afford the fees. When I quit, it became clear that he was very disappointed that I had left and obviously he had had a regard for my playing that I had not acknowledged. But I was already headed in a different direction, and shortly afterwards I met someone who became a significant influence on my early musical career.

This was bassist Tim Bell. In 1947, when I started work on the Mecca circuit with Freddie Barratt's band, my first fully professional employment as a musician, I met Tim, then one of the most in-demand players in the dance music field. His sister at that time worked as accountant/cashier at a Mecca venue (Streatham Locarno, as it was then) and it was she who introduced me to her brother. I immediately began studying with him. Tim came from a musical family: his father had played bass before he retired and Tim's brother, Billy Bell, was well-known on guitar and banjo. (Tim eventually emigrated to South Africa and recently passed away.) He was most helpful as a teacher and introduced me to what was then a revolutionary method of bass fingering, in which all four fingers of the left hand are used – playing semitone intervals. In turn, Tim had learned this from his studies with James Merrett senior, who had originally been a 'cellist. Old Jim (as he was known) had reasoned that, as with all stringed instruments, the space between the notes gets shorter as you go higher up the fingerboard. Thus you could easily adapt 'cello fingering to the bass in the higher intervals. The traditional method of fingering that used the third finger only as a kind of support for the little finger, could be dispensed with in the upper positions. Though a small revolution in playing technique, it was a significant one. After studying with Tim for a while, I was advised by him to continue my studies with Old Jim. He was *the* bass teacher in London and the doyen of classical bass playing. Both men helped me immensely and what I learned from them stood me in good stead – especially when I later emigrated to New York. I gained quite a lot of admiration (and music work) on account of this added facility. Incidentally, James Merrett's son (also called James) taught this to a later generation of musicians (among them Dave Holland), and this (then unique) method of fingering (using all four fingers of the left hand – as semitone intervals) has now become more or less standard among many players.

By the time I was nineteen, I could play the double bass reasonably well. I practiced like mad at least four hours daily, while at the same time working six nights and five days a week. Only the young have that kind of energy. By 1947 I had become a full-time professional musician. I had also become hooked on the music coming from the USA.

It's difficult to imagine or describe that world of the mid- to late 1940s into which jazz penetrated. This was decades before rock or pop music. Jazz, in the twenties and thirties, was dixieland or swing, and most of what we had been exposed to was polite versions of American music re-created by English society bands. During my employment at the Palais de Danse, I first heard the music of Charlie Parker. This was a 78 r.p.m. disk brought over from the USA by an enterprising musician, who was then working on one of the transatlantic liners. (Even several years after World War II, very little American jazz was available in British music shops.)

The two sides were "Billie's Bounce" and "Now's the Time." What now sounds so clear and logically creative sounded strange then, but enticing. Even more intriguing were the early trio records of Lennie Tristano, made about the same time (1947). What sounded to our ears like strange weird harmonies emanating from this piano, bass and guitar trio also had the enticement of sounding improvised, so unlike the classical music that I had been taught was the "only real valid" music. Jazz and swing music was considered decadent. Relatively untutored, I had accepted this dictum without question. I had regarded my own enthusiasm for jazz and swing merely as youthful waywardness. At that time I lacked the technical ability of the professional orchestral player and this, combined with opinions that jazz was merely decadence, instilled a lack of confidence in my own skills that took many years to overcome.

Both Tim Bell and Jim Merrett had helped to increase my confidence as well as helping me to improve my bass playing. But what they were teaching me began and ended with how to play the bass. Nevertheless, although Tim was a dance band player and did not consider himself a jazz bass player, he was a very open person. He enjoyed listening to the few jazz recordings that were finding their way to the UK in those days. It was through Tim that I first heard Charles Mingus on a recording he made with Lionel Hampton's orchestra (in 1947) entitled "Mingus Fingers." For me that was the first time that I had heard the bass featured as a solo instrument. Not long after that I heard Ray Brown, playing with Dizzy Gillespie's orchestra, featured in a tune called "One Bass Hit." Looking back, those two records were a milestone for me as an aspiring jazz bass player, but there was no one in the UK who could help my development in this direction.

When, in the summer of 1949, I eventually visited New York as a ship's musician and met Lennie Tristano, I found someone who had a grasp on the music and who could also teach it. Here was someone who took jazz seriously, not in a stuffy way, but very practically. So, at twenty-one years of age, I arrived in New York for the first time. It was a turning point for me, and it renewed all my excitement in being a professional musician. By then the dark memories of World War II were giving way to the discovery of the new music. Jazz – the new jazz – which tempted yet puzzled the ear and focused my attention on America.

This was the time when those incredible sextet records of Lennie Tristano, Lee Konitz, Warne Marsh, Billy Bauer, Arnold Fishkin and Harold Granowski were first released on 78 r.p.m. recordings. To me these were the epitome of the new jazz, which had entered a new territory of great musicianship and creative talent. Even then, however, I had no inkling of what times were to follow, studying, playing and recording with such musicians and forging the links that persist to this day with two survivors of that original group, Lee Konitz and guitarist Billy Bauer.

2 my early experiences of new york jazz

Despite my education-induced inhibitions, the appeal of the new jazz led me inevitably to the New World, and to the city of New York which, more than any other city, provided the milieu for that explosive musical creativity that came to be known as bebop. A chance opportunity changed the entire direction of my life, when I auditioned with another musician friend, Frank Abbot, for a contract on the *Queen Mary*. As fortune would have it, he secured the contract on the liner. When, in turn, he offered me a job with his band, I accepted, without dreaming what a change this would bring about in my own life.

In this day and age it is not easy to convey the impressions of New York as it was then. The five and a half days on board the *Queen Mary* were exciting enough for us young musicians, who had never before left the austerity of post-war England. Even traveling cabin class, we were plunged into a world of luxury we had never before experienced. We ate in the cabin class restaurant with the full meal service given to the passengers. There were three classes – first, cabin and tourist – not unlike air travel today. The cabin class service was similar to business class: waiter service with such luxuries as fillet steak, three-course meals and a change of menu each day. In England, we had left behind food rationing that in many ways was worse than it had been even during the war years. Meat, butter and sugar could be bought only with ration cards and were severely restricted; the ration for butter was just two ounces per week. Sweets were severely rationed and I remember that on this first trip, one musician – the alto saxophonist Bruce Turner – took full advantage and bought a two-pound pack of Cadbury's chocolate bars (unseen during the war). Within two days it was all gone!

My twenty-first birthday occurred during this first voyage and arriving in New York that misty morning in late July, gliding up the East River at 5 a.m., we were all on deck to catch our first glimpse of Manhattan, despite having had less than four hours' sleep. After the ship docked at Pier 90 at the foot of W 50th Street, it seemed an eternity before we received clearance to go ashore. We finally walked down the gangplank about noon into the heat of a New York summer, 100 degrees Fahrenheit in the shade. Though the area around the dock was somewhat seedy, it was amazing to us to see the lines of parked automobiles, mostly covered with thick city dust (there were then few cars in England). In those days huge solid-tire trucks plied to and fro, loading and unloading from the docks. Virtually the entire West Side waterfront from 14th Street to the upper Fifties was dockland (a scene very well depicted in Elia Kazan's 1954 film *On the Waterfront*, starring Marlon Brando). The Cunard ships, the French and US lines, all docked around this area and there was a constant flurry of activity, much like it is now at international airports.

We spent our first day seeing the sights of Manhattan and cooling off in the huge stores such as Macy's and Gimbels, which had the luxury and novelty (to us) of air conditioning. Then came the visit to the Empire State Building on 34th Street, at that time the tallest tower in New York. Emerging on the eighty-sixth-floor outdoor balcony, the view was awe-inspiring and the muted hum of the traffic far below just added to the grandeur of it all.

Returning to the ship for evening dinner, we excitedly discussed our adventures in this wonderful city, before disembarking again, this time to hear the jazz music that we had only dimly heard on scratchy 78 r.p.m. records. So overwhelmed was I by the sights and sounds of the day that I no longer remember which musicians and which bands I heard on that first trip; those experiences are mingled with visits to the clubs of 52nd Street in succeeding trips. I do seem to recall hearing John Kirby's band – perhaps playing in the first of the clubs we visited on that famous street. I also vividly remember the club called the Three Deuces, where I heard Charlie Parker, Max Roach, Bud Powell, Nelson Boyd and Fats Navarro. This was on one of our early visits – Fats died the following year. I saw and heard him twice. The second time I heard him play he had lost so much weight that his nickname was, sadly, no longer appropriate. He was one of the truly great bebop musicians and one of the music's legendary improvisers, but he made very few recordings and so it's hard to realize the impact he had at the time. It was also on one of those early trips that I first heard Erroll Garner, playing solo at the Three Deuces.

Our stay in New York was so brief – a maximum of two and a half days – that we wanted to cram so much into the time; we hardly slept. The clubs would close at three in the morning. A cab back to the ship, a breakfast at 3.30 a.m., then up at eight or nine to explore New York, go shopping (one way to make a little cash was to take back small luxuries to war-damaged, ration-restricted Britain), and again to the clubs in the evening. Those clubs were the center of jazz in New York and a revelation for jazz lovers. The famous 52nd Street was in its heyday. From Sixth Avenue toward the East Side (before the area had given way to skyscrapers), both sides of the street still retained New York's traditional brownstone houses, like many of New York's uptown residential areas. At one time these had been affluent dwelling places, but by the forties most had been converted for commercial use, many of them becoming jazz clubs.

The strength of New York jazz was something I had hardly realized from listening to records alone. The experience of hearing the music it live was almost overwhelming. As visiting musicians, what we heard on those nights in 52nd Street had such a profound effect that several of us decided, within a year or so, to emigrate to New York. Pianists Ronnie Ball, Dill Jones and Lennie Metcalfe, and altoist Dougie Fordyce (whom I subsequently lost track of) were among those who went to live and work there. Prior to our visiting New York, pianist George Shearing had already made the move from the UK and was playing with his trio on 52nd Street. Others, including guitarist Dave Goldberg, also went to the USA. Later on, vibist Victor Feldman and pianists Eddie Thompson and Joe Shulman (formerly known as Joe Saye) also made the move, irresistibly drawn by the music and the New York life. In addition to those who went to reside in the USA there were a number of other British musicians, some of them subsequently well known, especially on the British jazz scene – Ronnie Scott, Benny Green, Johnny Dankworth – who all worked on the transatlantic liners so that they could hear American jazz live.

The London club Ronnie Scott's was opened by Ronnie and his partner Pete King, inspired by Ronnie's visit to New York's original Birdland. Other British musicians who took advantage of those transatlantic crossings specifically in order to study with American players included alto player/clarinettist Bruce Turner, who studied with Lee Konitz; bassist Pete Blannin, who studied with Arnold Fishkin (at that time Lennie Tristano's bass player); and tenor saxophonist Gray Allard, who studied with Warne Marsh. (Gray later said that he had a seven-hour lesson with Warne that took him twenty years to assimilate.)

The year 1949, when I took my first trip, marked *the* peak year for jazz in New York, and 52nd Street, the greatest ever street of jazz clubs, was at its best. In those days there were far fewer jazz musicians, and with all those clubs open on 52nd Street there was a considerable amount of work in New York. Clubs would open at about 9 p.m. We would often walk there (and take a cab back at three in the morning). The feeling was of a special place – you weren't there by accident; it had a sense of purpose. It was busy. It was lively. It was buzzing. But then, in New York at that time, everything was buzzing with all kinds of activity, especially in the mid-town area. Despite this, it was not loud and although there were bright neon lights flashing everywhere, there was little rowdiness on the streets and little noise spilling out onto the sidewalk. It was not like now, with music blasting out onto the streets in club areas. For one thing, sound equipment in those days was far less powerful than it is today. And New York was safe for tourists. The term "mugging" had not even been invented, although, on the waterfront, victims of gangland battles were frequently recovered from the murky waters of the North River.

On 52nd Street itself, the clubs were located in semi-basements. From street level you would walk down half a dozen steps into the club itself. The bandstand would be at the far end. There would be a bar at one side and the rest of the room would be given over to tables and seating, for which there was some kind of cover charge or minimum fee. Drinks were kind of expensive – especially for us – during that time the exchange rate between sterling and US dollars changed, to the detriment of sterling. We seldom had enough money for more than one drink. When we took the first contract for the job on the ship, the pay had been US$40 a week (there were US$4 to £1 at the time). During 1949, the pound was devalued to US$2.8. So, at a stroke, our pay was effectively reduced to US$28!

But the club owners were very understanding, knowing that we had come from overseas especially to listen to the music. They would allow us to just stand at the bar and nurse our drinks, and we stayed as long as possible to listen to the music. We could go and hear Charlie Parker's group at the Three Deuces, Coleman Hawkins at the Famous Door, and then Lennie Tristano's sextet playing at the Orchid Room. Finally seeing and hearing these great creative jazz musicians live, instead of trying to appreciate them in spite of the limitations of 78 r.p.m. record players, was incredible, but to go and see them all in one night was overwhelming.

At the time we had no idea that all these former brownstone houses, converted into clubland, would soon disappear, to be replaced by the tall steel towers that today constitute mid-town Manhattan. Only the reminder "Swing Street" on today's street signs (which I noticed the last time I was there in 2000), indicates that over half a century earlier some of the most revolutionary jazz was being created there. Alas, within a couple of years all this had disappeared to make way for "growing New York." But none of this was apparent during that hot New York summer of 1949.

By then bebop, the musical revolution spearheaded by Charlie Parker and Dizzy Gillespie, had become familiar to our ears. Bebop (or rebop as it was briefly known) was a logical development from swing. However, its innovative approach extended harmonic concepts beyond the usual seventh chords; often the melody line would move beyond sevenths into ninths, elevenths and thirteenths. For example, a C7 chord (C, E, G, and B) would be extended to D, F sharp, A, and C. So while the rhythm section would be playing a C7 the soloist might be extemporizing on a D7. It was musically logical, but to unaccustomed ears gave the impression of playing in two keys at once. In some ways it was a gradual transition. For example, Charlie Barnet's band, playing an arrangement of "Skyliner," included a passage where each horn played a different note of a thirteenth chord – holding each note so that at the end of the phrase the entire chord sounded altogether. Though numerous individual examples like this could be given – suggesting that this was nothing new, that it had all been done before – the important point was that there was an overall change of emphasis in the music.

When Ray Noble composed "Cherokee," the melody of the middle section (the bridge) began with the ninth note of the chord. The ear was left only briefly in suspense, as the melody descended into familiar territory again. The bebop approach to jazz tended to leave you hanging, wondering did the improviser really mean that? There was a kind of outrageousness about bebop. Thelonious Monk, one of the initiators of the new music, would often play stridently in such an outrageous fashion. This was also reflected in his tune titles, which had a dadaist or surrealist outlook ("I Mean You," "Well You Needn't"). Possibly the main reason why jazz has so few enlightened followers is that the improviser is creating a line upon a concept of the original melody, while the melody may not itself be stated. Musicians are expected to be familiar enough with the idiom to be able to mentally hear the unstated melody and/or the harmonic structure. It takes great skill and deep understanding of the music.

Prior to bebop and even swing, jazz accented the first and third beat of a four-four bar, but bebop reversed that by putting the accent more often on two and four, with the additional freedom to play accents in previously unexpected places. But what seemed even more exciting and entirely new were the sounds created by the Lennie Tristano sextet. The group consisted of Lennie on piano, Lee Konitz on alto saxophone, Warne Marsh on tenor, Billy Bauer on guitar, Arnold Fishkin on bass and Jeff Morton on drums. Their entire approach to the music was totally different from anything I had previously heard. First there were these incredible lines (these were alternative melodies, usually more complex and more appropriate for the new idiom) which replaced the original standard melodies generally used by jazz musicians. Led by the two saxophones, they played with the technique and finesse of classical quality, but with the feel of improvisation. The excitement of the lines led into equally exciting improvisation, eighth-note ideas, giving way to eighth-note triplets, which in turn gave way to sixteenth-note ideas. Instead of relying on my description, it is best to listen to those 1949 recordings. They sound as fresh and revolutionary as ever. The rhythm section played with a smooth, even pulse, thus allowing the soloists greater freedom than was possible even with bebop rhythm sections.

Jazz has always been in a constant state of development since the very first recordings early in the twentieth century, but there have been certain creative peaks. The development of bebop through Bird, Dizzy, Thelonious, Bud Powell and Lennie's equally extraordinary approach to improvising – all within the space of a few years – is one of them. It was a remarkable surge of creativity that developed in New York from the mid-forties through to the early fifties.

This was the time of the Cold War, with all the uncertainty and anxiety that it engendered. During 1951, when I went to live in New York, the air-raid sirens were sounded every day at noon, to remind people of the apparent danger of the Soviet threat. The popular idea that jazz musicians lived a life entirely separate from the stress and political realities of everyday life is a myth. Though we seldom participated in everyday political reality, whether national or international, we were all very much aware of it but felt helpless to do anything about it. One only needs to listen to comedian Lennie Bruce's recordings from the late fifties to realize that jazz musicians were very aware of the world within which they lived. Somehow the bebop movement reflected this: it was frenetic compared to the gentler excitement of swing. There was a kind of unspoken (or rarely spoken) feeling about those times. The more articulate musicians, such as Lennie or Bird for example, were very concerned. When Eisenhower was elected President of the USA, I remember Lennie expressing concern that now a military general was at the helm, America from that time onward would be committed to being a military state. Was this view wrong in any way? Few ordinary Americans were as perceptive at that time.

But the musical creativity of that era gave us all some kind of strength against the materialism and militarism that was the post-war America. We realized that we were doing something special, that something was happening in the world of jazz, though the outside world was unaware and uncaring. The sense of foreboding, from living in a world in which we might all be annihilated without warning, was very real and very present in those times. (Not that the threat has disappeared, but we have become deadened to it today – though it is subliminally there in everyone's psyche.) In retrospect this presents a depressing picture, of a belief in something special, later totally sidelined by politics and by commercialism.

Of course we were all concerned with financial survival, and even in the late forties and fifties earning a good living as a jazz musician was not easy, despite that fact that there were gigs to be had. But, being young and without family responsibilities, life as a jazz musician was extremely exciting for me. What we may have lacked in affluence was compensated for by our enthusiasm for the music. My own search centered on how to develop further as a jazz bassist. I could not have made a better choice than studying with Lennie. Word had gotten around that Lennie "taught jazz." Before long, there were a group of us young Britons studying either with Lennie or other members of his group.

On our second voyage, early in August, there had been a change of personnel among the musicians and a new band had been hired to play for the entertainment in first class. One of these new musicians was the British piano player Ronnie Ball. We had played gigs together in London and Ronnie (who was a few months older than I) was one of the younger generation of British musicians who wholeheartedly embraced the new bebop discipline. During that second trip Ronnie and I went to hear Lennie Tristano's sextet at the Orchid Room.

In the intermission Ronnie, being a piano player, introduced himself to Lennie and asked if he gave lessons. Lennie already had a student group, of which Lee Konitz and Warne Marsh became the most noted. I also talked to Lennie, and both Ronnie and I arranged to study with him at his house in Flushing, Long Island, as did pianist Bill Le Sage, who played in the cabin class band, and with whom I shared a cabin. Initially I felt some hesitation about studying with Lennie. Since he was a piano player and blind, I wondered whether he would really be able to help me, a bass player (an instrument that Lennie did not play).

My excitement in playing in a jazz group was often tempered by hesitation when playing standards with which I was only partially familiar. In much jazz of that time the double bass – the bull fiddle, as Americans often referred to it – was just a rhythmic thump, often masked by the louder thump of the bass drum. Other jazz musicians seldom listened to the bass; they were more intent on their own contribution to the music. By this time (the late forties) the walking bass line had taken over as the fashion in bass playing. Preceding that, bass players were expected to play two notes to a bar or, if four to a bar were required, each note was repeated once. In that era – the swing era – a bass player was expected to play the root notes of the chord, similar to the figured bass of classical and baroque music. The new freedom in bass playing – that developed with bebop and the walking bass line – was a more scalic approach. This gave more punch to the music and allowed the soloist more freedom; the soloist was thus able to develop beyond the confines of simple harmony. All went well provided, first, that the bass player was competent and familiar enough with the piece being played and second, that if not so competent, his ramblings were mainly overshadowed by a heavy bass drum. That situation allowed many would-be bass players to become involved in the music without undue criticism being directed at them.

There is a tale about one such bass player who had been employed for years in a well-known British band. One day, however, the drummer's bass drum pedal broke and, for the first time, the inadequacies of the bass player's choice of notes became woefully apparent. The bandleader, questioning the bass player, discovered, to his horror, that he had just been thumping away regardless of any musical consideration (obviously looking the part). So, despite the years of acceptance, he was then summarily dismissed!

As I had studied piano and violin, I was competent as far as playing within the harmonic structure was concerned, but in trying to blend my knowledge as it existed at that time with the newer concept of a bass line on a scalic pattern, I would sometimes tie myself into knots, sailing away merrily until suddenly I would land on a note painfully at odds with the flow of harmony. Whether or not others noticed this was of secondary importance to me. For me it was like traveling at sixty miles an hour and then, without warning, hitting a brick wall. The basic reaction to such situations was one of playing safe – which after a while became boring. I longed for that freedom of expression in bass playing that I had heard, for example, in Ray Brown.

At that time I was focused on the belief that being a musician merely meant becoming a better player technically. At first I did not find what I was looking for in taking lessons with Lennie. It then became apparent that I was trying to run before I could walk. It soon also became apparent, when studying with Lennie, that technique was only one aspect among the many that one needed to develop to become a good jazz musician.

On our first meeting, Lennie asked me to play something. I felt somewhat exposed – in those days the double bass was regarded as an accompanying, not a solo, instrument. I remember playing something that showed off my classical technique. This did not seem to impress Lennie unduly. Though in many ways (even in those days) I did have a better technique than many American jazz bass players did, I felt I lacked the ability to play a good melodic line with a swinging beat. I soon found, in the lessons with Lennie, that developing this was no easy matter. In fact it meant examining the very fundamentals of music. I remember Lennie asking me to play a scale. It soon became clear to me that playing scales was not a mere technical exercise, but real music making. Prior to this, I had regarded scales as an elemental task in becoming familiar with the instrument. Played as music – this shed an entirely new light on the subject. Lennie then had me playing scales, rhythmically, with a jazz feel and pulse. When I had mastered this new approach, in later lessons Lennie had me playing scales in all keys, and was not satisfied until I could play them, even in previously unfamiliar keys, with equal ease. (For those who are interested, Chapter 10 goes into more technical details of Lennie's teaching.)

The only way in which I can convey the importance of what Lennie was doing is to set it against the awareness of jazz music in those days. Many things that are now accepted in understanding jazz were not yet realized in those days.

I found studying with Lennie in the early days somewhat disconcerting. When he asked me to play something, I responded by showing my technique: how I could do things on the bass that were unusual, at least in those days. Jazz bass players at that time were not expected to have the technique of symphonic players, and when asked to play something my reaction was to demonstrate how fluent I was. As I later realized while studying with Lennie, such an approach completely missed the point. Lennie was trying to show me how to make deeper contact with the music, not merely demonstrating skill, like the ability to show how fast or fluently notes could be played. He always emphasized the need to make contact with the music. Just to play one note with real profundity is something of which a beginner is seldom aware.

Most of the tuition I had received prior to studying with Lennie concentrated on technique. This was especially so with the bass. Being such a cumbersome instrument, classical music training concentrated on the student developing the technique to master those passages in well-known symphonic works that demanded extra practice and study. Thus the allegro passage in Beethoven's Fifth Symphony or the complexities in Richard Strauss's *Til Eulenspiegel* were central to classical training for the double bass. Indeed such parallels in classical tuition apply to other instruments, and are central to classical training to this day. Such abilities impressed Lennie little. To add to the picture, the classical music profession regarded jazz in those days as a bastard form of music – tolerated only (if at all) as some kind of childish amusement. But Lennie, with great strength of character, taught his students with as much conviction as if he had been president of some revered academic institution. Though he did not have a school in the formal sense, in a unique way he *was* the president.

There was, however, one aspect of his teaching that I found somewhat intimidating. In the early days, before he established his Manhattan loft studio, he taught from his home in Flushing, Long Island. This meant that students awaiting a lesson could easily overhear what transpired between teacher and preceding student. Despite being a musician confident about playing in front of an audience, I was still somewhat shy, and in this situation I found it difficult to be frank about any problems I was experiencing with my playing. Additionally, in the early days, I found it difficult to accept the fact that the apparent simplicity of Lennie's tuition could produce the results I so clearly longed for. For example, that mastering scales and learning to play intervals diatonically on the scales themselves could lead to an instinctive understanding of harmonic flow seemed, on the face of it, unlikely. In fact it was only the strength of Lennie's insistence that carried me through this period of doubt or disbelief. Lennie at that time had many students and, interestingly, while I was editing this chapter, I came across a comment by Leonard Feather that reinforced my own assessment of Lennie's teaching at that time.

> In New York I recorded Lennie Tristano and Art Tatum. I had begun studying with Tristano, traipsing out once a week to his Long Island home, where he tested my ear on recognizing chords, and showed me how to voice harmonic concepts of my own. He was an invaluable teacher. On our date he made only two tunes, but since he recorded so little for the major labels they were valuable documents of a heterodox talent. (Feather 1986: 109)

By some fateful irony it was Lennie's teaching that eventually led to his becoming less popular. This sounds incredible today, now that jazz courses are well established in many countries, often being included in the curricula of colleges and universities. In those days, the view was that the ability to play jazz was a gift. You either had it or you didn't. Claiming that it could be taught was considered presumptuous. Actually, Lennie never "taught jazz." He would not "train" people in the conventional sense. He would not change their playing. He just helped them to be better musicians, but in their own way. What was remarkable about his teaching was his grasp of what was needed to gain confidence to venture into the world of jazz improvisation. And to reach that goal one needed thoroughness. Most musicians were fluent in the "easy keys" but began to be very hesitant in the less familiar ones. This often led to students quitting study with Lennie, because they could not admit to themselves that they were lacking in certain of the rudiments of musical knowledge.

Lennie expected people to stretch themselves musically. He did not suffer fools gladly, although he seldom got riled. There was one occasion concerning a bass player employed in "Geraldo's Navy," as the *Queen Mary* bands were called, after the bandleader and organizer of the bands, "Geraldo" (Gerald Bright). This bass player was considered grossly deficient by the other musicians with whom he played. He was also extremely opinionated about other musicians, in inverse proportion to his own abilities. This became intolerable to his fellow musicians, and so they persuaded him to take lessons with Lennie, in the hope that he might improve. Apparently the bassist was overawed in meeting Lennie. Unlike some in such a situation, he immediately became extremely voluble. "I'm so glad to meet you Mr. Tristano; I think your playing is incredible. I am amazed at your incredible technique. I don't know how you have been able to become such a virtuoso; but don't you think if you played the melody sometimes, you would have many more fans and you would become so much more famous?" Apparently he continued for some time in this vein, his patter getting faster as his nervousness increased. Eventually he stopped and there was a long pause, which must have seemed like a lifetime. Lennie just sat there, and finally, in disbelief at what he had heard, exclaimed "Wow!" Not another word was uttered. Thus ended the attempt by this Geraldo's Navy band to enlist Lennie's help.

Those of us studying with Lennie and his associates would take a lesson each time we arrived in New York, which was about every two weeks. Clearly, in the space of one lesson – say forty minutes or an hour – there would be seldom time to play all the things Lennie had asked us to do during the previous lesson with him. Supposing, for example, I had been practicing thirds built upon the scales. To play these in all keys could take some time, leaving less time for other aspects of the work. So Lennie might suggest a couple of keys, say playing thirds on the scale in the keys of Db or A. While playing these at home or on the boat, I might feel perfectly at ease. In playing them for Lennie, however, I might falter here and there. Excusing myself, I might say that while doing these at home I had felt I knew them perfectly. What I didn't realize is that any tension that I felt during a lesson only pinpointed a weakness in my playing. Later, when I came to teach others, I realized this and made allowances accordingly. But it is only when you have reached a significant point of playing ability that, despite possible nervousness, the playing is not affected. It was all credit to Lennie's approach that you began to realize this yourself. Then, as part of a lesson, he might ask me if I had learned any solos during the past week. (In those days most of the recordings were 78s.)

I would put the record on the player and sing along with it – perhaps getting pretty close to singing the solo I had studied. Then he might suggest, "How about singing the solo without putting the record on?" It soon became apparent that no matter how well I thought I knew the solo, inevitably there were gaps in my knowledge. Despite hearing it in my head, I could not sing certain parts of the solo. It was one thing to be able to sing a solo while it was playing on the record player – it was OK to hear something in my head – but to be able to sing that solo without the support of the record playing it back, this really determined how well I knew it. Even if I knew how to sing the solo reasonably well – enough, anyway, to begin to play it on the bass – singing the solo without the support of the record player was the ultimate test. I particularly remember learning Bird's "Billy's Bounce," which took a number of months.

Sometimes students suggested writing down the solo as an aid to learning; Lennie would point out that the essence of learning a solo was to learn to sing it first. That made sure the music was in your head. Learning to play it after committing it to memory not only made the learning task easier, it also made it more meaningful. Sometimes he would insist that you didn't even attempt to learn to play the solo until you had mastered the ability to sing it note for note without the record player for support. After having learned a solo that way, you discovered that, when playing the solo, the fingers just found their way around the notes. Thus you began to develop an instinct to play what you heard. What Lennie was trying to do was to get you to absorb the music as part of yourself. Then, when you begin to play, the music comes from you as part of yourself, and not just a studied imitation of another player.

As mentioned earlier, another aspect of the jazz discipline is that of learning tunes – "standards," as they are called. A standard, for a jazz musician, is usually one of the popular tunes from the thirties onward, often by composers for Broadway shows, such as Jerome Kern, Cole Porter, and George Gershwin. These provide the foundation for improvisation. You needed to become familiar with the melody of a standard. Similarly, when you can sing the melody, then you can learn to play it. Few bass players developed that ability, seemingly more interested in being able to play exciting time and wild solos. But learning the melody is, as I later discovered, the greatest aid to learning to play a swinging bass line accompaniment. In fact, learning the melody becomes important for all instrumentalists.

And the bottom line for all of this is practice, always an arduous task. We faced particular difficulties in those days. During our transatlantic voyages, it was hard to find suitable places to practice on the *Queen*

Mary. We were allocated a place on "G" Deck. This was a huge dungeon at the very bottom and rear of the ship, "aft," as they say. The floor was duckboards. The propeller shaft ran at a thirty-degree right angle right through this dungeon. The walls were the steel plates of the hull and sweaty with humidity. Visualize this: with illumination restricted to a few naked light bulbs, the noise was incredible, like living with uninterrupted thunder. Whoever dreamed of sending the musicians to this hellhole to practice must have had a weird sense of humor. After a few attempts, during which I could not even hear my acoustic bass against the noise of the ship's propellers, I gave up trying. There was hardly anywhere else to practice, but even then my masochism had its limits.

But the trips were worth it to be able to experience the jazz scene first hand. On December 15, 1949, the famous jazz venue Birdland opened. This New York club was promoted as the "jazz corner of the world." Charlie Parker (Bird) played there with strings. This was an entirely new concept in music: the originator of bebop accompanied by a string orchestra. Until that time a string section had not been used with modern jazz. Strings were associated with symphonic and film music. Though Paul Whiteman had used a string section, this had been an earlier and more formalized style of music. Bebop was regarded as a rebellion in jazz; at least that is the way we viewed it. To have Bird, with his remarkable improvisational freedom, being accompanied by Hollywood-style strings; to us it seemed outrageous, yet somehow beautiful and appropriate. And it is this quality that you could find in the jazz clubs at that time.

The first night at Birdland that Bird played with strings, he seemed a little hesitant, but on the second night he really took off. I was lucky enough to be there both nights. Sometime later, recordings of that group were released. His playing on "Just Friends" was especially superb. I believe that of all his many recordings, Bird finally said "Just Friends" was his favorite. It was that record that he played for his doctor the night before he died.

No discussion about New York in the late forties would be complete without a detailed description of Charlie Parker. And this book about Lennie Tristano would provide an unbalanced picture of jazz if the significance of Charlie Parker's music to Lennie were not discussed. Known as Bird or Yardbird (the former name springing from the fact that his music was as free as a bird and the latter referring to his fondness for chicken), Parker was born in 1920 – a year and a half Lennie's junior. Bird's music was a huge influence upon Lennie. Many other jazz musicians, influenced by Bird, closely imitated his style. It is clear that as Bird developed there were certain stylistic aspects of his playing that enabled other musicians (particularly saxophonists) to imitate him. But, for Lennie, it was not merely Bird's style but his incredible ability to improvise that was important. For Lennie, the core of jazz was improvisation and it was Bird's freedom in that respect that most influenced and fascinated him. To his credit – though one can hear Bird's influence in his playing – Lennie realized that it was Bird's thoroughness that enabled him to develop such an extraordinary ability. There is a story, which I believe to be true, of Count Basie's drummer Jo Jones throwing a cymbal at Bird when Bird was a fledgling jazzman. One suspects that what Bird was doing was so far beyond Jo Jones's swing era concept of jazz that it enraged him and that he threw his cymbal at Bird under the conviction that here was an impostor. Ira Gitler believes that the real reason was that Bird was not that efficient as a player in those early days, though I suspect that a combination of both reasons might have been responsible for the incident. Far from being discouraged, Bird went home and practiced until he had established the ability that led to his subsequent recognition. In a radio interview with saxophonist Paul Desmond, Bird related how he was living at his mother's house and practiced many hours a day for a few years. In fact, he said, the neighbors made efforts to get his mother to move, because of his persistent practicing! No doubt Bird was incredibly talented – but it was not talent alone that led him to develop a music so significant and so beyond the world of jazz before him. He worked incredibly hard.

Lennie also realized that there were other musicians who were especially significant in developing such abilities to improvise. He heard it in Lester Young's playing – Lester well deserved the name "Pres," the president of jazz. Bird also acknowledged his debt to Pres, having studied Pres's recorded solos. Lennie always enthused about his playing.

No doubt it was also Bird's openness to all the influences around him that led him to respect Lennie and Lennie's direction, which was different again from that of the beboppers. I suspect, too, that the affinity between the two men was also cemented by the fact that they were of the same generation – for the respect was mutual. And indeed Bird was respected purely for his music. Unlike Dizzy, for example, whose reputation grew not only from his playing but from his comedy and from running a big band, Bird just played and played mostly with only rhythm sections. For him it was the *music*, wherever it was happening.

Though Bird made those wonderful recordings with strings, his approach on these recordings hardly differed from that of his small bands. Always the focus was upon improvisation. Both Lennie and Bird delighted in moving the emphasis of their improvisations, so that it could appear that they were misplacing the beat. Such innovations were very hard on the rhythm section. It was Lester Young who first played around with the time in that way and presumably both Bird and Lennie had been fascinated by Pres's ability to do this and had likewise developed these not insignificant abilities. Try playing a melody commencing other than on the traditional starting point, and unless you have first practiced this thoroughly, it will prove very difficult. The danger is that in stretching out like this you can easily confuse yourself. Accompanying such exciting musical gymnastics can also be confusing to the rhythm section, so they too can lose the place. A wonderful description of such an event is included in *Miles: The Autobiography*. Davis says:

> I was really happy to be playing with Bird again, because playing with him brought out the best in me at that time. He could play so many different styles and never repeat the same musical idea. His creativity and musical ideas were endless. He used to turn the rhythm section around every night. Say we would be playing a blues. Bird would start on the eleventh bar. As the rhythm section stayed where they were, then Bird would play in such a way that it made the rhythm section sound like it was on 1 and 3 instead of 2 and 4. Nobody could keep up with Bird in those days except maybe Dizzy. Every time he would do this, Max [Roach] would scream at Duke [Jordan] not to try to follow Bird. He wanted Duke to stay where he was, because he wouldn't have been able to keep up with Bird and he would have fucked up the rhythm. Duke did this a lot when he didn't listen. See, when Bird went off like that on one of his incredible solos all the rhythm section had to do was to stay where they were and play some straight shit. Eventually Bird would come back to where the rhythm was, right on time. It was like he had planned it in his mind. (Davis with Troupe 1989: 91)

Bird was such an incredible character. He could be difficult and hit on people for money for a fix and there are many stories about his antics and difficult behavior. For example, I don't know whether this is a myth or not, but rumor had it that Bird hired a horse and tried to ride it into Charlie's Tavern. There were a couple of places that became musicians' hangouts, in particular Jim and Andy's and Charlie's Bar, which were both located on the West Side, not far from Carnegie Hall. You can imagine the disruption of trying to take a horse into a small packed mid-town bar! That was sort of typical of Bird – always a challenger but mischievous.

But he was not the crazed drug addict, as people now like to portray him. Though he became hooked on narcotics, this should not detract from how diligently he studied, working hard at his craft; he was head and shoulders above other jazz musicians at the time. He lived a precarious existence partly because of how jazz is viewed, and seldom found consistent employment – and when he did it was mostly "on the road."

These realities have not really been given due recognition and the popular press tends to regard him as a maverick, though a jazz virtuoso. He read widely and was very concerned about young jazz musicians getting into drugs. For example, he laid into Red Rodney when he found out he had gotten into drugs seriously. He was always his own man and he was aware that he was different from the others. He would never be constrained. He knew he was special in music, but was not arrogant about it. He just knew it.

Bird was always thought of as doing outrageous things – the story also goes that he peed in the telephone booth in Birdland and for that he was subsequently barred from the club. I don't know for sure whether or not this actually happened, but if it did, was it because he got so far out of it that he mistook the phone booth for the toilet or, with his particular wild sense of humor, was he repaying a real or imagined wrong on the part of the owners? According to Ira Gitler, this did not happen at Birdland but either in Chicago or Detroit. But I do remember Birdland's manager, Oscar Goodstein (whom I liked and respected) telling me: "Bird was not a gentleman and I had to ban him on account of his behavior" when I had remonstrated with him about not employing Bird anymore. So maybe Oscar's decision was based on the Mingus incident related below.

Bird could be a charming man. In spite of all that had happened to him, he looked on the world with a wry sense of humor. He could be a real prankster. There was a musical but mainly friendly rivalry between him and Dizzy. An example of this was Bird introducing Dizzy at a concert as "my worthy constituent." On the surface just a kindly comment, but this would have irked Dizzy, because Bird was subtly implying that he was the Senator, a statesman, whereas Dizzy was just a constituent (though a worthy one). That was Bird's type of humor. But Ira Gitler believes it was just Bird affecting his high-falutin delivery – his put-on of fancy folks.

His humor could be unremitting but very clever. Another story concerned Bird and Bud Powell. Birdland was famed not only for its music but also for the diminutive Pee Wee Marquette, who announced the musicians and introduced them to the audience. Pee Wee had this shrill high-pitched voice – it can be heard on a number of jazz recordings made at the club. For those musicians who played at Birdland, it was well known that if you wished Pee Wee to announce you personally you had to tip him. "You take care of Pee Wee and I'll get your name right" was Pee Wee's greeting to the musicians who were about to perform. Thus Pee Wee amply augmented his salary. Not all of us would comply – maybe having complied once it got to be too much of a drag, or maybe musicians did not compensate Pee Wee sufficiently to deserve a mention. I remember playing in Paul Bley's trio at Birdland, and Paul omitted the obligatory donation. We were then unceremoniously introduced as the Paul Blaah trio.

But as to the occasion concerning Bird and Bud: Bud was forbidden to drink alcohol, being under supervision and medication (he had suffered a severe head injury due to an assault and this had induced symptoms of psychosis). But by amply taking care of Pee Wee and becoming Pee Wee's favorite, Bud received the drinks he wanted. Though Bird was the bandleader, when it came to announcing the band Pee Wee totally ignored Bird and repeatedly and enthusiastically announced, "Ladies and gentlemen, Bud Powell, the amazing Bud Powell, Bud Powell, the amazing Bud Powell." As the musicians left the stand, Bud walked out of the club, followed by Bird tapping him on the shoulder and repeating incessantly in mimicry "Bud Powell," "Bud Powell," "Bud Powell" all the way out up to the street! This was related to me by Ronnie Ball. However, Ira Gitler says that "the Bud Powell incident occurred over the microphone, after Bud left the stand on the night of the famous blow-up with Mingus on the last time Bird played at Birdland."

Despite the fact that Bird had a habit, mainly for heroin, and that he could hit on you for money, I got along fine with him. I knew Bird fairly well, having had the opportunity to play alongside him occasionally in some of those legendary "loft" sessions that used to be a feature of jazz in New York during the fifties. We also talked occasionally and once when Bird came to hear Miles Davis at the Down Beat Club on 48th Street (this was in 1952 – one of the few times I worked with Miles) Bird gave me the nod. (Of course I felt honored – I was a new face on the scene and he approved.) Above and beyond the fact that we all thought he was an incredible jazz icon, personally I liked him – a loveable rogue, if you like, but a man with great depth, a man of such contradictory behavior that he was banned from the very club that showed its respect for him by naming itself for him! In retrospect I wish I had hung out more with him. But as an immigrant, I felt wary of becoming too involved with anyone associated with narcotics, knowing that I risked deportation should I find myself so accused.

When the Birdland club opened it looked like a real departure. It was a larger club than the small venues on 52nd Street and it was on Broadway. It was as though for the first time a wider audience was taking bebop seriously. For a brief time it appeared that jazz was beginning to gain general acceptance. Shortly afterwards, an even larger venue opened called Bop City, but this closed after only a brief existence. Jazz was now on Broadway – and it was a bit like the difference in acceptance between off-Broadway theater and shows performed in the theater district proper.

Sometime in 1950 when, on one of our visits, Lennie's sextet was playing at Birdland, I had gone ashore to visit Lennie for a lesson at his house in Long Island. Afterwards, Lennie asked what I was doing that evening. I said I intended to go to hear his group at the newly opened club. His was one of the favorite groups at the time and appeared there on a number of occasions. He then asked if I would play the first set with the band, as bassist Arnold Fishkin would be late due to a studio session. I was over the moon, because this meant that I was being regarded as an ally, not merely as a student. It is one thing to hear the leading group of its time, but to join them and play among those incredible sounds took me to another world. I suppose that was the moment when I knew that my future lay in New York. It was certainly a boost to my confidence, and when I returned to London the buzz went around that Peter Ind had played with Lennie Tristano in Birdland. That did more than anything to increase my confidence in my playing.

3 living in new york – working with lennie in the early days

A year and a half after that memorable first visit to New York, I took my last outward voyage from Southampton – this time as an emigrant, arriving in New York on April 29, 1951. With today's world travel such a journey is virtually an everyday event. We can travel to anywhere in the world within twenty-four hours and Europe and New York were, until recently, less than four hours' flying time apart by Concorde. Travel in those days, however, was rare and exciting. It was a luxury that not everyone could afford. Commercial transatlantic flying began only at the end of the forties. Prior to that, sea travel was the only form of intercontinental travel. In 1951, Atlantic flying had not been long established, and it took eighteen hours, with stopovers in Iceland or Newfoundland. The majority took the five- or six-day journey by sea. It was a complex process – obtaining visas and changing money took considerable time and involved much bureaucracy. (Nothing like today!) And it was very expensive. For example, when I finally traveled to New York, I traveled tourist class on the *Queen Mary* and the cost, for a one-way trip, was the equivalent of over six weeks' salary. (At today's prices it would be the equivalent of paying almost fifteen hundred pounds for a one-way ticket if you were earning the basic annual minimum of twelve thousand pounds.) To save money for such a trip was not an easy achievement.

Emigrating (despite my familiarity with the Big Apple) seemed a daunting decision. Unusually, summer heat had already arrived. I had brought with me my three basses, and at the end of a hazardous journey by truck with all my worldly baggage, I arrived at a mid-town hotel and the bellboy snapped the neck off one of the basses in carrying it into the elevator. He immediately disappeared and I entered a dingy room with a view over an areaway. With one of my basses broken, it seemed an inauspicious start. I felt totally lost and lonely. It was a terrible feeling. It was a mediocre hotel that catered for people who were, shall we say, not at the peak of their career.

Those kinds of hotels exuded a depressing similarity – you entered the lobby and superficially it appeared luxurious. But entering the room

– painted in a color one of my friends described as "babyshit green" – an immediate aura of depression became apparent. The one window – giving the illusion that there is an outside world after all – had an outlook via which, by craning your neck, you could just see a patch of sky about fifteen stories above. Looking across, one met the view of similar windows encrusted with power station dust. Several stories below was a wire mesh that held innumerable numbers of used milk cartons, beer bottles, plastic containers, candy wrappers, condoms, and the odd sanitary towel. Truly a hallmark of civilization. I had taken this final step to emigrate. Christ – this was not the New York of Macy's and Gimbels, nor the New York of wonderful jazz. It was the New York of cheap liquor, of hard relationships, and of despair. Here I was – England seemed to belong to another planet – stuck here with just a little cash and one of my basses destroyed (or so it seemed at the time). I had certainly burned my bridges. But all this was soon forgotten as I entered that world of jazz.

By 1950–51, many of the clubs on 52nd Street were forcibly closed as the land was earmarked for future skyscraper development. The jazz world's loss was the real estate world's gain. There had always been a flux of jazz in different parts of New York, but the heyday of 52nd Street was the only time that jazz was located in one area. After that it was a case of playing wherever there were the opportunities. Uptown at Minton's, in Brooklyn at Soldier Meyer's and downtown in the Village, for example. I soon met and played with a number of the outstanding musicians of that time, many now legends of the jazz world, such as Miles Davis, Gerry Mulligan, Max Roach, Roy Haynes, Bud Powell, to name a few. It was a world within a world. I found a place in the jazz scene – kind of naturally. My association with Lennie and the new introductions that came from that, and from those who associated with him, helped enormously.

I also had the advantage of having developed a classical technique on the bass. The majority of players in those days were not that schooled, and so I attracted quite a lot of attention. Many years later, just before he died, I met Charles Mingus in Holland. I was in Holland with my own band, with saxist Bruce Turner, as I recall. I had known Mingus well since those early days visiting New York (back in 1949). He was playing in the Bimhaus in Amsterdam, but was by then in poor health. We were in the dressing room, when he said to me, "You know this, and I know this – you were the first cat to play all that high shit on the bass." Gratifying, really. I had first met him when I was in Noah Wulfe's bass shop on West 49th Street. I was trying out some basses, having learned to play both parts at once of the first half of a Bach two-part invention. Hearing such unusual musical dexterity, a voice boomed out, "Who's that?" and that's how we met. We became friends until his death in January 1979. So I had this technical advantage, stemming from my early days with James Merrett, but many bass players were far ahead of me in their conception. And what I desired was to develop that kind of conception.

My goal was to be able to play time like Ray Brown and solos like Oscar Pettiford. It took a number of years, not only to develop something like that kind of ability, but also to find my own voice; more precisely, to recognize what that was in me. Others could hear something individual in my playing, but consciously for a while I was trying to escape that, believing it was something to be ashamed of.

It also took some time before I came to understand that those players who were original were expressing their inner self. This meant that they had overcome their self-consciousness – and found their own voice. Invariably, those who make a place for themselves by imitation of an accepted style have not taken that difficult step to be themselves in their music. And more than anything I owe it to Lennie's initial guidance that I reached those kinds of levels of freedom in jazz.

If your material expectations were not high, it was easy to live during those days. With the help of my new friends Warne Marsh, Ted Brown, and Don Ferrara (all students and associates of Lennie), I found a rooming house on Broadway and 76th Street that was home to many musicians. Rents were reasonable. Warne, Ted, and Don were living there, as was guitarist Sam Herman and pianist/vocalist Blossom Dearie. At that time, Blossom was very young and had just come to New York. I remember her wearing white ankle socks and saddle shoes. We were good friends and she reminded me of that rooming house when I met her a few years ago, after hearing Martin Taylor play. She was playing the piano back in those days, but it was much later that she developed into such a celebrated chanteuse, accompanying herself tastefully – her playing was always tasteful. But I remember her simply as a young girl, like the rest of us fresh New York residents.

The rooming place (later known as the Hevro) was huge. Each apartment consisted of maybe ten rooms and the one that we shared was owned or rented by two Hungarian ladies whose claim to fame in show business was that one of their nieces worked with Phil Spitalny's all-girl band. We all lived very modestly – scuffling was a permanent way of life. ("Can you lend me a deuce or perhaps a five. I'll pay you tomorrow.") All such loans were on trust and the trust was never broken. A week's gig in New York (probably about $100) would, with care, give money enough to live modestly for two or three weeks, even a month taking especial care.

Rent was $6 a week, $7 would buy a week's food, a lesson was $5 and there was money left over for transportation. A subway ride was 15 cents and a cup of coffee a dime.

Although we were poor, it was easy living. Then there was the loft scene. These former warehouse buildings (mostly located downtown in the area south of Houston Street – these days known as SoHo, South Houston), could be rented cheaply, which was their main attraction. Ironically, nowadays, rents there are phenomenal and only the rich artist can afford that kind of exclusivity. But it was in such locations that much of the development of bebop occurred. There were jam sessions going on all the time.

Some were serious rehearsals – Neal Hefti trying out new arrangements, Gerry Mulligan getting together ideas for his quartet. Neal was rehearsing arrangements that were destined for the Basie band. Gerry was rehearsing his piano-less quartet, I remember, which was unsuccessful in New York, but when he went to the West Coast and met up with Chet Baker, it became a great success. Some were merely get-togethers for the fun of improvising. Playing with these groups taught me much, but the most enlightening and enjoyable were the sessions organized with Lennie and his musician associates.

In those days, though, the music was the core of our friendship – it was not merely professional but social as well. Even before Lennie established the studio, we would get together as a group of friends – we would visit him at his house in Flushing, and talk, maybe smoke a little pot – just discussing the music scene, or books that fascinated us and, later on, particularly Wilhelm Reich's writings. Sometimes politics would be the topic. The discussions we had at those gatherings were erudite – so much so that they hardly seemed political at all. Maybe it was our youth, but there seemed no need to hold back opinions – one could express ideas freely without risk of offending.

From the beginning some of us would get together informally and play at Lee Konitz's house, in Elmhurst on Long Island. Also during the summer of 1951 we played – Lennie, Lee Konitz, Warne Marsh, and the drummer Jeff Morton – at Rudy Van Gelder's house in Hackensack, New Jersey. Rudy, who was originally a professional optometrist, had developed a keen interest in sound recording and had converted part of his house into a studio. It was all very informal; we played in the living room and Rudy had the control room adjoining this, but such luxurious surroundings impressed me greatly. What a tremendous contrast – this modern home with all its furnishings – compared with the dowdiness of the Britain that I had so recently left. Later, he was to design and build his now famous studio, in Englewood Cliffs, New Jersey. Several years later I was to record again at Rudy's studio – in 1957 and 1958 – with Lee Konitz, Sal Mosca, Don Ferrara, and the drummer Shadow Wilson. Shadow earned his nickname from his beautiful light touch with brushes, creating a very open pulse that just made you want to play. I have fond memories of him from that time – he was a very gentle, unassuming man whom life had not treated easily. Not too long afterwards he left this world. Listen to him on those recordings with Lee's band and also with the Count Basie band on a track called "Feather Merchant" – the touch is so sensitive and yet commanding.

Shortly after my arrival, Lennie had secured a small loft property downtown on the East Side, located between First and Second Avenue. He transformed this into a recording studio and a place to teach and to play. I believe that Rudy Van Gelder advised in the purchase of recording equipment and Rudy's brother Joe helped in the construction. Also several of us students gave a hand. Maybe such things could not happen nowadays – people would expect to be paid. Much more was done on a helping-each-other basis then; it would never occur to people to be paid for this sort of work. Lennie also purchased a Steinway grand piano – but was initially very dissatisfied with the instrument. Whether or not the Steinway people were able to adjust it to his satisfaction or whether Lennie had it changed for another, I cannot remember. But I remember he was most offended when the Steinway representative assured Lennie that that particular instrument had been recommended by none other than Jose Iturbi (a popular classical piano player of the day). Lennie was fully aware of his own abilities as a pianist, and to be compared in any way with Mr. Iturbi, Lennie evidently regarded as insulting.

The studio was a second-floor loft building above a sheet metal workshop. The entrance was at the top of a steep flight of stairs. Lennie had it divided into two sections, the smaller section becoming the control room where the recording equipment stood and the main room housing his piano, with a couple of movable sound screens – as aids in separation during recording sessions. At the far end was a small kitchenette with an air conditioner mounted in the rear window. There was also gas heating for winter times. I seem to remember the walls being painted a creamy color and wall-to-wall blue carpeting. In addition to a couch, there were maybe a dozen or more folding metal seats, padded and finished in a salmon color. Very simple yet tasteful and quite luxurious for those days. All of this was done as Lennie directed – he was able to visualize exactly what he wanted. A remarkable man. The atmosphere was very peaceful and Lennie always spoke in a quiet but authoritative voice. It set the tone. Often students would emulate his manner. One seldom saw Lennie ruffled.

This place was a musical haven and was Lennie's studio for teaching and recording. It also became immortalized as the title of one of his superb lines, "317 East 32nd St." Sessions were held regularly on Wednesdays and Saturdays – the only exceptions were when Lennie had out-of-town engagements. We would often play for twelve hours or more, daylight arriving long before tiredness set in. There was always a regular core of musicians: Warne Marsh, Ted Brown, Lee Konitz on saxes, Willy Dennis on trombone, Don Ferrara on trumpet, Billy Bauer on guitar, Al Levitt or Jeff Morton on drums. Ronnie Ball, Sal Mosca, Lloyd Lifton or Phyllis Pinkerton (all piano players) would share the piano chair. Phyllis not only studied with Lennie but also helped him financially during the early days when Lennie's studio was being constructed. She also recorded with Charles Mingus – in 1952 at Lennie's studio on a recording released on Mingus's Debut label. Mingus would often come by or pianist Paul Bley, sometimes Stan Getz or bassist Arnold Fishkin. There were others – associates or students who dropped by: psychiatrist Steve Silverman, pilot Bob Publicker (both pianists), trumpeter Cy Platt, singers Sheila Jordan and Natalie Reimer. I remember the jazz critic Jack Maher studied drums with Lennie, also drummer Tom Wayburn, who made a recording with Lennie at his studio – later released on Jazz Records. Tom was originally from Michigan, a math graduate who came to study with Lennie. I heard recently that he is now the Executive Director of the American Policy Institute in Houston.

It was at Lennie's studio that I first met Sheila Jordan – that wonderful vocalist whom Bird called "million-dollar ears" because of her incredible accuracy of pitch. Actually, there were fewer women instrumentalists in those early days but I remember playing with tenor saxist Judy Tristano, Lennie's first wife, also pianists Judy Seiden and Phyllis Terrazano (who later married Ted Brown). And sometimes the Bird himself would come by. Then there was the Armenian Band – the Norikes (New Dawn). These were second-generation Armenians whose parents had fled to the USA after the Turkish massacre in the twenties. Two of the band members, clarinettists Steve and Sudan Baronian, were studying with Lennie at the time. The oud player Chick Ganirnian has since passed on. Sudan, however, is still very active and runs a group called Taxim playing Armenian and other ethnic music – and he still travels the world with the group.

Sometimes percussionists Max Roach or Roy Haynes would stop by. Then there was photographer Bob Parent and other musicians outside our particular circle. One day, while we were playing, two guys came in, unknown to me. They watched and listened and even danced all around the piano while we played. I was introduced to them as Lenny and Willie. I realized later that they were Leonard Bernstein and Willie Capell. Bernstein was amazed at Lennie's playing, saying excitedly, "How does he do it, how does he do it?" Many years later when Lennie Bernstein visited the Bass Clef, my club in London, after one of the concerts he had conducted at the Barbican, I reminded him of that time. He said, "How we miss him and what a wonderful influence he was on all of us."

I remember also meeting sculptor Julie MacDonald at Lennie's studio. She had just completed a wonderful wood carving of Bird. This was conceived as a bird but with Charlie Parker's face and his stance as though he was holding his saxophone – it conveyed just how Bird looked and played. This had pride of place in Lennie's studio for some time.

Regular jam sessions were held once or twice a week at his E 32nd Street studio – we always referred to these events simply as "sessions." Some might be spontaneous – Lennie would phone or we got to know by word of mouth, much like other loft sessions. Communication was less formal in those days. In contrast to other loft sessions, where people would come by whether invited or not, Lennie always made it clear that his were invitation-only. This had the advantage of avoiding situations where someone (usually a not very talented player) hogged the music and accordingly spoiled the vibe, a situation frequently encountered in the less disciplined loft sessions. Lennie often recorded these sessions, sometimes as frequently as once a week.

Monday nights at Birdland usually featured informal groups of players, contrasting with the other days of the week when set groups would be hired for a week at a time. The management had a policy of posting the names of the musicians for the following Monday outside the entrance. As a jazz musician, you were expected to take note of this, which was manager Oscar Goodstein's way of letting you know you were hired. (This did not, of course, apply to Bird etc.) So I would find out whether my name was on the board either through the grapevine or simply by passing by. I did miss one such notice once – and it didn't improve my reputation! But it was a small scene in those days. Since Birdland had the edge on all the other clubs (and almost everyone would be keen to play there) the management considered that posting your name outside was sufficient.

At Lennie's studio loft, there was always a pot of coffee going and we would pop around the corner to the deli or the bagel shop, if we were hungry. Often sessions would begin at 9 p.m. and we would play right through to the early hours, sometimes until 9 or 10 a.m. the following day. It was easygoing. Since there could be ten or twelve musicians (at least), some would sit out and then we would change round. If too many played in a jam session it just crowded the music too much. Sometimes Lennie would suggest who should play, but we often just changed around after a few numbers. This is the way it happened then. It was not such an ego scene, with everyone pushing to play or unwilling to let others play instead. I can recall this happening only once at Lennie's. Lennie calmly insisted that the offender stop, and that was that. Later on in jam sessions, such ego hustling became commonplace, although even in the early days one could sense that this was becoming a trend in the free-for-all loft sessions. To combat this, musicians such as Bird would start to play in unusual keys to throw the intruder off the scent. Later on in the fifties, when loft sessions became popular, a younger generation of musicians came who would just be pushy, determined to play at all costs – seemingly oblivious of the subtleties of a change of key. Strangely, I cannot remember any of those people becoming well known.

Lennie seemed to love such marathons as these all-night jam sessions, as, in fact, we all did. Not that we played continuously all the time: we would take breaks and discuss things, not always musical subjects either. But marathons they were, with far more playing than happened during a gig. So many of these overnight sessions were recorded, yet I wonder what happened to the tapes?

During the summer, if the weather was good, some of us would drive after these all-night sessions to the beaches on Long Island: Coney Island, Brighton Beach, Far Rockaway, Long Beach or even as far as Jones Beach. After having breakfast and a swim, we would sleep on the beach for a few hours and then return to Manhattan ready to play again – either a gig or more jamming. Regretfully, Lennie would not join us on these trips; he always preferred to return to his home in Flushing. It is perhaps unsurprising that with such closeness between musician friends, rivalries would develop over love relationships, and sometimes this cast a shadow over what would have ideally been pure musical association. Lennie was a decade older than most of us and, as the leader of this social/musical group, inevitably became something of a father figure for many. But I never viewed us as a group of disciples, as some people have tried to claim.

In November 1951, Lennie invited Roy Haynes and myself to his studio. He recorded the session and released it on a 78 r.p.m. record. After we had recorded, he superimposed a second piano line upon the first. The resultant tracks ("Passtime" and "JuJu") made jazz history – one improvisation overdubbed upon another. Such was the novelty that the critics were totally puzzled, even questioning how Lennie managed to record such complexities with only two hands. It was only some time later that the realization dawned that one line was overdubbed.

Apparently this was not the first time multi-tracking had been used. There were, of course, the Les Paul and Mary Ford recordings, but these were more in the nature of arrangements, not freely improvised, as were Lennie's. When the critics finally deduced the fact that Lennie had overdubbed another improvisation upon the first, they implied it was cheating. I am grateful to Ira Gitler for pointing out that Sidney Bechet (years before tape) played all the instruments on a recording of "The Sheik of Araby." How was this achieved? Presumably with a series of disk recorders – a virtual miracle of technology in those days. However, when, many years later, Bill Evans used a similar approach by multi-taping it was heralded as revolutionary – forgetting that recording of Sidney Bechet and the tracks by Lennie. Also, with Bill's tracks there was no carping about cheating. Today, almost fifty years later, after much has evolved in recording techniques, such criticism would be viewed as naïve. Those two tracks of Lennie's, released initially on a 78 r.p.m. recording, were the very first overdubbed and improvised jazz recordings ever made.

It is an indication of Lennie's ability to conceptualize that he was the first to apply such revolutionary concepts to jazz. As with so many new things, afterwards people say, "How obvious – why wasn't it done before?" But it took an original clear thinker to conceive of such an idea.

I continued my studies with Lennie. In the early days, Lennie had worked gigs pretty frequently and teaching time had to be organized around that. But even in those early days, the late forties and fifties, he realized that he would not be able to earn a living from playing alone, unless he compromised his playing. So over the years, more and more time was spent in teaching to the point when gigging became a comparative rarity. At one time he might start his teaching day at ten in the morning and continue right through till one or two the following morning. As I said, he seemed to love such marathons.

But Lennie always treasured time to himself and began to restrict his teaching in the studio to one or two days a week. For the rest of the time he played, listened to music or to talking book tapes.

I have mentioned the lack of privacy when studying with Lennie at his home in Flushing. But when he started teaching at the Manhattan studio, this problem was resolved, as the soundproofing between the main studio and the control room was good. He normally used the studio control room to teach – except, of course, for piano players – and if students arrived early they would then wait in the control room. This gave musicians such as myself the privacy to feel free to express ourselves and outline our problems. Sometime later, Lennie's brother Michael moved to New York, and Michael sometimes used the studio control room for his psychotherapy practice. A trained psychologist, very much influenced by Wilhelm Reich's teachings, Michael – like many practicing therapists at that time – was focusing on helping his patients to reach and express repressed emotions. All this predated such concepts as the "primal scream" and group therapy sessions. So, while Michael was using one room in Lennie's studio, Lennie would frequently be teaching music in the adjoining room. Apparently, one afternoon, when Michael was with a patient (and while Lennie was teaching next door) the patient let out a bloodcurdling scream. Despite the soundproofing, this was clearly audible both to Lennie and to the music student. "Did you hear that?" said the student in considerable alarm. "What?" said Lennie in his most disarming manner, continuing to teach as though nothing had occurred. Classic Lennie! Then the scream was repeated. I don't know the outcome of this, but suspect the music student felt reluctant to continue study-ing afterwards. Shortly afterwards, Michael continued his practice else-where in New York.

In addition to playing and being recorded, I developed an interest in recording itself. Though still playing a lot, I also began to record ses-sions and concerts. Tape recording was a rapidly developing area of work. Recalling again that memorable November evening in 1951, when Lennie had recorded the session with Roy Haynes and myself, he recorded it on his Presto tape recorder, the latest equipment at that time. Tape recording was then a new process, although many of the studios were still work-ing with direct disk recordings. For those interested in the early develop-ment of tape recording: when Allied armies advanced into Germany at the end of World War II, they discovered that the Germans were using recordings made from a magnetic signal on paper tape or on wire. A few of these machines found their way to the USA and, by the late forties, tape machines were being manufactured there. Most of these machines were OK for speech, but the wow and flutter made them less suitable for recording music. However, by the end of the decade, professional tape recorders were manufactured that rivaled the disk recorders which, tradi-tionally, had been the standard recording medium.

The leading maker of recording equipment in those early days was the Presto Corporation. They were previously known for their disk recording equipment but, by 1950, Presto had developed a professional new tape recorder that was state-of-the-art at that time. It had significant advan-tages over disk recording because you could record up to half an hour at a time and, with tape splicing, editing became an easy task. Subsequently Ampex became the leader in the field (a company founded, incidentally, by Bing Crosby). When Lennie later purchased an Ampex machine I bought the Presto recorder from him and this formed the nucleus of my studio – this was in 1956. Some historic records were made on this machine. I believe that when Charles Mingus recorded some of his music for his Debut label this was done on the Presto recorder. When I purchased it from Lennie, I recorded the *Real Lee Konitz* album for Atlantic Records, a recording that since its initial release has never been out of print. A second album recorded at that time I recently released on Wave. In turn, when I bought Ampex equipment the Presto passed from me to the pianist Sal Mosca, who I believe still owns it.

Looking back, the recording with Roy Haynes was a highlight for me of what were regular loft sessions. I saw Roy in London recently (in 2001), playing with his own group at the Pizza Express jazz club in Dean Street in London's Soho. He is still an incredible player, very much influenced by the Latin scene. We had a wonderful night listening to him. Though fifty years have passed, he still remembered the recording session with Lennie as a special occasion. Those loft days in New York were special musically, but were just one aspect of a very interesting and stimulating era. Many musicians were not only focused on their music, but on a wide range of creative and philosophical thinking, which naturally influenced their playing.

4 other influences on jazz musicians and artists during the fifties

Visualize the New York cultural scene as it was in those early post-war years. Jazz was a major aspect of New York life, as the pages of the *New Yorker* magazine testified. It was the popular music of the day. From Benny Goodman's band at the Rainbow Room in the Rockefeller Center, to the venues in Greenwich Village, jazz abounded. And jazz musicians were so much a part of the culture, mixing with artists, sculptors, photographers, and writers, discussing new ideas and interested in the wider world around them.

Lofts, rented mainly by artists and writers, were frequently the location for those legendary all-night jam sessions discussed in Chapter 3, and although a less public aspect of the jazz scene, were very much a part of New York jazz life right up until the early sixties. Rents uptown were high, but the areas from about 23rd Street right down to the Wall Street area contained numerous former manufacturing buildings taken over by artists, writers, and sometimes by jazz musicians. In those days rents were low. That was their main attraction, but they also provided a tremendous space in which to play and live. I had rented a loft in Astoria on Long Island in the mid-fifties and then, in 1960, moved to loft premises in Manhattan. I rented a loft on E 2nd Street (between Avenues B and C) for $75 a month and, when the following year the rent went up by $10 a month, I thought this exorbitant! Hot in the summer and cold in the winter, these were huge areas – rooms of 2,000 square feet or more and drafty as hell. But with few neighbors, one could play all night. Chances were that any neighbors within earshot were also enjoying the freedom of the night-time.

As previously mentioned, during 1951, the air-raid sirens were sounded in New York every day at noon, reminding people of the apparent danger of the Soviet nuclear threat. Most people remembered life before the nuclear era, and despite previous terrors and the evils of two world wars, still regarded the pre-nuclear times as safe compared with the Damoclean sword of possible nuclear devastation. Though we have become used to living with the reality of nuclear weapons, it is a mistake to believe that jazz musicians were so focused on their world as to be immune from such worries. Though our lives as jazz musicians may in other respects have appeared carefree, it was not a thoughtless existence but a time of great concern. Emerging from World War II, we faced, for the first time in recorded history, a genuine fear of annihilation. Though these fears have not been realized, it is important to acknowledge that such anxieties were widespread in those immediate post-war years. Since then, newer generations have emerged with different priorities and different outlooks, and there is an understandable tendency to view the past from the perspective of present-day reality.

Jazz in those days was the music of the cognoscenti, at least in America. Though the US jazz fraternity was in many ways a disparate group, its members were linked by their dedication to the music. Inevitably cliques formed, yet at that time these had not hardened into factions. Debates in those days were much more open, there was much mixing and loyalties and viewpoints were less rigid. It was later, around the time of the third Newport Jazz Festival (in 1957), when the event was disrupted, that factions emerged that have (I think) never been resolved.

Though there were always issues about commercial jazz and how restrictive it may have been in terms of creativity, commerciality was seen more in terms of popularity than of style. Louis Armstrong was popular, as was Benny Goodman or Tommy Dorsey's band, playing at the Paramount in Times Square. These were not always jazz bands, yet frequently jazz musicians would be found playing in them. In many cases musicians would feel apologetic about taking such employment, yet the need to earn some kind of a living sometimes gave them little choice. Compared to later times, living was easy. For many, life on the fringe was at least possible. Some found the solution in the "day gig" scene, though such work was generally taken reluctantly and always regarded as a temporary solution. Trombonist Willie Dennis took temporary employment as an attendant at the Museum of Modern Art, as did saxophonist Bob Ryman. There was a time when trumpeter Buck Clayton worked as an elevator operator. A musician might have notable recordings to his name, yet still the problem of how to earn a living was ever present. Despite these difficulties, there was usually hope that a break would occur and fame, if not fortune, would make life easier. And apart from the odd day gig, life was not divided up into the nine-to-five routine.

Life was a twenty-four-hour business. In this world of jazz the loft scene was an essential component. Jazz was not just restricted to gigging in a nightclub. When the buzz of traffic eased, this was the time for the jazz community to come alive. And the loft scene had a life and an identity of its own. Walls displayed the ragged freedom of expression of a De Kooning or Pollock, or the photos of Eugene Smith. I might play alongside Elvin Jones, or Jay Cameron or even Bird, with Warne Marsh playing alongside bassist Eddie de Haas. All manner of styles and attitudes would blend – a boiling pot of jazz, art, and photography.

What is never mentioned and may be almost forgotten are the conversations. What did take place that helped to form the attitudes and opinions of that era? Jazz is popularly thought of as a product of drugs, late-night living and racy lifestyles. Most of the so-called drug culture of those days was pot smoking, if anything. Not everyone partook of stronger substances. Such issues can get overblown by the media and writers; it seems to be what they like to focus on. As an example of this, compare such a portrayal of New York then with today's picture in the media of apparent heavy recreational use of cocaine by City workers, implying that this is widespread – do you see how exaggerated a picture it can be? The phrase "drug-crazed" points as much as anything to orthodox society's refusal to acknowledge the deeper reality of the jazz world. Some players used substances such as cocaine or heroin to blot out the distractions of audience insensitivity. Was this drug-crazed? I don't think so. Living in New York during those times was as exciting and inspirational as Paris must have been in the twenties. It was also a very thoughtful time. To see all this as a result of drugs is really to demean the creativity.

Little of this real "scene" has been recorded. It is as though, being so far outside mainstream America, hardly anyone thought it worthwhile to capture either on film or on tape the reality of the loft scene, to document what a rich cultural seam it was. One exception is the book of the photographs of Eugene Smith, published by Thames and Hudson, containing many pictures of sessions held at David Young and Hall Overton's loft at 821 Sixth Avenue in downtown Manhattan. For a while Duke and Sheila Jordan rented a loft at W 18th Street. I remember it was there, one day, that Duke said to me, "Want to hear my new tune?" and he played "Jordu" for me, on his old upright piano. At one time Allen Ginsberg lived down the street on 2nd Street. Film-maker Howie Kanovitz made a film at another loft downtown in about 1960. A whole host of musicians joined in – Elvin Jones and I made up the rhythm section.

Lennie Tristano's loft on E 32nd St (unlike many) was very well appointed, warm, comfortable and soundproofed, more like an up-market recording studio, but those of us who rented less salubrious loft space did what we could to make for some comforts. Overall, though, the atmosphere was that of those who "dropped out" of the comforts and conformity of America. Toilets were partitioned by hardboard, and antiquated stoves and fridges at one end of the loft served as a kitchen. No one was actually supposed to live in such places, but in the main we lived without harassment. As well as jazz gossip, who's playing where, etc., there was a lively interest in art, in poetry, and in what were regarded as fringe subjects. mysticism, psychoanalysis, Reichian therapy and, in particular, the writings of Wilhelm Reich himself.

The term "fringe" had not come into use at that time, though it does convey something of the picture of New York life among the jazz and alternative culture that flourished so strongly then. For although we did not in any way regard such interests as "fringe," we were living beyond the confines of conservative America. For those of us involved in such interests there was the absolute conviction of the truth embodied in the underground literature of the time. Little of this was seen as subversive. Some publications – *Neurotica*, for example, published by Jay Landesman and G. Legman – poked fun at orthodoxy. The *Village Voice*, Greenwich Village's newspaper, also reflected many of these views of alternative society. The McCarthy hearings were viewed by the alternative culture and many other New Yorkers as being dangerous and undemocratic, yet the Soviet threat was also seen as real and Communists viewed as a clear threat to American democracy. Many prominent Americans fell prey to the McCarthy trials. The Fifth Amendment, originally conceived as a democratic safeguard, when invoked, was automatically presumed to signify that the user was guilty of subversion. The legendary jazz musician and harmonica player Larry Adler spent the rest of his life in the UK in protest against that witchhunt. Larry made the harmonica a real jazz instrument and showed that even a simple musical instrument could produce good jazz. He was renowned for playing Gershwin's Rhapsody in Blue on the harmonica. Always outspoken, he was a great raconteur and a prolific writer, especially in the UK satirical publication *Private Eye*. Frequently he worked at Pizza on the Park at London's Hyde Park Corner and respect has finally been shown for his contribution by the naming of the downstairs club "Larry's Room" in his honor.

Though America is now seen in a very different light in today's world, I cannot stress enough the fact that (Senator McCarthy notwithstanding) Americans, whether of the world of the jazz and literary underground, whether Democrat or Republican, had complete faith in the concept of American democracy at that time. The immediate post-World War II Western world still regarded Americans as heroes who had saved the world from fascism. The black community, though frequently treated as second-class citizens or worse, still kept faith with the federal government in Washington, and predominantly black bands, such as Duke Ellington's and Dizzy Gillespie's, went on US governmental promotional tours overseas. Such was the innately felt security of orthodox America that even with the McCarthy witchhunts alternate views of underground, jazz-oriented society did not seem worthy of US government attention. It seemed that each side of the social divide lived its life unaffected by the other.

One could devote an entire volume to the jazz fraternity in New York during those post-war years, partly because so little has been written (it was a lived, rather than documented, existence), perhaps simply because it was so creatively rich. Of course that New York existence, the music, the literature, the art — the initial freedom of it — all began to change. Like most social change, it was gradual and almost imperceptible. During the fifties, jazz was still *the* music of the day; the rock era had not yet dawned. Though tempered by the everyday reality of life, hope for a future recognition of jazz and other creative endeavors loomed large. In the early fifties, with scuffling as a way of life for many, but with a camaraderie around music and ideas, it was not easy to see a future of certain individuals being picked out by the establishment for fame and success, while others, possibly equally talented, were being left high and dry.

Jazz was regarded as essentially American. Though those of us from austerity Britain embraced jazz, there were quite marked differences in ability and approach. It took me at least a couple of years to shake off my British reserve. America prided itself on being the land of the free, and in many ways it was. Despite the country's many obvious imperfections, I experienced a freedom there the likes of which I had not previously known. Indeed, it also seemed at that time that the persecution of black people was being overcome. The New York jazz scene even spearheaded this movement, with people mixing freely. There was no hint at that time of the "political correctness" that replaced this genuine mutual respect. When I read of Francis Newton's description of jazz (discussed in more detail in Chapter 11), being divided into schools – black, white, cool etc. – I wonder if he ever had any inkling of what it was really like in those days of the early to mid-fifties? For the reality was that of musicians dedicated to the music; it meant a lot of hard work practicing, getting together and talking about issues we saw as important, coupled with the everyday struggle to get gigs or suffering the demoralizing effect of taking temporary mundane "day gigs," usually low-paid, unskilled work. The focus was on playing whenever and wherever. I am reminded of the story of the jazz musician taking temporary employment at a circus, cleaning elephant dung from the animal pens. When his friends heard of this, they were horrified. Why did you take a job like this? Surely you could get a regular job with better pay? "What! and quit show business?" was the response.

Visualize the world without rock or pop music; television was black-and-white and not the universal entertainment of today. There were no fax machines and no Internet. International telephone communication was erratic and expensive. Travel was by road or rail (flying was expensive – in noisy and slow piston-engine planes. Jet travel did not start until late 1958.) When I flew from New York to the UK in 1959, not all the planes were jets and going in a jet then was comparable to going on a Concorde flight. The cover of Sinatra's *Come Fly with Me* LP depicted an Eastern Airlines, piston-engined Stratocruiser. The very words of the song convey something of the unusualness, luxury and excitement of travel by air. Flying in those days was special, and did not involve huge queues waiting, like cattle, to be transported to the other side of the world. Life was lived more locally. There was more personal contact, hanging around together, finding out what was going on by word of mouth and going around different places just to see what might be happening.

Unlike much of the academic world, which often teaches subjects from an intellectual ivory tower standpoint, these topics were very much a part of our life and interest. Just as twenty years earlier topics would have concerned the rise of fascism and Roosevelt's "New Deal," discussion among jazz musicians might center around the politics of the day: the execution of the Rosenbergs; the McCarthy hearings; the development of nuclear weapons, including the feared possibility and subsequently the reality of hydrogen weapons. As previously mentioned, the issues regarding racial freedom were also much discussed. In literature, the writings of D. H. Lawrence, of Dostoyevsky, of Freud, of Henry Miller, the poetry of e. e. cummings and Kenneth Patchen were the topics of the day. Some of these were new publications and provided a real sense of dealing with fresh ideas.

A much-discussed topic concerned the writings and work of Wilhelm Reich. Until 1954, few knew that Reich had been targeted by an arm of the US government (the US Food and Drug Administration, FDA). For those of us who followed his work closely, there were not only the books – *The Function of the Orgasm, The Cancer Biopathy, Character Analysis, Ether, God and Devil, Cosmic Superimposition, The Mass Psychology of Fascism, The Sexual Revolution* – but also the *Orgone Institute Journals*, which came out regularly, sometimes even quarterly. You could buy his books in any good bookshop or take out a subscription to the journals.

While there were many who influenced our thinking in those days, I would like to focus more on Reich, not only because of his significance, but also because he had a particular influence on the lives of Lennie, myself and some others in the group. In those days Reich was highly regarded as a psychiatrist and scientist. After all, less than a decade earlier, he had been a respected lecturer at the prestigious New School for Social Research. For those of us who followed his work at that time there was no hint of the future actions of the FDA in 1954, when the agency obtained a court injunction effectively prohibiting his research. Many prominent people included Reich's writings in their libraries, and those with whom I discussed these issues were certainly convinced of the legitimacy of his work. Nevertheless, because much of his research centered on sexuality and the sexual function, you could see a certain reluctance and hesitation on the part of many to discuss these ideas freely! It was Reich's work, in fact, that foretold or perhaps even triggered what we now look on as the sexual revolution. Such discussion was, however, just part of the more open debate among jazz musicians and artists at that time.

A number of jazz musicians were also in therapy with some of the physicians Reich had trained. There was a tacit view that becoming freer or less repressed would be an aid to letting go and improvising jazz. Maybe we were somewhat too optimistic in expecting psychotherapy to do the work for us. Although there were undoubtedly benefits from therapy, this was no substitute for genuine music practice and playing.

There was a marked influence upon many people of the writings of both Sigmund Freud and Wilhelm Reich. A refugee from Nazi Germany, Freud had died in the UK in 1939. His writings, by the early fifties, had virtually become part of mainstream psychology. Reich, on the other hand, was still actively working and continuing to develop his ideas, and a number of his books, particularly *Character Analysis*, were required reading in many American colleges and universities. He too had fled from the Nazi persecution. During those war years and beyond, he had trained a team of medical doctors in his science of orgonomy. With an established reputation in New York as a lecturer, therapist and researcher, his work was at the forefront of psychiatric development. By 1950 he had moved to new headquarters in Rangeley, Maine, continuing his work there. Having been introduced to his writings by the drummer Jeff Morton, I remember trying to contact the Orgonomic Association and found a phone number located in Forest Hills, Long Island, only to find that the move to Maine had already taken place. This was in 1951.

Lennie had been immensely interested in these developments in psychiatry and also in what Reich had described as bioenergetics and, on occasion, in the early fifties I would read to him from some of Reich's books, such as *The Function of the Orgasm* or *Character Analysis*. These were unavailable as talking books. I would often visit Lennie at his East Side studio and sometimes, as I entered, I could hear this high-pitched Mickey Mouse voice coming from the record player: Lennie would be playing his talking books at twice the recorded speed. He was very perceptive, very sharp, and as is often the case with blind people, he could be very quick in terms of hearing. I would walk into the studio; there would be no lights and this little high-pitched voice from space would be reading Dostoyevsky or whatever and Lennie would say, "They read so slowly – I want to get on with it."

It was in 1953, I believe, that Lennie wrote to Reich, offering, on our behalf, to give a free concert for him and his co-workers in Maine. Lennie was so moved by Reich's insights and strength of conviction that he felt it would be good if we gave something of ourselves in appreciation. But Reich courteously refused this. At that time we did not realize the serious situation Reich and his associates were facing, both on account of the incredible nature and danger of his research and also from the threat against his work by US government authorities. Rumors then went around that Reich was under investigation by the FDA. There had been an article published in one of the psychiatric journals by a freelance journalist by the name of Mildred Brady claiming, among other things, that Reich and his associates used to masturbate their patients, that they used a device called an orgone accumulator that made their patients "orgastically potent" and that Reich was allegedly profiting by this activity. It was a typical smear article. Appearing in a professional psychiatric journal gave it a spurious stamp of authority and, without knowing the background of how the article came to be written and even more how it came to be printed in an official publication, one can only surmise why it was done. This was not long after the McCarthy hearings.

But later on we realized that the article was merely the beginning of a campaign to discredit Reich. In 1954, the FDA issued an injunction against Reich claiming that his research was fraudulent, and the injunction in effect forbade further research. (I got a copy of the injunction because I was very concerned about what was happening.) A trial date was set, then deferred. Reich was then informed of a further date, but this was then changed again without Reich being notified. Subsequently, he was arrested, found guilty and jailed for two years in Lewisburg Federal Penitentiary. A colleague, Dr. Michael Silvert, was also arrested and jailed for one year. After Dr. Silvert's release he was found dead – an apparent suicide. Reich died in prison just one week before being due for parole. The official verdict was heart failure. Meanwhile, his books were seized, taken out of the bookshops and burned in New York City's Gansevoort incinerator. Book burning in America in the mid-fifties – an incredible and unbelievable event, yet true. Imagine how Reich must have felt, having already witnessed book burning in Nazi Germany.

What a shift in thinking there had been! Reich had been known worldwide as a pioneer in psychiatry. He was originally a younger colleague of Freud, but their paths went separate ways when Reich began to concentrate on the somatic aspects of neurosis and psychosis. This had led him to investigations concerning the nature of life energy functioning and an understanding of universal principles of life energy flow. His discoveries are described in his books in a straightforward manner and though a different orientation and outlook is required to appreciate them fully, they are not that complex. To those who studied his writings carefully, the logic of his presentations was clear, and with a few simple tools could be confirmed by anyone. The impact of Reich's work upon many within the artistic, musical milieu in New York at that time cannot be overestimated. It is an aspect of what went on during those times that is virtually never referred to by the critics, but, for example, when Bird was in Camarillo State Hospital in California in the late forties, he read a number of Reich's books and was thereafter a staunch advocate of his concepts. Bird talked to Ronnie Ball and me about this, because we were interested in Reich. This must have been in 1953 or '54, a couple of years before he died. As I recall, we were in a bar next to Birdland – one of those mid-town bars. While I talked to Bird at the various loft sessions, this was the only time that I remember us sitting together in a bar, so it stands out in my mind. He said that they had Reich's books in the hospital – he mentioned *Character Analysis* and *Functions of the Orgasm*. Bird's view was that Reich was correct in his understanding of neurosis and that his approach to such problems through orgone therapy was valid. Nevertheless Bird felt that it was too late for him personally. Bird died in 1955, at thirty-four years of age.

Many others were interested in Reich and it would often be a topic of conversation. I remember Dave Lambert, the jazz singer (of Lambert, Hendricks and Ross) talking about Reich. Dr. Simeon Troppe (an associate of Reich) was the psychiatrist who was most popular in treating musicians. I know he treated Gil Evans as well as Lambert. I met Simeon later, after I returned to London. He phoned me, having read my book *Cosmic Metabolism*, and we became good friends – as it turned out, this was to be the last year of his life.

As I mentioned earlier, in 1952 Lennie's brother Michael had also moved from Chicago – their city of origin – to practice psychology in New York City. A number of musicians, myself included, underwent therapy with Michael, while others went to some of the doctors that Reich had trained. It was not just Lennie's associates alone who sought such help. Other musicians outside Lennie's circle and artists such as Willem De Kooning, the famous expressionist artist, also sought help.

When Reich was jailed, it threw the artistic and psychiatric world into turmoil. Reich's work and concepts had been of immense interest to many, but his jailing caused many to doubt his work rather than doubt the established authority of the US government. By this time, his work had taken him into the realm of weather control: there are remarkable reports of rainmaking, in Reich's journals, in the state of Maine, and of the diversion of a hurricane from New York City. His work seemed to many like science fiction come to life. Many of us followed those developments and I was one of the few who repeated some similar experiments to ascertain for myself the validity or otherwise of Reich's concepts. My own experiments confirmed what Reich had written and it was very sobering to realize not only the extent of his research but also the enormity of what had happened to him and his co-workers. My own experimentation, confirming his work, left me outside the pale of "normal" society. Most people just stopped talking about him (even if they had agreed with his ideas before) or just shrugged and said maybe he had been wrong after all.

I discussed these events in detail with Lennie. He and his brother Michael were among the few people I knew who seemed able to grasp the enormity of what was happening. Nowadays the world is less naïve about governmental credibility and that of world leaders. We live in a far more cynical world, the majority considering that corruption can penetrate virtually all aspects of politics and that economic interests compromise political veracity. Just look at all the recent marches against the Iraq war in March 2003 – with placards clearly seeing this as a war about oil and who controls it.

Not all scientists get the recognition they deserve. For example, Tesla's work on electricity is seldom recognized and Immanuel Velikovsky was vilified because of his insights into geology, archeology, and astronomy, so Reich's incredible discoveries were to be curtailed – no matter at what cost to Reich, to his associates, and to the truth itself. I found that people were shocked or at least uneasy about what had happened, but their reaction was mainly to shrug their shoulders and carry on as usual. The virtual absence of press coverage gave people an excuse to move on to other things, as though nothing of real import had happened. This blow to academic and scientific freedom passed unchallenged. Much of Reich's earlier work had already become accepted within psychiatry. Yet just as Tesla's discoveries concerning electrical energy – such as the generation of AC electricity – are used without credit being given him, so it was with many of Reich's discoveries. But the psychiatric world evidently was in no mood to accept the realization that psychosexuality had a real physical energetic basis. When Reich was able (through his research) to link the laws of life energy to those of the cosmos, it was regarded as outrageous. The solution was to brand him either as a charlatan or as having gone crazy.

Though I never met Reich, it was clear to me that he was a brave and dedicated individual who would not allow social pressures to deter him from his work. He continued his research right up until the time he was jailed.

Of course there have been other innovative searchers after truth. I think of Oswald Spengler, Rudolph Steiner, Sigmund Freud, Immanuel Velikovsky – to name just a few who have influenced me – but Reich was in many ways above anyone else in importance to many jazz musicians and artists in that New York scene. Not necessarily those who made it big, like Buddy Rich or Benny Goodman for example, nor all musicians, but for many who felt themselves to be outside of mainstream America, totally outside, who were concerned about the life around them, and whose belief in the jazz music scene was paramount. The music was the key to it all for them. You can see how the play *The Sideman* illustrates a jazzman's total obsession with playing jazz improvisation, detrimental to his marriage, his kids and his own comfort. Doris and Rufus Reid (the bass player) had bought us tickets to see the play on Broadway, so we were interested to see subsequently that it was coming to London. But publicity for the play in the UK focused more on the fact that a young soap actor was starring in it rather than on what the play said about jazz – which says much about modern-day interests.

Back in the fifties there seemed to be much more depth, much more interest in non-material matters, and Reich and his group were part of this – "telling it like it is" – so honestly. Reich really was a symbol of someone who did that no matter what the consequences – and that is what jazz is about! I can't answer for every other jazz musician and for how they saw it individually, but there had been a strong following – a very strong following – of Reich and his ideas. I remember reading these to Lennie and he exclaimed, "What a great scientific innovator. What a motherfucker!" For Lennie, it was his strongest praise; his way of saying that here was a challenger, a down-home, straight-talking man. Typically for Lennie, he focused on what was said, not on how people presented themselves.

The vilification of and subsequent silence over Reich's work is, for me, a most significant example of the distortion of history. So much so that if you mention Reich's name to today's generation it's unusual to find anyone who has even heard of him. It is sobering to realize that what we are taught as history contains omissions of extreme importance. In those days the West accused the Soviet bloc of rewriting history – but the blatent demeaning and obfuscation of Reich's work should remind us that America and the West also have much to answer for. Though a much smaller and different circle of influence, Lennie's contribution to jazz has been similarly distorted and evaded, particularly by those self-appointed jazz critics who have taken it upon themselves to decide who's who in the world of music. You have to ask why.

5 lennie and the changes in jazz from the fifties

As the fifties moved on, America woke up to the realization that it had its own unique artform – that of jazz. For jazz, this was to have particular consequences. In a market-focused, commercially oriented country, what was it going to do with such an enticing "product" as jazz? These were changes one would only really reflect on later.

There were also changes going on within Lennie's world. Many of those musicians who had gathered around him were beginning to go their own ways. Although in the early fifties Warne Marsh had remained in New York, Lee Konitz, who had been such a key member of Lennie's sextet, had in 1952 joined Stan Kenton's band as featured soloist. In 1953 Lee formed his own band with Jeff Morton, Ronnie Ball and myself. None of us had been playing exclusively with Lennie, our association being mostly at the twice-weekly sessions at Lennie's studio. Ronnie Ball and Sal Mosca (being pianists) obviously had to forge their own links with the jazz world. Ronnie had been working with guitarist Chuck Wayne and also gigging frequently with Bird. I had been working with Paul Bley, Jackie McLean and Donald Byrd and on several occasions with Miles Davis. Like all jazz musicians, I did a whole variety of one-off gigs – with musicians Hank D'Amico, Joe Puma, Bill Evans, Tony Scott, Philly Joe Jones, Eddie Costa, Hal McKusick, Carmen McRae and even on one occasion with Billie Holiday. Everyone was busy playing a variety of gigs. I also stopped taking lessons with Lennie about the time I went on the road with Lee.

George Wein was then promoting Lee as a lead musician. George (a pianist from Boston) came from a wealthy family. He had been running a club in Boston for some time, the Storyville Club, first located in Kenmore Square and then later in the Copley Square Hotel near the Back Bay area. This area has now completely changed; in those days it overlooked Back Bay, which was the tangle of railroad tracks outside the main Boston station. Since then this has all been built over. Some of the former railroad tracks have become a motorway and the rest has become part of Boston's financial center. But in those days the Storyville Club was the center of jazz for Boston. When I look back at the Storyville, and all the other jazz clubs of the time, they were very basic set-ups. It is a real irony that the people today who want to relive or re-create those days would not have cared to set foot in clubs such as Storyville as it was. The jazz clubs of those days would be seen as too down-home, too seedy and certainly with none of the up-market design features that make today's clubs the "in" places to be seen at! It always amused me when I ran the Bass Clef that people would say how they loved the way it re-created the atmosphere of a jazz cellar from the fifties and then would ask why I didn't have matching tables and chairs.

Anyway, George Wein promoted a number of musicians and also ran a record label, Storyville Jazz. A couple of Lee's albums were recorded on Storyville – *Lee Konitz at Harvard Square* and *Konitz* – and these were my first LP recordings.

The club was frequented by a number of wealthy people who were jazz aficionados. Among these were the Lorillards – Louis and Elaine – who were extremely wealthy as tobacco heirs (Old Gold etc.) and lived in a grand mansion in Newport, Rhode Island. Most of Newport's residents were right-wing, conservative New Englanders. Not so the Lorillards: loving jazz and enjoying a freer social life than many of their neighbors, the impression was that they were envied for their extreme wealth and frowned upon for their lifestyle, including, of course, their love of jazz. When I was in residency at the Storyville Club with Lee's band, George Wein, Louis and Elaine Lorillard were engaged in a discussion that I now realize I was fortunate to witness. There had been some previous publicity in the *New York Sunday Times* about jazz, claiming that it was a uniquely American artform. If I remember correctly it was Louis who said, "What we need is a jazz festival." (George Wein said it was Elaine. He also remembers another Englishman being present – though I don't recall anyone else being there at the time.) Following this fateful conversation (early in 1954) Newport Jazz Festival was born, and plans went ahead for the first event. Both Lennie and Lee Konitz had a high profile in jazz in those days, and it seemed inevitable that Lennie's group would appear at the festival – as indeed happened. Lennie's sextet – Lee Konitz (alto), Warne Marsh (tenor), Billy Bauer (guitar), Jeff Morton (drums) and myself (bass) – were invited to perform there during the three-day festival.

George Wein organized it and it was in the summer of 1954 that this first festival took place. As I recall it, it was held at the Lorillards' Newport estate, though the jazz publications list it as being held at a tennis club at Newport. Was the location changed after the first year? I had never visited an executive ghetto before. Imagine: everyone going to the festival had to go through the estate's security check before being admitted to the Newport estate. It was a huge area of affluent residents living in their New England mansions, the kind one sees depicted in Hollywood movies. The festival was a great success and received huge press coverage. Jazz (it seemed) had become accepted as part of American culture. I remember a kind of exultation among many musicians – believing that finally the underdog image would give way to some respectability and a reasonable standard of living. Young, and enjoying the relative success, which had come to me so easily, I didn't for one moment think ahead to future times, for it would have been difficult to raise a family on the kind of money I was able to make from my jazz adventures. In retrospect, it was one of the most carefree times in my life. Even so, I was somewhat suspicious that all the brouhaha over America's newly discovered artform would benefit only very few. Time has proved the truth of this – success has been enjoyed by those who marketed themselves or employed agents and managers for the purpose. Lennie, I feel, was one of those left out of this particular rat race.

However, at the time of Newport, Lennie was still regarded as a key player. When we played I remember feeling a conviction that I was part of something special – a music that was the true avant-garde of the day. Not that this was stated explicitly. Lennie always manifested supreme conviction, not only in his playing, but also in his demeanor. He never wooed his audience; he merely conveyed his conviction in his playing. He has been criticized for not relating to the audience. This seems an odd comment to me. In later years Miles Davis was criticized for turning his back upon his audience. For some this was pure arrogance. Whatever the real reason was, this was understandably construed (rightly or wrongly) as Miles's disdain for his audience. But in Miles's case, the audiences seemed to accept this, even liked it in some weird sort of a way; the psychological aspects of adoring someone who is disdainful of you seem to me to be deeply woven into the psyche of the jazz fans of that later era.

Lennie, however, was not arrogant or disdainful. All his attention was focused on the creation of the music itself – whether or not an audience was present. The open-air stage at Newport could have been a recording studio as far as Lennie was concerned. Whereas he would acknowledge applause, he would never become emotional about it. It was as though he let his playing transmit the inspiration and that was all that mattered. Lennie always conveyed total technical mastery – whatever he wanted to play, he played. Rarely did any trace of technical difficulty manifest itself, no matter how complex his performance. And this seemed also to be true of the other musicians, particularly Lee Konitz and Warne Marsh. As I see it, Lennie's influence on both Lee and Warne was very strong. Warne always acknowledged this, right until the end of his life. On the other hand, it often seemed that Lee (though also influenced) was striving to reach out in other directions.

But we were all there together at the time of that first festival. The Newport Festival had something of the air of a circus about it. It was certainly festive – perhaps never before had so many jazz musicians congregated and socialized together. But it was a gathering of some very disparate social groups and people with very different outlooks on life. Picture respectable, affluent Americans alongside nonconformist, alternative living jazz musicians and fans. It was an odd mix. But after all these years I remember little about the music that was played. The overwhelming impression was the setting, the socializing and the awareness of a new kind of social event. There was a fête-like atmosphere. A story that sums up the odd contrasts for me is of George Wein and Louis Lorillard strolling through the estate, when they came upon Lester Young sitting in the grass rolling a joint. Bearing in mind that smoking pot was viewed as highly illegal in those days, George coughed and said to Lester, "Pres, what are you doing?" To which Lester replied, "Well, isn't this a festival?" "Of course," said George. And Lester said, "Well let's be festive then."

And festive it was: the weather was fine, the music was good and it felt like new beginnings. However, in some ways, Lennie's group seemed remote from this festivity, as though it represented the "serious" aspect of jazz. My impression was also less than objective. It was not always easy to accompany Lennie. His complexity of rhythm – superimposed on the standard 4/4 jazz beat – challenged rhythm sections of the day. The temptation was not to listen to what he was doing and instead to pound away, bass and drums together, to maintain the beat. But such an approach was far from satisfactory for it merely led to the rhythm section "tightening up" – and the jazz beat needs to swing and not become compulsive. Drummer Jeff Morton and I had perhaps more experience in playing with Lennie than any other rhythm section, and we also had the advantage of being held in high regard by him. Nevertheless, it was not an easy gig. My memory of our concert at that first Newport Festival was a combination of the challenge it imposed and the pride I felt in being part of it. As far as I am aware there was no recording of it. It would be fascinating to be able to hear it again.

But another lingering impression of that first jazz festival is that it marked, to me, the division between jazz as serious creativity and jazz as commercial entertainment. I remember also the polite curtness of the guards at the entrance to this executive ghetto on Rhode Island, the clowning of Dizzy Gillespie contrasting sharply with Lennie's pleasant seriousness, and the overall feeling of the invasion of jazz into one of America's most wealthy and exclusive domains.

Bird was never invited to that first Newport Jazz Festival. It is difficult to know why – after all, Pres and Dizzy were invited. Maybe it was because Bird could be difficult and had been going through a bad time. Lennie berated George Wein for not inviting Bird. Lennie said that Bird was the natural king of jazz improvisers at that time. I find myself wondering whether this lay behind the failure to invite Lennie for subsequent Newport Jazz Festivals. But maybe it was felt that the seriousness of Lennie's music was out of place in such a festive atmosphere. I'm only guessing. But for Bird it was too late. In March 1955, Lee's quartet had a long residency at George's Storyville Club. Maybe to make amends, George had invited Bird to join the quartet. It would have been Lee Konitz and Bird (the two leading alto soloists of that time) with the rhythm section of Ronnie Ball on piano, Jeff Morton on drums and myself on bass. When the time came, Bird didn't show up. I remember us wondering and grumbling about it – "What's with Bird? Doesn't he want to play with us?" Three days later we heard the news: Bird was dead. It was many years later that I heard that, far from not wanting to play with us, Bird's last words were "I've got to get to the gig, man." That is what I heard, but, as ever in jazz history, there are always myths and counter-myths.

A somewhat different story emerges from Ross Russell's book *Bird Lives*.

> "You're ill," the Baroness said firmly, and insisted on calling a doctor. "No, don't call a doctor," Charlie said. "I'll be okay in a few minutes." He explained he was on his way to Boston to play a gig at Storyville for George Wien [*sic*]. He would appear as a single, using a house rhythm section that Wien had provided. He knew it wasn't much of a gig. The new agency had gotten it for him and he had to make good, show up for all the sets on time, and play well. (Russell 1972: 349)

Contrast this statement with that from *Bird's Diary*, a carefully researched book written by Ken Vail about Bird's life over the last ten-year period and quoting from the Baroness.

> Wednesday 9th March 1955. Charlie Parker sets off for Boston to play an engagement at Storyville where he is due to open on Thursday. He stops off at the Stanhope Hotel on Fifth Avenue to visit Baroness Pannonica de Koenigswarter, known to her many musician friends as Nica. Nica realizes something is wrong and she calls a doctor. This is Nica's account. "He had stopped by that evening before leaving for Boston,

where he had a gig at Storyville. His horn and bags were downstairs in his car. The first thing that happened which was unusual was when I offered him a drink and he said no. I took a look at him and I noticed he appeared quite ill. A few minutes later he began to vomit blood. I sent for my doctor who came right away. He said that Bird could not go on any trip, and Bird, who felt better momentarily, started to argue the point and said that he had a commitment to play this gig and he had to go." (Vail 1996: 173)

Being part of the group that was to play with Bird at Storyville, I knew what it meant to Bird, and Lee and Bird knew each other well and greatly respected each other. And yet the mythmaker (in this case Ross Russell) implies that Bird thought "it was not much of a gig." The unanswered question is why Russell felt it necessary to demean the engagement. For this not only demeaned the musicians he was engaged to play with – the Lee Konitz Quartet – but also George Wein, who ran the most prestigious jazz club in Boston. It also demeaned Bird himself by implying that Bird was only considered good enough to be employed on gigs of little account at the end of his life.

After Bird died, Lennie really felt his loss. I was working with Lee away from New York (either still in Boston or in Toronto) by the time of the funeral. But Lennie talked to me a number of times about Bird and the funeral, after I returned. It was obviously a sad time and a period of reflection for Lennie. He had always respected him – he had always seen Bird as the greatest improviser. Also, Bird had been his contemporary and had died at such a young age.

Lennie often talked of Bird's funeral and of the pallbearers stumbling and almost dropping the coffin. Lennie was a pallbearer along with other jazz musicians: Max Roach, Dizzy Gillespie, Sonny Stitt, Louie Bellson, and Charlie Shavers. Leonard Feather and Teddy Reig were also pallbearers. Lennie said that he knew intuitively that the coffin was about to drop and he put both his hands on the coffin to prevent it from falling. However Ross Russell, describing the funeral in very critical terms, attributes the steadying of the casket following the stumbling of the pallbearers to "a Herculean effort on the part of the powerful Mr. Reig" (Russell 1972: 361). Teddy Reig was previously described as "the hip artists-and-repertoire-man, resplendent in a shiny gunmetal-blue silk suit."

However, according to Robert Reisner, "At one juncture, they dropped the casket. By some mysterious intuitive process, Tristano stuck out his arm at that precise moment and caught it" (Reisner 1974: 223). You wonder about mythmaking, which can so distort reality. Not everyone, however, focused on the negative aspects, which effectively downgraded Parker and his contribution. "A few months after his death *Down Beat* readers elected Charlie Parker to the Jazz Hall of Fame, the fourth musician so honored. And Charlie Mingus commented, 'The musicians at Birdland had to wait for Charlie's next record to find out what to play. What will they do now?' " (Russell 1972: 367).

Lennie's tribute – the incredible "Requiem" to Bird on the *Tristano* album – is, for me, one of the most moving blues tracks of all time and a fitting tribute to Bird and his music. On the last chorus Lennie recorded an additional track of right-hand tremolo, which added still further to the sense of awe that Lennie's music could evoke.

When Bird died in March 1955, as I saw it, it marked the start of a great change in the direction jazz was taking – a change that none of us was aware of at the time. Some saw it as coincidental. Other musical influences and approaches began to come to the fore, with less focus on improvisation and more stylistic changes. It was as though Bird's influence focused everyone on improvising and when Bird died many jazz musicians said, "Bird is dead, we cannot follow that – he was too great." It also meant that some jazz musicians stepped out of the shadow of Bird's aura and into the limelight. And apart from Lennie and many of those who were greatly influenced by him, it seemed that improvisation became secondary, and formalized arrangements – as with the Modern Jazz Quartet – became the main focus for the music. And despite some great recordings to come, one could sense that in this new world of jazz, Lennie's (and Bird's) influence was waning.

There were also changes within our group of musicians. With hindsight, I suspect that Lennie felt disappointment that his most talented students went their separate ways. Also, this was the time when Lennie lost his E 32nd Street studio. I believed that it was demolished to make way for skyscrapers but, according to Safford Chamberlain, this was due to difficulties with a new lease. My memory is that, after 1955, the area became derelict, awaiting demolition. Later, in 1962, according to Safford, this area was cleared and new construction – a huge apartment block called Kips Bay Towers – replaced the old buildings.

Lennie moved to a house in Palo Alto Street, Hollis, Long Island. He created another studio on the top floor. A number of his students, me included, again helped in the conversion work. As ever, Lennie had designed in detail what he wanted and carefully planned how the space should be used.

Though Lee and Warne did play with him again from time to time in the fifties and sixties, both had begun to work as leaders of their own groups by the mid-fifties. Such a change was almost inevitable, but the sessions at Lennie's studio lost something as a result. Those times when they worked together again were few and far between. When, in 1956, Lennie released (through Atlantic Records) his album *Tristano* with such now well-regarded tracks as "Lineup," "East 32nd St," "Requiem," and "Turkish Mambo," it also included music recorded at the Confucius restaurant in mid-town Manhattan with Lee, giving a rare glimpse of how Lennie sounded live in a club. The rhythm section this time was Gene Ramey on bass and Arthur Taylor on drums.

Other changes were afoot. As jazz gradually found an accepted place in America, commercialism began to take over. It was not a sudden change. The world of jazz embraced so many facets, even in those days. It was not simply about an earlier golden era being replaced by commercial interests. There had been package tours: Norman Granz' s "Jazz at the Philharmonic," for example. However, following the successes of the Newport Jazz Festival, more festivals sprang up – Monterey and others. Also, over the years, more jazz tours took place; American musicians were regularly traveling to Europe. Then Russia opened its doors to the US State Department tours, featuring leaders such as Duke Ellington, Dizzy Gillespie, or Louis Armstrong, all adding to the worldwide spread of jazz.

The US jazz club circuit continued. Some cities such as Boston, for instance, had established clubs that were a regular source of gigs for traveling small group combos. Then there was the recording industry, which was rapidly expanding in the fifties, providing work for jazz musicians, the bigger labels – Atlantic, RCA, Colombia, Emarcy – signing the best-known groups. Other labels, such as Blue Note and Riverside, concentrated on finding new talent, providing opportunities for up-and-coming young black musicians or promoting musicians who, despite having influence on other jazz musicians, had not yet established a wider public appeal.

Despite all this activity, there were always musicians who failed in one way or another to capitalize on their talent. Ironically, so often those who follow in their footsteps have an easier time of it, at least in mastering the art of playing jazz. The musical vocabulary of jazz has taken at least a half-century to develop, and that period during the late forties to fifties was possibly the most creative period of jazz improvisation ever known. Looking back over the years, it's hard to realize that bebop used to irritate people – as though music of that idiom was anti-social rubbish. Also, during the time of the late forties, when the new creativity in jazz became known as bebop, it upset many of the older jazz fans, who viewed it as an impurity. One of Bird's great records, for example, was dismissed because the critic at the time had detected a "squeaky reed"!

It is easier for us today to look back half a century and to realize that despite the differences, bebop really was a continuation of earlier jazz improvisation, and not some maverick attempt to destroy what had previously been developed. And this is also the case with Lennie's music.

With the consolidation of the jazz vocabulary, it became more commercialized and bebop became more accepted. The criticism leveled initially against bebop in the late forties and fifties then changed toward a new tolerance, that accepted all jazz – sometimes apparently without regard for merit. It seemed to me, having watched bemusedly the level of sniping that had gone on before, that the critics finally became convinced by the musicians and jazz aficionados' acceptance of the new music. Also the critics, unwilling to be proved wrong again, became more careful in their reviews.

Jazz reviewing then became more cautious and less independent. But it seemed odd to me, despite the wider acceptance of bebop, that Lennie was often a target for negative reviews. To my cost I found this to be true, after one critic, John Mehegan, accosted me in 1956 about this. I had recently made those jazz rhythm tracks with the drummer Jeff Morton. These were for Lennie's use, as both Jeff and I had previously gone on the road with Lee Konitz's band, and we could no longer be at our regular twice-weekly sessions at Lennie's studio. Within a few years, such recordings had become commonplace – and were marketed extensively as "Music Minus One." But ours were the very first jazz rhythm tracks ever recorded.

Lennie had used a couple of these tracks for those unique recordings, "Line Up" and "East 32nd St" on the Atlantic album *Tristano*. When D.J. Symphony Sid played them on his late-night jazz program on WNEW, these tracks had taken the jazz world by storm. Again Lennie – always an innovator – had used these up-tempo tracks to develop his improvisational skills. Lennie had often impressed on us the value of slow improvisation. This allowed ideas to come through with less difficulty over technical limitations. In other words, it was easier to allow one's improvising ability to develop by doing it slowly. Explaining this, Ira Gitler quoted from my *Looking Out* album:

> Bassist Ind explained overdubbing and speeding up tapes on the back of his *Looking Out* LP. "I accomplished this by making a rhythm tape or bass line tape first," he wrote, "then slowing the tape to half speed and playing slow improvisation with the slowed-down tape. By re-recording the resultant two tracks at the slow speed and then playing them back at the fast speed, the original tracks return to normal and the improvised track becomes twice as fast and is raised one octave into the cello

> range... Speeding up an improvised line does not improve a bad line, nor does it cover bad notes, rather it accentuates both of these." ... The last thought is true enough. (Gitler 1966: 239)

Lennie had taken a rhythm track that was recorded at a fast tempo and slowed it down to half speed – technically easy to do by then, as it just meant playing a tape at 7.5 IPS that was originally recorded at 15 IPS. The tempo dropped but the key remained the same, only sounding an octave lower than normal. When the combined recording of the original track and the slow improvisation was played back at the 15 IPS speed the original rhythm tracks sounded as normal and the overdubbed track sounded one octave higher and twice the speed. Lennie didn't discuss how this was done and, like the previous tracks "Passtime" and "JuJu," recorded some four years earlier, he let others figure out how it had been done. At first the reaction was that this was phenomenal playing executed on some new kind of piano. For Lennie had played mainly a single line in the lower register of the piano, so that on playback it did not sound abnormally high. Taking a tune that was usually played at a fast tempo – and then improvising on it slowly – gave one a chance to find new directions in playing. It also required considerable skill. Often when playing at a fast tempo the excitement and difficulties of executing the notes cleanly interferes with the creative flow. And it was this realization that led Lennie to make those unique tracks.

When this new album (*Tristano*) was released in 1956, I was playing at the Hickory House. When John Mehegan came in one evening, he invited me to the table he was sharing with his lady friend. After complimenting me for my playing on the new album, he asked me how it had been done. I explained how Jeff and I had made the tracks for Lennie to practice with for the times when we were on the road. He wanted to know also on what sequence was "E 32nd St" based. Unsuspecting, I told him, and shortly afterwards there appeared a scathing review of Lennie's playing, implying that Lennie had somehow cheated with what he had done. It gave the impression that he, the critic, had worked out for himself the chord sequence – which actually was on a standard tune ("Pennies from Heaven") originally in a major mode but changed to a minor mode. The critic failed to hear for himself what the changes were and then panned the record as though he himself had figured it all out. (This is not the only time a critic has described something that didn't happen: recently I was amused to see an article about a performance I played with Lee in London – the critic there had been so inventive that the piano player in the previous part of the performance had now become part of our trio and somehow we had lost our guitarist!) The experience with John Mehegan taught me to be somewhat more circumspect in my dealings with the press from then on. When he read the review, Lennie asked me about it, and I told him what had happened. He was none too pleased. Lennie always wanted others to figure out for themselves what was going on.

After Mehegan's review was published in *Down Beat*, Warne Marsh quickly came to Lennie's defence and wrote to the magazine, "I feel obligated to point out that John Mehegan's eloquent appraisal of Lennie Tristano's recording technique on 'Line Up' and 'East 32nd Street' is eloquently incorrect ... however I don't hope to be able to illustrate this to John as long as he insists upon regarding Lennie's music as a personal challenge, rendering him incapable, of course, of simply listening to the music" (Chamberlain 2000: 99–100).

Though times were changing for jazz music and for Lennie and for the group of musicians associated with him, I failed to realize it. There was still plenty of music work for jazz musicians. Though the cost of living began to rise, without commensurate increases in pay, I had regular work during 1955–56 at the Hickory House. This was the last of the 52nd Street jazz clubs, owned by John Popkin. He was very good to the musicians he hired and always respected them. I was part of the trio (along with Ed Thigpen) led by pianist Jutta Hipp, whom Leonard Feather had discovered playing in a club in Duisberg in Germany. Recognizing her unique talent, he arranged for her to come to New York, and it was on this, her first American engagement, that we played together. It was a good time for me musically and financially. I earned a regular salary for almost a year. I had a nice apartment on Riverside Drive. I was starting to record more with Lee Konitz, and I began to feel secure in the jazz world. There was also a double album of Jutta and her trio recorded by Blue Note.

All this obscured for me the changes that were happening in the jazz world. It wasn't simply that improvisation had ceased, it was more the case that improvisation was no longer at the center of things. Musicians formed groups with the specific aim of getting a hit record. Even I was offered the chance. In the mid-fifties, while I was still working in Lee's band, Joe Glaser and George Wein had approached me, offering to take me under their wing with a band of my own. Joe, along with George Wein, was managing Lee's band at that time and he was of course also Louis Armstrong's manager and agent. He had some well-known connections and I felt that that scene was too heavy for me. My personal aim was to develop further as a musician rather than taking that route. I had already seen that not everyone offered this opportunity succeeded. I suppose I wanted success on my own terms, so I declined the offer. I failed to realize at the time that such an offer was unlikely to be repeated!

Even Lee Konitz (not the most commercial of jazz musicians) specifically tried to record a track that might become a hit. He recorded a very melodic "Crazy She Calls Me" and "Stairway to the Stars" on an album for Verve with the hope that this would get air play. But, although those two tracks are very beautiful, they did not get the hoped-for commercial attention.

Though I continued to work, it was becoming apparent that there was less work available generally and another generation of musicians was arriving on the scene: Horace Silver, Jackie McLean, John Coltrane, Sonny Rollins and Canonball Adderley, for example. (You can see that years later a similar phenomenon occurred on the rock scene. At first there were relatively few bands – the pioneers of the new music – but, as the popularity of the music increased, more bands formed than could be accommodated by what then became known as the music industry.) The newer generation of jazz musicians formed its own coteries.

During the next few years, the Musicians' Union, which had formerly been a closed shop, began to lose its grip. Previously, it had been impossible to obtain work unless you were a union member. A number of bars, especially in the Greenwich Village area, began to encourage live music jam sessions, for which there was little, if any, pay. It was, however, another arena for jazz musicians to play in. By this time more musicians were openly flouting the union. Taking work below union rates caused a free fall in earnings generally.

By the early sixties, there were significant differences between those who were successful, establishing national and international reputations, and others, working on the fringe of the scene, striving for a piece of the pie. So much has been written about black (and white) jazz – but what remained unrecognized was the emergence of so many new jazz musicians generally and the resulting lack of working opportunity. This created a situation of severe competition, which was reflected in the music. Jazz became hard, hard bop, racially divided in a way not seen before. Whereas the racial divide had previously been a social phenomenon, it now became a commercial phenomenon. It too reflected the growing competitiveness of American life. The influence of the hard, unforgiving commercial music (promoted by the music business) became reflected throughout the world of jazz. It has also, I fear, contributed to the diminishing popularity of jazz in recent years.

Bird did not live to witness these changes. Lennie did. By 1959, even though he was still working gigs – for example, playing at the Half Note, back again with Lee and Warne and various rhythm sections as well as touring that year – he was concentrating on his teaching. Only one new recording of his was released. During this period I was also recording freelance as a recording engineer/studio owner, coupled with a residency along with Al Schackman and Ronnie Ball at the Den and the Duane Hotel on Madison Avenue. It was around that period, 1959 to 1961, that I offered to record Lennie. I was well aware of his reluctance to record unless he had total control of the recording. I offered to record and give him the tapes to do what he wanted with them. As I saw it, at that time he had recorded so little and it seemed wrong for such wonderful music not to be recorded. But he had refused.

On one occasion, when Lennie was not playing at the Half Note, but the rest of the group were with Bill Evans on piano, I recorded it for Verve. This record was subsequently released. Occasionally there would be live radio broadcasts at the Half Note. One, scheduled during one of Lennie's engagements there, stays in my memory. But Warne had obviously arrived late. What we heard was an elaborate introduction by an overawed announcer, effusively announcing Lennie as the high priest of jazz, when in the background sounds of the club could be heard clearly. Then Warne's voice, rather apologetically, says (presumably to Lennie), "I called your house." Really weird – the announcer so in awe that he almost sounds castrated with nervousness, and then back to earth with Warne's apologetic comment! I don't recall any music being played on that particular broadcast. Sometime later, a TV film was made with Lennie and the group at the Half Note.

The fact that Lennie recorded so little was something of a disappointment to the many of us who recognized his incredible abilities. But when in 1962 *The New Tristano* was released, this more than compensated for the wait. This is arguably the most incredible jazz piano recording ever made. The entire album is recorded at normal speed with no overdubs. The track "C Minor Complex" is an incredible *tour de force*. Lennie said later that he wanted people to realize that, although he had overdubbed tracks on some previous recordings, he could also play like that live!

As I mentioned in Chapter 3, those earlier experiences in playing and recording with Lennie at his studio had sparked my interest in recording and I was focusing more and more on this. By the time I bought Lennie's Presto recorder (the one on which he had recorded those very first piano overdubs, "Passtime" and "JuJu") in 1956, I had created a small home studio in my Riverside Drive apartment. From that time on I always kept a studio for recording. When I moved out to Astoria, Long Island, this was first in the basement of my home, but later I rented small loft premises above a shop. Rather than becoming a commercial musician, I augmented my living as a jazz musician with sound recording assignments

By the late fifties, I had my own studio with Ampex state-of-the-art equipment. I had gotten more and more into recording. In 1957, following my father's death, I received a legacy of about $7,000. I used this money to purchase and equip my studio, after returning from a stint in Florida with Buddy Rich. I had made a number of recordings at the studio with Lee and Warne and also with the Armenian band, with whom I was gigging at that time.

In 1960 I moved from the Astoria premises to a loft on E 2nd Street, Manhattan. This was much roomier (about 1,600 square feet) and I was busy with the studio – recording for a number of jazz labels. After having completed a year's residency at the Den, I then started working with Roy Eldridge and Coleman Hawkins, with pianist Tommy Flanagan and drummer Eddie Locke. These were busy times and I seldom played with Lennie in those years, apart from on some rare occasions at the Half Note. However, in the spring of 1961, when I had an unfortunate run-in with a New York policeman (not, I should say, about narcotics), Lennie without hesitation came to court on my behalf as a character witness.

But my life was beginning to change then. In the summer of 1961 I was ill, partly through overwork and partly due to the stress of the court action (I was eventually acquitted). This was also the time I met my future wife, Barbara. I went to Europe in 1962 and reunited with Barbara in London, where we married. In November of that year our daughter Anna was born. We returned to New York in 1963, but finding playing and work conditions difficult, we moved to California in June of that year, only to find that opportunities to play jazz in Big Sur were not so great either.

Big Sur is very beautiful and we lived there for three years. During that time I had played with Lee Konitz, who was then living in Salinas (Monterey County), and for a while Warne Marsh came to live there. We used to meet on Sundays at Kim Novak's house in Carmel Highlands with the guitarist Al Schackman (who was later Nina Simone's manager), with whom Kim was then having an affair. Kim recorded a number of these Sunday-afternoon sessions; I wonder if she still has them. Also during that time there was a TV documentary about Kim, and some footage was made at Eduardo Terrella's House in Big Sur, which featured the music of Lee, Warne, Al Schackman, myself, and the LA drummer Larry Bunker. I know this was transmitted as some people in Australia once told me they had seen it. But video recorders were virtually non-existent in those days, so I suppose the only hope of finding it is in locating the film company who made it. During the recent Denver Jazz Film Festival (very ably organized by Tom Goldsmith), where we saw some incredible footage of Bud Powell, I informed the two jazz archivists who were there– Michael

Chertok and Michael Cantor – that such a film exists. Maybe they will be able to track it down. (It seemed, when I was writing this book, that many aspects of the jazz life in New York had been lost. Let's hope someone rediscovers them.)

By 1963 it didn't seem to matter whether jazz swung or not – it had gone into eclipse, with the beginnings of the rock era and the start of discotheques. It was also clear by this time that unless you had established a commercial reputation as a jazz musician, there were few gigs to be had and pickings were lean. There were still jazz clubs, to be sure but, despite increasing inflation, these paid even less than during the early fifties. From the point of view of the jazz musician, rock music appeared crude and unskilled. Jazz musicians sometimes found work in recording studios, but often merely to give backing to rock stars. This was especially so in the UK. It all gave rise to much bitterness and disappointment among jazz musicians, apart from those who had succeeded in maintaining a high profile.

Jazz had developed a class system. There was the hierarchy: Miles Davis, Ella Fitzgerald, Nina Simone, Carmen McRae, Sarah Vaughan, the Count Basie and Ellington bands, Dave Brubeck, Stan Getz, Jazz at the Philharmonic, Newport All Stars etc. If you were fortunate enough to be included (even as an accompanist) a good or at least reasonable livelihood was possible. If not, you might have recourse to teaching which, by then, was beginning to be considered a legitimate occupation. To join the hierarchy at this late date in jazz development, you could seldom rely on talent alone. You had to become a personality, and find a very good promoter or agent. This was not so easy, especially given the competition of the rock and pop world. Music was becoming theater first and foremost; musical content was secondary. Though I am well aware that some aspects of pop and world music have genuinely enriched musical development, the other side of this coin is that a simple, even trite melody can with suitable promotion become part of modern folk tradition. The beauty and subtleties of the kind of lines and improvisation that Lennie created are lost in the proliferation of commercial music. Many people believe that this music of Lennie's is worthy of far greater attention than it has received so far. I regularly receive emails and correspondence from people who say so. My hope is that, eventually, after the wheel has turned full circle, the beauty of this music will again be recognized and reach a new popularity.

There have now been eighty-plus years of jazz development, with creative endeavors reaching higher and higher, through Louis Armstrong, Lester Young, Charlie Christian, Roy Eldridge, Charlie (Bird) Parker, Bud

Powell, Clifford Brown, Lennie Tristano, Lee Konitz, Warne Marsh, and many others. As the music soared to ever greater heights of creativity and subtlety, it obviously attracted attention and interest. Commercial interests utilized this for their own means, to make money – using whoever would suit their purposes and promoting easy-listening music. This has meant that some of the greatest talents in jazz have been overlooked. Lest such a view be dismissed as one-sided (or sour grapes), I should point out that Bird, for example, is probably revered largely because of his early death and wild living. Put on one of Bird's great records before a group of jazz lovers. My guess is that before thirty seconds of the music elapses they will no longer be listening, but talking.

Clint Eastwood made a movie about Bird. It is said that Mr. Eastwood loved Bird's music and that this was what motivated him. In making the movie they used Bird's recordings and with today's technology they isolated Bird's playing from the old recordings and re-recorded his music with present-day rhythm sections. Possibly that was considered a technical necessity, so that this could be synchronized with the actors' performances. But to a jazzman's ears it sounded artificial – particularly if you were familiar with the original recordings. One of the strangest examples (to me) occurred where they had taken a recording of Bird playing with Lennie, having erased Lennie's playing from the track. I had never had the opportunity to hear those tracks as they were originally recorded, but from the kind of tempo alone it was obvious to me that it was Lennie.

As with many jazz movies, *Bird* only confirmed for me the general public attitude toward jazz as being attractive because of its anti-social, outrageous loucheness – born of the underprivileged and belonging to the other side of the tracks. To me the film was only a caricature of the reality of a great musical tradition and represented the musical freedom of the fifties and sixties in a very superficial way. But of course, as is well known, Hollywood and reality belong on different planets. Bird lives in his recordings. Lennie lives in his recordings – let's listen to their music.

It is pertinent to recall the opinion of Paul Goodman, co-author of the book *Gestalt Psychology*, that the media control opinion not by out and out censorship, but by swamping alternate views with massive output. I feel that Lennie's concern and conservatism about his recordings have played their part in his comparative obscurity today. On the other hand, virtually all his recordings are masterpieces of improvisation – in many ways, they are still avant-garde (in the true sense) even fifty years after they were made. Fortunately, there are enough people around who still appreciate his music, despite his relative obscurity. Michael Cuscuna of Mosaic Records has recently released a boxed set of Lennie's Atlantic recordings, which include his most prominent associates, Lee Konitz and Warne Marsh. One of Lennie's recordings, apparently lost for years, concerned a concert in Toronto in the summer of 1952. We flew from La Guardia to Toronto and played for a jazz society there – which was recorded. The personnel were Lennie on piano, Lee Konitz and Warne Marsh on saxes, Al Levitt on drums, and myself on bass. This recording was released thirty-five years later. I think it was the longest time ever that I waited to be paid for a recording. Though the recording quality leaves much to be desired, the music is a valuable addition to what little has been preserved.

For me, life moved in a completely different direction. In 1966 I returned with my family to the UK and commenced teaching and playing gigs in London. In 1967, after having started the teaching courses at Leeds Music College, I had the opportunity, through Bernie Cash, of inviting Lennie to play at the Harrogate Festival. It was not easy to entice Lennie away from his home in New York and of course there was his teaching schedule to consider. I remember his insisting upon an air-conditioned hotel. In those days air conditioning in British hotels was unheard of. The climate was seldom that warm anyway. Even the best hotel in Harrogate, the Grand, could not boast of such modern technology. So for a while it seemed the concert would not take place. There was also considerable opposition, as the jazz committee wanted to book a more "commercial" jazz artist. But the gods were with us. Unable to convince Lennie that air conditioning was not a necessity in Britain, I finally said to him, "Bring a sweater – you'll need warm clothes." And so, on meeting him at the airport and then in the car to Harrogate, we were all the while exchanging news about New York and about the UK etc. Finally, the night of the concert arrived. All seats had been sold. There were two sets – the first with an English group, Bruce Turner (alto), Chas Burchell (tenor), Dave Cliff and Derek Phillips (guitar), and Bernie Cash (bass). All were great admirers of Lennie and had carefully rehearsed some of his "lines." Then, for the following set, Lennie and I played together. Finally, as an encore, we all played together. It was a memorable concert.

To my knowledge, unfortunately no recordings were made. Maybe someone in the audience recorded it secretly on a cassette – but nothing has come to light. It turned out to be the last time that we played together. After the concert a group of us went back to the hotel and talked for hours. It was a highlight of my life, as I'm sure it was for the others. Lennie had often said that although he was no showman he could always be entertaining among friends and that night was no exception. We were all busy talking.

By about 1 a.m. Lennie said, "Is anybody hungry?" It was then that we all realized that we hadn't eaten for hours. Whereupon Lennie rang for room service. You have to remember this was post-war England, with little idea of, or inclination for, service in its hotels. Lennie, however, with his American background, called room service just expecting it to arrive. We, being used to the English attitude, foresaw problems and waited apprehensively. A few minutes later, a man appeared in a rather well-worn tuxedo. "Yes sir – you rang?" Lennie said, "My friends and I are hungry. We would like something to eat." "I'm sorry sir – kitchen's closed," came the reply. "Kitchen's closed?" said Lennie incredulously. "Yes sir." "But why?" said Lennie. "It's 1.15 in the morning," said our room service friend. "But surely a hotel is expected to cater for its guests?" said Lennie. "It's not for me to say," came the reply. "But don't you believe that a hotel should cater for its guests regardless of what time of day it is?" asked Lennie. (All of Lennie's questioning was said in a quiet respectful manner – no offense could possibly be taken by our room service friend.) Nevertheless, room service was beginning to get rattled. "I don't believe in anything," he said. "You don't believe in anything?" said Lennie. "That's right – I don't believe in anything." "You don't believe in God?" asked Lennie. "That's right." "Do you believe in money?" asked Lennie. Room service – by this time weakening somewhat: "Yes, I believe in money." "Well we believe in food," said Lennie, holding up a fifty-dollar bill in front of him. "If you get us what we believe in you can have what you believe in." And in minutes a huge spread arrived, which was shared with relish by all. When recently I related this to Lennie's daughter Carol, she exclaimed, "*That* was Lennie!" Lennie was always disarmingly open and very perceptive; perhaps this story of the evening at the Grand Hotel, Harrogate, conveys more than anything the strength and calmness of Lennie's personality.

During Lennie's visit to the UK in 1967, we had a good opportunity to talk about past times and what we had experienced. Lennie had seldom felt satisfied with the rhythm sections he had used. When he stretched out, with his multiple rhythms, most rhythm sections would tighten up, unable to follow the complexity of his lines. Also Lennie used to like to "lay back on the time," as though it were a cushion. Erroll Garner was also notable in this respect, and it tended to make the rhythm sections slow down. One can hear this clearly on some of Erroll's recordings. But Erroll did not embark on the kind of rhythmic adventures that Lennie enjoyed. Lennie expressed his surprise at why he had not asked me to play more with him in those latter years of the fifties, and he spoke well of the rhythm section of Jeff Norton and I, which was good to hear. But by the time we had talked about this I had moved on. I had already spent several years in California and then the UK.

We met again briefly – during the summer of 1973. I had been on a trip to the USA with my family. He was very welcoming and though there was no opportunity for us to play together at that time, we had a wonderful visit. He died in 1978, at barely sixty years of age. I don't know the cause of his death. I know that there was talk about taking out his eyes, due to infection or deterioration. But I don't know the details. Recently Ted Brown told me that he recommended studying with Lennie, toward the end of Lennie's life, and it seems he was drinking heavily at that time. (He was not a drinker when I knew him.) Ted said that Lennie had a bottle of spirits always by his side. He once asked Ted to play something – an exercise – and when Ted had finished he found that Lennie had nodded off. (It is very sad for me to write this, but I need to give a balanced picture.) I will say that the impression I have got was that in those later years he was not well enough to continue teaching but presumably had to earn a living. Lennie's death was a shock to us all. With someone of such personal strength, it's hard to realize that they're no longer around. But those few records – now re-released on CD – are always there to remind us. He was a musical genius and a great teacher. I like to think that, as is the case with Johann Sebastian Bach, whose music lacked appreciation for so long, the time is coming when the real worth of Lennie's contribution to jazz will be fully appreciated.

6 lennie's influence and what happened to his associates from those fifties days

We have discussed what happened to Lennie, as far as I am aware, after those days when we played together. But what happened to all his associates with whom we worked and played during that time? I have kept in touch with some and contacted others to try and piece together this part of Lennie's legacy. Safford Chamberlain's recent book about Warne Marsh, *An Unsung Cat*, is the first book written about one of his close associates. Safford knew Warne personally and the book is a very informative and sympathetic portrait of Warne's life. It also includes insight into Lennie's life and personality. Ironically, this is the first book to be written about Lennie – though I believe he has been the subject of at least one PhD. Lee Konitz is, of course, well known in the jazz world (and a biography is being written of him). Clearly in a book of this size it is not feasible to include more than a brief pen portrait of his other associates as I knew them, and what I have heard and seen since.

Lennie's uncompromising spirit is undoubtedly one reason why he is less well known than he deserves to be. Many of his close associates had a similar outlook. But the problem of how to earn a living challenged not only Lennie but all of us. Several of his associates are major jazz talents in their own right, yet with the possible exception of Lee, they have not received anything like the recognition they deserved.

For those, including myself, who sustained the belief that we had a prime duty to the spirit of the music alone, it has meant an uphill struggle to survive. Of all of us, Lee has been the most successful; still considered avant-garde by many, he is one of the most prolific of jazz recording artists.

Lee Konitz (b. 1927)

The alto saxophonist Lee Konitz is certainly the most recorded, and arguably the most prominent, of Lennie's associates. Born October 13, 1927

– just a fortnight before his tenor sax colleague Warne Marsh – he was, like Warne, a most precocious talent. These two young musicians were a very powerful duo at the time of the seminal recordings with Lennie.

At just twenty-one years of age he had recorded with Lennie's Sextet, those most wonderful sides "Wow" and "Crosscurrent" and it is not only the mastery of his playing on the lines but the improvised solos that evince total maturity. Reminiscing about the early days of Tristano, Lee spoke about Warne: "There were times when [Warne] really felt like a brother, for moments, mainly because we had this mutual affinity with Lennie." Their musical rapport he described as a kind of "magic," a "mysterious" something that "was really special." (Chamberlain 2000: 280)

In addition, the same year, he had recorded sides as a leader with guitarist Billy Bauer and played as a soloist on the memorable album led by Miles Davis, later issued as *The Birth of the Cool*.

Despite this early success and the well-deserved recognition it engendered, it remained a difficult time for Lee financially. Gigs, though fairly frequent, did not pay that well, at least not well enough to enable him to raise and keep a family. After emigrating to New York, and awaiting my Musicians' Union card (six-month US residency being required in those days), I obtained temporary employment at the office of the British Information Services in the Rockefeller Plaza. Lee, whom I had already met and played with (at that memorable evening at Birdland with Lennie's sextet in 1950), was in need of some "extra bread" and really struggling, and I managed to find some day work for him at that establishment. It was an interesting introduction for Lee to quaint English habits: "They spend all day saying 'Good morning,'" he said. Fortunately for Lee, this was of brief duration – a hiatus in an otherwise successful career. This was May 1951.

Lest one believe that artistic success equates with material success, consider how he was viewed by the renowned jazz critic Joachim Berendt, at the very time Lee was experiencing severe financial difficulties.

While all the other instruments during the great days of bop produced important musicians in addition to the leading representative on the respective horn, the alto saxophone had to wait for the start of the cool era for a considerable figure to emerge: This was Lee Konitz, who came out of the Lennie Tristano school. The abstract, glittering alto lines played by Konitz around the turn of the forties on his own and Lennie Tristano's recordings later became more singable, calmer, and more concrete. Of this change, Lee says that then "I played more than I could hear" … Konitz has absorbed and incorporated into his music many of the jazz elements since then – and some of Coltrane and of free jazz

> – and yet he has always remained true to himself. He is one of the really
> great improvisers in jazz. (Berendt 1983: 239)

Ironically Berendt fails to point out that Lee was part of the very first free jazz improvisations ever recorded – a decade before the so-called "free jazz" movement took the limelight. So who influenced whom?

During 1951, we used to meet regularly and play sometimes at Lee's house in Elmhurst, Long Island. We were often joined by Sal Mosca on piano, Willie Dennis on trombone, Don Ferrara on trumpet, and Warne Marsh and Ted Brown on tenor saxes. From time to time there were some gigs, and in 1952 Lee left to go on the road with the Stan Kenton band. During that stint with the band Lee recorded some wonderful solos – which sound outstanding and fresh to this day. While in California with the Kenton band, he recorded, with Gerry Mulligan and Chet Baker, an album for promoter Dick Bock at the Los Angeles club The Haig. This was the famous piano-less group, with Gerry on baritone sax, Chet Baker on trumpet, Carson Smith on bass and Larry Bunker on drums. After leaving the Kenton band in late 1953 to form his own group, he found a new manager in pianist George Wein, running the Storyville Club in Boston. This resulted in my joining his group and several albums were made, the first being recorded early in 1954. Simply entitled *Konitz*, this ten-inch LP really established Lee as a leader. In addition to Lee, there was the British pianist Ronnie Ball, with whom I had worked in the UK and on the *Queen Mary*. Jeff Morton was the drummer, with myself on bass. Following this Lee took the band to Boston, where we spent some time in residency at George Wein's club Storyville, then located at the Copley Square Hotel in Boston's Back Bay area. In addition to *Konitz*, two ten-inch LPs were made at that time on George Wein's Storyville label; one featured the other personnel listed above, the other had Al Levitt on drums and Percy Heath on bass. These have since been re-released on the Black Lion label.

During this time Lee took the quartet on the road, and we played at the Colonial Tavern in Toronto, the Blue Note in Philadelphia, the Comedy Club on Pennsylvania Avenue, in Baltimore, in Washington DC, and in the Crystal in Detroit. During that year we also played opposite Louis Armstrong at Basin St West with Velma Middleton (vocals), Arvell Shaw (bass), Trummy Young (trombone), Ed Hall (clarinet), and Barrett Deems (drums). That reminds me of a story I heard recently about Barrett, who led a big band in his later years. I remember him from that gig (about 1954): at that time, Barrett seemed quite a character, giving the impression of being an affluent and reformed hobo. I remember that he had a Mickey Mouse pocket watch encrusted in diamonds, the legs of which went round and told the time. But that was way back in the mid-fifties.

By the late nineties, Barrett – by then well into his eighties – married a young saxophonist in his band. She was over forty years his junior. A British jazz critic congratulated him on his marriage, then asked Barrett, "Are you concerned at all about the disparity in your ages?" Barrett replied, "If she dies, she dies."

In December 1954 we drove (Lee, Ronnie, Jeff, and myself) to Hollywood and were resident first at the Tiffany Club and later at Maynard Sloate's Modern Jazz Room till the end of January 1955. Driving back to New York in early February we were booked to play at a club in Kansas City. We arrived to find a foot or more of snow and a police notice pinned on the club door announcing its closure, necessitating a weary drive back to the Big Apple to new pastures. Shortly afterwards, I left Lee's band for what turned out to be a year's residency at New York's Hickory House. We nevertheless continued to play together from time to time. I remember one memorable evening at the Cork 'n' Bib in Hempstead, Long Island, when in addition to Lee's group Billie Holiday was appearing. This was in 1956 – during the time the infamous cabaret card requirement was in force. A zealous New York police ruling meant that no one could obtain a cabaret card to work in New York City if they had a police record. One unfortunate musician, who had been picked up several years before in the Deep South and had been jailed merely for hitchhiking, was therefore unable to work as a musician in New York City. By 1956, Billie Holiday had been in and out of jail a number of times for possession of narcotics. Of course this prevented her too from working in New York, but when word got around that she was due to appear at the Cork 'n' Bib, people came from all over to hear her. She brought with her her accompanist, Mal Waldron, but we also had the good fortune and privilege to accompany her on some of her tunes. This was the first and only time for me – and I believe for Lee also. A night to remember.

In February 1957 Lee was invited to bring his group to Pittsburgh to play at the Midway Lounge in the Golden Triangle. The group was initially a quartet with Billy Bauer on guitar, drummer Dick Scott and, on the weekend, trumpeter Don Ferrara joined us. Lee had recently recorded for Atlantic Records on an album called *Lee Konitz in Hi Fi*, with Don on trumpet, Sal Mosca on piano, Shadow Wilson on drums and myself on bass. The Pittsburgh gig proved popular, and when the owner invited us to stay for another week, Billy and I drove all the way back to New York on our day off to pick up my recording equipment. We taped for much of the following week. The result of this was the album *The Real Lee Konitz*, subsequently released by Atlantic Records. The following year (1958), after a stint with Buddy Rich in Miami, I rejoined Lee's band at the Greenwich Village venue, the Half Note. We made a number of recordings there – none of which has yet been released, apart from one I recorded for Lee and Warne in 1959 with Henry Grimes on bass and Paul Motian on drums. This was released on Verve. As I discussed in Chapter 5, in February 1960 I relocated to a loft studio in Manhattan's East Village. This became the location for many jazz recordings. There were a number of recordings in which Lee participated. Recently we have discussed the possibility of releasing some of these.

During the sixties Lee continued his prolific recording career, but our paths divided again after I returned to the UK in 1962. I met Lee again in 1963 after I had moved to Big Sur, California. Lee had moved to Salinas, in Monterey County, and we had a surprise meeting after Lee had visited the Big Sur restaurant Nepenthe, enquiring as to the possibility of music work. Bill Fasset (painter Kaffe Fasset's father), who owned Nepenthe, pointed over to our house on the opposite mountain and our meeting led to us working together frequently in San Francisco and San Jose. Big Sur was a meeting place for many artists and musicians during the mid-sixties and guitarist Al Schackman moved there briefly during 1964 and 1965. In 1965 Warne Marsh also moved to the area and we all used to play together on Sunday afternoons at Kim Novak's house just south of Monterey in Carmel Highlands.

After that time in California, our paths did not cross again until 1975. Lee had been booked to appear at Ronnie Scott's Club in London. Meanwhile, Warne had gone to Denmark to play concerts for the Danish Jazz Society. I suggested to Lee that we team up together. I contacted drummer Al Levitt, who was then living in Paris. We re-formed, with the addition of the British guitarist Dave Cliff. During the remainder of that year and most of 1976, we toured Europe – sometimes with Warne, sometimes as a quartet – playing Lennie's lines, plus those of both Lee and Warne. During that time a number of recordings were made, some for the Danish Storyville label, some for an Italian label and one that I personally recorded and subsequently released on Wave. As an example of how jazz politics intrude into the music, I have described some aspects of this tour in Chapter 11 of this book.

During the final quarter of the last century Lee was very successful indeed, becoming one of the most prolific jazz recording artists. We played together briefly while I was running the Bass Clef Club in London, and we played together again in November 2002 at the Queen Elizabeth Hall, on London's South Bank. For me it was a very enjoyable reunion – fifty-two years after we first played together with Lennie's group in New York's Birdland.

Warne Marsh (b. 1927, d. 1987)

Born October 26th, 1927, Warne Marsh, tenor saxophonist, was one of the original members of Lennie's sextet. He came to New York from his birthplace, Los Angeles. Warne's father, Oliver Marsh, had been a well-known Hollywood cameraman. With a relatively affluent background, Warne was not so subject to the financial pressures that Lee had experienced during his early professional years. The fact that they came together and played so remarkably – and were virtually the same age – makes it appear that their early professional years indicated a kind of destiny. In some ways Warne reached musical maturity after Lee; on the early sextet records Lee's playing sounds far more assured. But as the years passed by, Warne developed a clear direction of his own, though Lennie's influence was always detectable. He never received fame as a major jazz artist in his lifetime and experienced lean times during the early fifties, but he recorded prolifically, mainly for small, independent labels. Later he moved back to California, but despite his growing reputation he found it necessary from time to time to take mundane work (cleaning swimming pools etc.) between music gigs.

When he first moved back to California in 1956 he led his own group there (with fellow tenor saxophonist Ted Brown, pianist Ronnie Ball, drummer Jeff Morton and bassist Ben Tucker). You then began to hear the mature Warne, an improvising talent second to none. One early recording in particular stands out. This is the Metronome All Stars session of 1952. Warne played a superb sixteen bars on "How High the Moon". For sheer improvisatory inventiveness it stands out from all the other solos. Already, in those days, you could begin to detect that jazz such as Warne was creating was going beyond popular taste. For commercial success, it was just too good. Nevertheless, Warne has developed a considerable following over the years, which has gradually increased since his death in 1987.

But during the early fifties he lived mostly in New York, playing the occasional gig and jamming frequently at Lennie's studio. Sometimes, also, we would rent a studio to give us more opportunity to play. In 1955 Warne and Lee recorded for Atlantic Records, with Ronnie Ball (piano), Oscar Pettiford (bass), Kenny Clarke (drums), Billy Bauer (guitar), and pianist Sal Mosca on one of the tracks. Out of print for a long time, it is now again available as part of the six-CD set of the former Atlantic Records catalogue of Lennie and his associates. Another album for Atlantic featured Warne as leader, with a rhythm section of Paul Chambers and Philly Joe Jones. In 1959 Warne again returned to New York. In the summer of that year, Lee and Warne rented my Long Island studio for three months, while I took a trip to Europe. Always introspective in character, music was almost his sole interest (apart from pinochle and chess).

"He had the kind of analytical mind that made him an advanced chess player and that in music led him to exploit unusual time divisions and manipulations of meter. One of his girlfriends, wondering at his choice of jazz as a profession, expressed a common attitude when she said, 'He could have been a nuclear physicist' " (Chamberlain 2000: 4).

Shortly before I left on my European trip, I helped Warne put up some of his pictures in the studio. I stood on some steps with hammer and nails while Warne held the picture over his head. In a totally dispassionate voice he said, "You won't hit my head with that hammer, will you Pete." This was a man of very few words.

> Family members have said that as a child Marsh did not talk until very late, perhaps as late as three and a half or four. He understood perfectly well, would follow directions, such as "Go get Aunt Minnie's straw hat," but he did not speak. When pianist Susan Chen, his student and colleague and lover in the early 1980s, asked him about it, he replied in characteristically laconic fashion, "There wasn't much to say." (Chamberlain 2000: 3)

I was not surprised when the only contact from him, after I sent him the completed tape for our record, was a terse postcard: "Release record, send tape." Hence the name of the Wave vinyl album and CD.

He was also a straight-talking person. Again from Safford Chamberlain's book, one quote sums this up:

> In a lecture for the Composition Department at the Norwegian State Academy which prided itself on its modernity, Marsh gained the enmity of many in the audience when a student asked his opinion of Arnold Schoenberg. After a motionless interval of ten seconds, he said, "Schoenberg was probably the worst crock of them all, because he was the first composer that managed to write music to death." Another student asked, "Mr. Marsh, what do you think about improvisation on quarter tones?" Quarter tones can be played on string or wind instruments but not on the piano, which is limited to the half tones on the chromatic scale. To answer the question, Marsh walked to the grand piano in the room, played middle C, and asked the student to sing a C major triad (C-E-G). The student did so, but with imperfect pitch. "If you can't do that," said Marsh, "why bother with quarter tones?" (Chamberlain 2000: 253)

Warne continued to spend more time in New York during 1960 and 1961. This was the time when I had relocated my studio to the East Village in Manhattan. Trying to achieve the most natural recording conditions, I used to put the tape on at seven and a half IPS (fifteen CPS) – which with long-playing tape gave us an hour and a half of uninterrupted recording time. After setting a balance on the mikes, I lowered the input so that even if someone suddenly played too loud, the recording would not distort. This had the disadvantage of increasing the signal to noise ratio, but I felt it was worth it if we could obtain recordings without feeling the usual pressure of limited time or interruptions from a recording engineer. The two albums that I recorded of Warne and subsequently released on Wave – *Jazz from the East Village* and *Release Record, Send Tape* – were recorded that way. Now that I have released this music on CD, with the aid of digital remastering, the quality obtainable is superb. Some reviewers have described these two CDs as containing the best of Warne's playing. I feel this was because the tape ran without interruption, there being no intrusion at all on the playing.

I left New York late in 1961 and did not see Warne again until June 1963, when I moved to Big Sur, California, and then met up with both Lee and Warne again. We played together for the following few months as described above.

After that time in California it was not until 1975 that we met again and both Warne and Lee embarked on those European tours. Following that, Warne returned to the USA, and also spent much time in Scandinavia playing and recording. I saw and heard him only once after that. He played with pianist Lou Levy for a few days at London's Pizza Express jazz club.

His remaining years were spent in California and were a prolific time for him, both for work and for recordings. He died on December 18, 1987 while playing a gig at Donte's in Los Angeles. Rumor has it that he had just finished playing a solo on "Out of Nowhere" when he fell back into the drums and died instantly of heart failure. (But Safford Chamberlain's account differs; Warne "finished his solo, sat on his stool, then abruptly stepped off it and staggered, gently laid his horn on the floor and lay down on his side" (Chamberlain 2000: 268). Everyone realized that he had had a heart attack. Phyllis Brown, tenorist Ted Brown's wife – who was also a part of our group in the early days – said that in the last months of his life Warne had suffered so badly from heart problems that his wife Gerry had to carry his sax on to the stand for him. Yet he continued to play as though totally inspired and physically fit. He was just sixty years of age.

Sal Mosca (b. 1927)

Sal, born April 27, 1927, was from Mount Vernon, New York, and has lived there all his life. He was very much a part of the group and from the mid-fifties onward we used to meet regularly to play as a duo as well as playing at the numerous sessions we held all through the fifties and early sixties. He had also been a student of Lennie's and though Lennie's influence is clear in his playing he is very much an original creator. In addition to some of the early recordings he made with Lee for Prestige Records, he has recorded a number of albums under his own name. I released a couple of albums featuring him during the late sixties, initially recorded during my sojourn in New York. Much of this music was recorded live in a nightclub, the Den at the Duane Hotel on Madison and 37th Street. He is also featured on the first of the Wave albums, *Looking Out*. Sal has continued to play and teach throughout the years, and is highly regarded as a musicians' musician. Despite his high artistic merit, he has not yet attained the recognition he deserves. When I last visited him in the summer of 1999 at his Mount Vernon studio, a decline in health meant that he was not playing or teaching at that time. Since then his health has improved and I hear that he is now playing jazz again.

A story that illustrates that we were all living lives as well as focused and deeply committed to our music: in the mid-fifties, I used to like to get away from the city from time to time – from the pollution, the noise, and the general stress of city life – and would often take a day or so off and drive up to New England and camp overnight. On one occasion, Sal with his young son Michael, then five years old, came with me on a trip. We took about three days and drove up to Vermont to one of the most beautiful and verdant areas out on the East Coast of America. In order to get back to New York City on time, we left really early, about 4.45 a.m. About fifteen minutes later, we found ourselves driving through a sleepy Vermont town and Michael spied an old fire engine on show outside the fire station in the middle of town. We stopped to let Michael look at it and before we realized what was happening Michael had climbed up on the engine and was ringing the fire bell like crazy – an ear-piercing sound. Sal grabbed Michael and we took off like a rocket, having woken up half the township. A case of jazz musicians waking people up to music – even as family men! (Sal's son Michael, who is now the chief of police in Mount Vernon, New York, reminded me of this incident when I visited both Michael and Sal a couple of years ago.)

It is a sad but telling reality that in Joachim Berendt's *Jazz Book* – claimed by its publishers to be simply the best modern companion to jazz available – there is no mention of Sal, despite his numerous recordings and the strength and beauty of his playing. This is also true of trumpeter Don Ferrara, pianist Ronnie Ball, tenor saxophonist Ted Brown, drummers Jeff Morton and Al Levitt, and bassist Arnold Fishkin. With the exceptions of

Don, Jeff, Arnold, and Al, the others all had significant recordings released under their leadership. Don was the featured trumpeter on Gerry Mulligan's recording *Gone Fishin'* and also featured prominently on several of Lee Konitz's acclaimed recordings. As for Jeff Morton and Al Levitt, there are numerous recordings that showcase their respective talents, but despite this Berendt did not think fit to recognize this.

Ronnie Ball (b. 1927, d. 1984)

Like myself, Ronnie was an émigré from the UK. He was born on December 22, 1927, and was originally from Birmingham, in the Midlands, but came to London as a teenager and quickly emerged as a new jazz talent on the London scene. He formed a trio with drummer Tony Kinsey, also from Birmingham. He played with Ronnie Scott, Harry Klein and many of the musicians who were influenced by the new bebop movement taking place in the USA. In late summer of 1949 he obtained employment on the *Queen Mary*. Ronnie's time on the liner coincided with mine and we spent some great times playing and jamming after hours. Ronnie was very meticulous about his approach and used every available opportunity to practice on the pianos in the lounges after the passengers had retired for the night. It was through Ronnie that I realized the great advantages of consistent practice.

I believe he was the first of us to commence his studying with Lennie: as I described in Chapter 2, we both went to hear Lennie's sextet at the Orchid Room on 52nd Street and Ronnie introduced himself to Lennie. In 1952 he obtained his immigration visa and went to live in New York. Once he had his union card, he was soon playing in the New York jazz clubs alongside many of the jazz luminaries of the time. Also he was regularly at the sessions organized by Lennie at his studio. He contracted a mild form of TB at that time, but after a spell in hospital, he completely recovered and soon became in demand. The New York Club scene was still strong during that time, even though the era of 52nd Street was virtually at a close. During that time Ronnie worked with Chuck Wayne, with Bird, and many other well-known musicians.

Ronnie and I joined Lee's band in 1953 and we traveled around the States, working a week here and a week there, New York, Philadelphia, Detroit, Boston, Toronto, Cleveland, Los Angeles, Baltimore, etc. Unlike today, bands in the fifties usually traveled by road. Usually this would be a station wagon with bass, drums and horns in the back, together with personal baggage, while we would takes turns driving. Going to the West Coast from New York could take several days, although the first time I went there (in Lee's band, with Ronnie and Jeff) we drove to Columbus Ohio (600 miles), played a gig there and the following day set out for California. Ronnie was not a driver, so Lee, Jeff, and I would take turns each time we filled with gas; we would change only when the tank was virtually empty. From Columbus, Ohio, we reached Hollywood in fifty-two hours (a distance of about 2,400 miles). When we climbed out of the vehicle we were so tired our legs collapsed under us. We did a ten-week stint altogether, arriving in December 1954 and returning to New York in February 1955. Ronnie had previously recorded three albums with Lee, the one entitled *Konitz*, a second recorded at Storyville and the third *Lee Konitz at Harvard Square*. Other recordings were *Lee Konitz and Warne Marsh* (June 1955), one with Mike Cuozzo, and another with Al Caiola, both in December 1955.

In February the following year he recorded again with Kenny Clarke, and in the same month, played on *The Jazz Message of Hank Mobley*. The following month he recorded his own album, *All About Ronnie*, with a band comprised of Ted Brown (tenor), Willie Dennis (trombone), Wendell Marshall (bass) and Kenny Clarke (drums). That June he recorded another album for Savoy with Mort Herbert, *Night People*. In the summer of 1956 Ronnie left New York again and went to live in California. He joined Warne Marsh's group at The Haig, with Warne and Ted Brown on tenor saxes, Ben Tucker on bass and Jeff Morton on drums. That band was very successful and some wonderful records were made, including one with alto saxophonist Art Pepper. He also played alongside guitarist Don Overberg and trumpeter Rolf Ericson.

At that time we were all in our mid-twenties. Playing jazz together can form bonds of friendship that in later years may stretch somewhat but are never entirely broken. This does not mean that there is any lack of professionalism, but the music conveys more than mere professional skill. In those days also we were quite aware of setting an added direction to the music – being part of something that was entirely new. It was not in any way negating what had already occurred, but it was pioneering. Listening to the recordings one can still hear that sense of excitement. For Ronnie and me it was also the excitement of acclimatizing to a new culture – in those days cultural differences between the UK and the USA were far greater than now. For us it was like moving up to a cultural front line. There was also our mutual interest in Wilhelm Reich's discoveries and writings to bind us.

During our stay in LA we worked at two clubs, the Tiffany Club and then the Modern Jazz Room near Hollywood and Vine. During one gig an astronomer from Mount Wilson came to hear us and was so taken with the music that he invited us to Mount Wilson in Pasadena to see the telescopes. By this time (1954) light pollution was seriously affecting the performance of the telescopes. We saw the sixty-inch Hooker reflector and the hundred-inch Hale reflector. These were being used for photography, but we did get a fine view of Jupiter from a smaller 'scope.

Leaving LA, the temperature was a balmy seventy degrees, but when we arrived at the observatory there was about three feet of snow and it was very cold – something we had previously not considered. Dressed in summer clothes, we felt chilled, but seeing some of the world's largest telescopes and having an astronomer explain their workings was a unique experience. We left about two o'clock in the morning. Shortly afterwards a snowstorm in the area cut off the observatory for several days – we were lucky for we would have missed our gigs had we stayed longer.

In 1955 Ronnie and I shared a Riverside Drive apartment in Manhattan. It had the advantage of having enough room for a studio. With my recording equipment and Ronnie's grand piano we recorded a number of sessions there. Though there were a number of rooms, it was not always ideal when wives or girlfriends became involved. I remember when Ronnie first met Rita – the lady he was to marry. Rita had ideas about decor. For us the place was just for sleeping, eating, and playing. As long as there were pots and pans, and bedding, everything was fine. I came in one day and Ronnie said, "Come and look at this." Their bed sported a new spread and five cushions, two big ones and, between them, three smaller ones. Without thinking I yelled, "Three kids!" That was the last thing Ronnie wanted to hear – but, sure enough, a few years later that's exactly what happened. The following year when Ronnie moved to LA, I too moved to a less expensive place in Astoria, Queens. Within a year Ronnie had moved back to Manhattan, on the Lower East Side. In December 1957, we drove to Florida to work with Buddy Rich's band. It was just a quartet with Flip Phillips on tenor. Buddy was the proverbial pain in the ass, but the music was good and very spirited. A live album was recorded at the venue in Miami Beach. Entitled *Buddy Rich in Miami*, it is still available, I believe. I stayed only for a couple of months and then headed back to New York. The new studio equipment I had purchased was ready for delivery. Later that year I recorded several sessions with Ronnie and Joe Puma on the new Ampex equipment. On his return to New York, Ronnie then worked with Kai Winding and J. J. Johnson, and I was then playing with guitarist Al Schackman at a new club called the Den. It was a trio gig and Ronnie came and joined us in 1959. (I believe this was just after he had returned from a European trip with Jazz at the Philharmonic.)

During the gig at the Den – which lasted almost a year – I recorded some of that music and used a track with Ronnie and Al on my album *Blues at the Den*. During that time I moved to a loft studio on E 2nd Street – just half a block from where Ronnie was then living. I had a really good studio there and we held many sessions. Some of this music with Ronnie was released on the Wave albums *Release Record, Send Tape* and *Jazz from the East Village*.

Ronnie was not only a remarkable pianist, but also a talented arranger and composer. Virtually all his compositions were jazz lines, some of which were recorded not only by him but also by Lee Konitz and Warne Marsh. These include "Ronnie's Tune," "Froggy Day," "Ronnie's Line," "Undersided," "Penny Packer," "Citrus Season," "Ad Libido," "Oops," "Ear Conditioning," "Quintessence," "Time's Up," "Earful," "Aretha," "Arrival," and "Coolhouse." In January 1960 Ronnie recorded with Gene Krupa's band and in June 1960 with Roy Eldridge. In 1961 he went on a tour of South America with Zoot Sims, Al Cohn, and others, recording an album with the group in Rio de Janeiro. Between 1960 and 1963 Ronnie recorded no fewer than six albums with vocalist Chris Connor. During that time Ronnie was also playing for Roy Eldridge and Coleman Hawkins.

I left New York in December 1962 and as I recall we didn't meet again. It's so strange how life takes different directions – only later one looks back and realizes a whole change has happened that didn't seem at all obvious at the time. I believe Ronnie spent more time arranging than playing in those later years. I heard he too felt disillusioned about the way the jazz scene had changed and work opportunities diminished. He died in New York in 1984, I believe of heart failure. One man – discographer Keith Pipkin, who lives in Birmingham – is also determined that Ronnie's music will not be lost. Keith told me how he discovered Ronnie's playing when he came across a copy of *Jazz at Storyville* by the Lee Konitz Quartet. Keith said that for him it was Ronnie's solos that were a revelation. I am grateful for the information he gave me to add to my memories.

Today this very underrated pianist from Birmingham is in danger of becoming a forgotten man. And to try and rectify this Keith has produced a complete discography (his contact address is at the back of this book). Birmingham should take pride in such a talented man. Keith Pipkin, having compiled the discography of Ronnie's playing, is trying to obtain funding to make more of his playing generally available. A final comment about Lennie by Ronnie himself. In an interview with Fukuda Ichiro in Japan, in the early sixties, Ronnie said, "I don't have any idol as far as pianists go; however, I really respect Lennie Tristano. Lennie is really great."

Don Ferrara (b. 1928)

Peculiarly, those of us who were recognized as associates of what was described as the Tristano School found ourselves, if not jazz pariahs, at least set apart from the world of working jazz musicians. It was not easy to understand why this should have happened. To improvise on the level that Lennie had reached and, for those of us who played with him, aspiring to raise our level, demanded more than having an instinct to play. One had to become totally involved in a musical self-development that was very different from that of most musicians, who seemed content to develop a style.

Among the jazz fraternity in general there was a kind of unspoken view that what was considered the Tristano School (a misnomer if ever there was one) did not belong to the real world. Gerry Mulligan, in particular, was outspoken in accusing Lennie of not waking up to the real world. Don Ferrara was viewed that way by many. His reaction was to keep developing his "chops." It is regrettable that so few recordings of his playing were released. Many of us earned extra income by teaching, because at least that felt less of a compromise. When we were still in our twenties, it was easier just to concentrate upon the music, but as we grew older it became a serious challenge: how to survive with as little compromise as possible. Teaching was another way to add to our income. Don concentrated on teaching but, as with the rest of us, there was little financial security.

Perhaps unthinkingly, we set ourselves apart, but also we became aware that we were also being set apart from the mainstream of jazz tradition. Don had enjoyed much success in his earlier years and from the time he was seventeen he played trumpet with some of the best big bands around. After being inducted in the US army, where he met bassist Red Mitchell – both being in the same army band – he also met Warne Marsh, who introduced him to Lennie's recordings. After leaving the army in 1947 he started studying with Lennie. Like most of us who studied, he was helped to find his direction by Lennie. Subsequently, Don became very busy working with Chubby Jackson and in 1950 joined Woody Herman's band. A year later, Don quit Woody's band and went to study with Lennie again. When I met Don in April 1951 (having just arrived in New York as an émigré), Don was already a legend, especially among those followers of Lennie's musical circle. Warne Marsh had recommended a rooming house on W 76th where Don, Ted Brown, Warne, and various other musicians were living, and that is where I found a place to live. We then started to play together frequently, sometimes at Lee's house and sometimes by renting a studio at Nola's in mid-town Manhattan.

By the mid-fifties, Don had joined Lee's band, with Sal Mosca on piano and myself on bass, usually with Dick Scott on drums, and he had played at most of the New York jazz clubs: Birdland, the Half Note and also a stint at Cafe Bohemia. He joined Gerry Mulligan around 1960, first recording with Gerry's sextet and later with Gerry's big band. I have a wonderful recording of the latter made at my New York loft studio in 1960, on which Don takes a magnificent solo. Contractual difficulties have prevented the release of this music to date.

He stayed in the New York area, playing and teaching, until 1972 when he moved to San Diego. He still plays and teaches. Ironically, it was not until June 2000 (at seventy-two years of age) that he was featured in an article in the UK magazine *Jazz Journal*. A great musician and trumpeter – and despite having made a number of notable recordings, he is not mentioned in any of the standard jazz reference books, some indication of how partisan the world of jazz is! I have in my archives a number of unreleased recordings of Don, and I hope I shall be able to release these eventually.

From 1956 until the end of 1961, I recorded many sessions, with Don, Ted, Sal, Ronnie, Willie, Lee, and Warne, mostly with Dick Scott on drums. These followed on from the sessions held at Lennie's studio on E 32nd Street. Don was one of the most frequently recorded musicians at my studio. I was concerned that these musicians were not getting the recognition they deserved. I felt that their music should be recorded, believing that eventually in later years their creativity would be recognized, and there would be a market for the release of some of these tapes. In Don's case, some of his greatest playing lies in this archive. Though there are many who do follow the music, all over the world, there are not yet enough of these enthusiasts to support commercial releases. What is notable is that those who are supporters are passionate about the music. I have tried to obtain funding to make it possible to release some of this music, but the British Arts Council tell me they are not permitted to support recordings already in existence, even if the recordings have not previously been released.

Don has perhaps had fewer recordings released than any of us: he does not have one recording released as leader. He is, however, featured on several albums with Lee Konitz: *The Real Lee Konitz*, released by Atlantic in 1958, and a companion CD recorded at the same time, at the Midway Lounge, Pittsburgh, in February 1957, *Peter Ind Presents Lee Konitz in Jazz of the Nineteen Fifties*. Another album is *The Very Cool Lee Konitz* – recorded, again for Atlantic, at Rudy Van Gelder's Hackensack studio in 1958. And then there are his recordings with the Gerry Mulligan band, notably his feature "Gone

Fishin'." Listen to the strength in his sound. As Lennie pointed out, Don has something of the intensity of Roy Eldridge, all the more remarkable considering his comparative lack of success. It takes tremendous strength of will to achieve that intensity, while facing a situation of scarcity of work opportunities. In the *Jazz Journal* feature, Don (in commenting on Lennie) enthused about working with him at New York's Half Note in 1962. He said it was the best time he had ever had playing.

Though I have always held the belief that eventually there will be a reappraisal and that the contribution of these musicians will find a rightful place in jazz history, there are few signs of this occurring as yet. Few deserve reassessment more than Don Ferrara.

Willie Dennis (William DeBernardinis, b. 1926, d. 1965)

Born in Philadelphia on January 10, 1926, Willie came to New York during the late forties. Like Don Ferrara he never made a recording as leader, and despite his unique and talented playing received little recognition. As Brian Priestley has pointed out, his work was never widely appreciated except by other musicians (Kernfeld 1988: 283). Brian also notes that some of his few recorded solos have been attributed to other players.

In 1946 Willie joined Elliot Lawrence's band. He also worked with Claude Thornhill and with Sam Donahue's band. He then studied with Lennie and there were a few rare occasions in 1950 when he appeared with Lennie's group in the newly opened Birdland. Willie was also a regular player at the loft sessions held at Lennie's E 32nd Street studio from late 1951 onwards, and it was at these sessions that we met. Some of the most exciting musical times I remember were with Lee, Warne, Don, and Willie playing some of those incredible lines composed by Lennie, Lee, and Warne. Lennie recorded some of this music but I have no idea whether the tapes still exist. Willie's playing was unique and he had a facility beyond other trombonists at that time. One of the difficulties of the trombone concerns the movement of the slide, which can restrict facility. As similar notes can be reached in more than one position of the slide, Willie developed a rare dexterity on the instrument, that came from a thorough study of all slide options. This enabled him to articulate with rapidity, often bypassing extreme movements of the slide.

Again, his studies with Lennie helped him to achieve such fluency. His playing was also characterized by a rare melodic improvisational ability. I believe that it was Willie's musical influence that brought about the popularity of the valve trombone, as other players tried to achieve similar fluency, achieving this only by using the valve instrument.

He worked and recorded with Charles Mingus, touring with him in 1956. In 1960 he joined the Gerry Mulligan concert band. He also toured with the Benny Goodman band. He was married to vocalist Morgana King. He recorded with Ronnie Ball on *All About Ronnie* for Savoy in March 1956, and subsequently joined the four-trombone band of Kai Winding and J. J. Johnson.

Despite his recognition by other musicians, Willie never achieved the success he deserved. His tragic death on July 8, 1965 in a car accident in New York's Central Park cut short a career that otherwise could and should have given him the wider success that he deserved. Joachim Berendt notes:

> Particularly individual was Willie Dennis, who died in 1965. He emerged from the Tristano school and was the actual trombone exponent of the Tristano conception. Since he formed most of his notes with his lip, he did not have to move his slide very much, and in this way achieved a fluidity on the slide trombone which few others have approximated even on the valve trombone. In addition, his tone gained much in singing grace. (Berendt 1983: 218)

Willie, along with Don Ferrara, Ronnie Ball, Sal Mosca, Lee, and Warne, often came to our informal sessions. Despite following our individual careers, we always maintained a musical and personal bond. I never saw Willie again after 1961 – and only heard of his death when I returned from California in 1966.

Billy Bauer (b. 1915, d. 2005)

Born in the Bronx of a German immigrant family, Billy Bauer's choice of profession soon became apparent, despite family misgivings. He played banjo as a child and changed to guitar in the early thirties. He first worked in a band led by clarinettist Jerry Wald, then in 1944 joined Woody Herman's First Herd. After the group disbanded in 1946 he played with Benny Goodman and Jack Teagarden. He enjoyed his most creative period between 1946 and 1949 as a member of Lennie Tristano's ensembles where he ceased to be purely a rhythm guitarist and quickly became an advanced bop stylist. He was known particularly for his fleet improvisations and his remarkably precise playing of unison thematic statements. He also played on those very first free-form Tristano recordings, "Intuition" and "Digression."

Meeting Lennie Tristano in 1946, from that time onward he was a close associate of Lennie's. His chordal work and improvisations set a new dimension in guitar playing, and added a new dimension to jazz guitar. He played with Lennie but didn't study with him – he had to work, and couldn't study "heavy," as he described it, but recognized Lennie's teaching skills.

"He told me why I should know it [scales, learning the instrument better] that well. He was a good teacher. He'd show you how to use these things to cut a couple of years off your development" (Bauer 1997: 92).

He can be heard on many of Lennie's early recordings between 1946 and 1949. He received awards from *Downbeat* and *Metronome* magazines and from 1947–53 recorded in the Metronome All Stars group with Charlie Parker, Dizzy Gillespie, Miles Davis, Lennie Tristano, and Fats Navarro. He also played with the NBC Staff Orchestra and taught at the New York Conservatory of Modern Music. In 1958 he traveled to Europe with the Benny Goodman Orchestra and performed and recorded fre quently with Lee during the fifties and early sixties.

His book, *Sideman*, gives a very interesting picture of jazz development in New York from the thirties onward as well as a real insight into his great personality. He celebrated his eighty-eighth birthday in November 2003 and still teaches at his Albertson, Long Island studio. We went to see him in 2001 and he managed to fit us in between giving lessons – so he is still going strong. He has also been the main publisher for many of the group's compositions, including lines written by Lennie, Lee, Warne, Don Ferrara, and myself. As the only one of the group that has written about that time himself, Billy's salute to Lennie in his book provides one of the few personal testimonies of this group of musicians.

> My time with Lennie did more for me namewise than any other period of my career. He did me a big honor by recording me with him. Certain people heard me... He believed in me. He let me publish his work. He told his students to put their work with me. He thought I was honest. I think I am. He recommended people to study with me. He thought I was truthful. I think Lennie was a truly great musician. Harmonically he rode his own orbit. "Thank you" for letting me try to fly with your orbit. (Bauer 1997: 92)

We visited Billy at his home, in May 2005, sadly he died just three weeks later.

Ted Brown (b. 1927)

Half of the Marsh/Brown tenor sax duo, Theodore (Ted) Brown comes from a musical family. His father was formerly a successful bandleader in the twenties and thirties. Ted is best known for his association with Warne Marsh; they played and recorded together in the mid-fifties in Los Angeles. He also featured prominently on Ronnie Ball's Atlantic album *All About Ronnie*, together with trombonist Willie Dennis. In addition to the albums with Warne, he has a CD, *Ted Brown Trio*, released on Gerry Teekens's Criss Cross label, and also recorded with Lee Konitz. Ted was a frequent player alongside Lee and Don Ferrara at the many sessions held at my former East Village studio in Manhattan. His wife Phyllis is a pianist and she also studied with Lennie in those early days. They have a son and a daughter, Anita, who continues the tradition as a pianist and arranger. Ted still plays and records – but also had a second profession in computer technology, from which he has now retired.

Arnold Fishkin (b. 1919, d. 1999)

A bass player, whom I first heard playing with Lennie's sextet at the Orchid Room on New York's 52nd Street in 1949, Arnold was nine years older than me. We nevertheless share the same birthday (July 20), and also have in common that we both started on violin at eight years of age!

As with Lee, Arnold had a family and had to make a living from jazz, so he was very much a working bass player. We never played together, both being bassists, and he did not participate in the loft scene; usually he was out working gigs. He played and recorded with such a wide range of people, including Bunny Berigan (1937), Jack Teagarden (1939–41), and Les Brown (1942) before serving in the US army. He then played with Lennie (1946–47), again doing so in New York (1948–49). He performed and recorded with Lee Konitz (1949–51) and with Ella Fitzgerald (1951). During the fifties through to the sixties, he was part of the staff orchestra of CBS and ABC and also made a number of recordings, for Don Elliot (1952), Billy Bauer (1953), Mel Powell and Tony Aless (1955), Howard McGhee and Lee Konitz (1956), Hank Jones (1958), and Toots Thielemans (1962). From 1966 he worked as a freelance musician in Los Angeles. Sadly, Arnold died recently.

Jeff Morton (Jeffrey Morton Haber, b. 1929, d. 1997)

Again one of the original members of Lennie's sextet, Jeff Morton previously worked with Max Kaminsky's band, and then briefly with Woody Herman. According to trumpeter Don Ferrara – who had also been with Woody – Jeff really swung that big band as though it were a small combo. Jeff of course was the drummer who made those first ever rhythm tracks with me that predated the music-minus-one recordings, and arguably it was from this that the ideas for pre-recorded rhythm tracks arose. Jeff eventually gave up playing to concentrate on photography. He later married the sculptor Julie MacDonald, best known for her remarkable sculpture of Bird. I last saw them in California in 1958 on my way back to New York, having visited Alaska. We corresponded for a while, but then I lost touch. Jeff later remarried and leaves a widow, Marcia.

Jeff Morton, who played very intensely, had by 1956 already moved to California, and though I didn't realize it at the time we were never to play together again.

Al (Alan) Levitt (b. 1932, d. 1994)

Al became a member of that group of musicians who studied and played with Lennie during the early fifties. He recorded with the quintet that Lennie took to Toronto in the summer of 1951 and also recorded with Lee on George Wein's Storyville label in 1953 (with Ronnie Ball on piano and Percy Heath on bass). For most of the fifties, he lived and worked in New York, playing and recording also with pianist Paul Bley. He then later relocated in Paris where he played with many other American expatriates and many prominent French jazz musicians. He also played and recorded with Lee and French pianist Martial Solal during the mid-seventies, and was a member of the group with Lee, Warne, and myself that toured Europe (France, Holland, Denmark, and Italy) during 1975/6 from which a number of recordings were made.

Al died in Paris in 1994. He was always very interested in art, and it was Al who encouraged me to visit the Philadelphia Art Museum while we were playing at the Blue Note in February 1953 with Lee's band. That visit had a profound effect upon me – it was the Centennial Celebration of Van Gogh's birth and was the largest exhibition of his work ever shown. Like so many jazz musicians, his interests extended far beyond jazz.

Dick Scott (Tox Drohar)

Though I knew Dick very well and we played together often I have few biographical details. I am puzzled when I reflect on this. Ironically, to my knowledge Dick doesn't appear in any jazz encyclopedias. Yet he deserves recognition, for he played and recorded with many well-known musicians: Lee Konitz, Bobby Hackett, Lou Stein, Marian McPartland, and Warne Marsh. Certainly those publications claiming to be encyclopedic need some revising. As it stands at present, if a jazz musician is omitted from such publications it is presumed that his contribution to the music is of little or no import. Though with today's proliferation of recordings this might be true, it certainly was not valid in those early days. In the fifties record releases were prestigious, and by association so were the participating personnel.

Dick and I first met at the sessions at Lennie's studio and he soon became a regular player in these and other sessions that we held. He married vocalist Betty Scott and they brought three children into the world in addition to two children from Betty's previous marriage. At that time he was in his early twenties and worked extremely hard to raise his family. But despite financial struggles he still remained cheerful and eternally good-natured. His drumming reflected this and was always sensitive to the musicians with whom he played.

One unfortunate event changed the direction of his life. In 1962 he and a friend were arrested for smoking cannabis. He was then incarcerated in a Long Island jail. They were both subject to serious assault, which resulted in his friend committing suicide. Upon his release, Dick went to live with the Cherokee Indians, and changed his name to Tox Drohar. Since that time he has lived a different kind of life. Eventually moving to Big Sur, California, he made his own drums and played with many different musicians, mostly involved with ethnic music.

In the late sixties, he went to France, where he has since spent much of his time. He visited England in 1967 and became part of a group featuring Chas Burchell, the legendary UK tenor saxophonist, with Dave Cliff on guitar and myself on bass. The group had a weekend residency at a pub in Chelsea, during which a recording was made, *No Kidding*. He and I also made a rhythm record for jazz musicians to improvise with, entitled *Your Friendly Neighbourhood Rhythm Section*.

When I was over in America in 1973, I visited Tox in Torrance, a suburb of LA. As ever, with Tox, it was an intriguing visit. He had the most beat-up Ford Fairlane that I have ever had the pleasure to ride in (and I am someone who still clings to an ancient Volvo 1987 which the garage has kindly asked me *not* to send to them for its MOT next year!) The highlight was a guided tour, passing the homes of Hollywood stars and being tailed by an LA squad car with me nervously worried that they might stop and search the car. Tox, for his part, as ever lived above such mundane considerations! Incidentally, I seemed to provide a lot of gasoline for it!

A large personality, perhaps the most concise picture I can give of Tox is that, bearing in mind I have long gray hair and a beard, when I met Tox I thought he was Jesus Christ. He was always the life and soul of the party, though the parties could turn out to be rather expensive. The most amazing picture I have is of Tox in a long coat, long boots and three-cornered (Napoleon-style) hat, standing in a puddle with a French nuclear reactor in the background.

Since returning to France he continues to play jazz and organize concerts – maybe he's settled down; he has written and occasionally sent me an ironic cartoon for my amusement. It is funny how the tradition of music continues – his eldest son Skip became a drummer and his daughter Carol visited me a few years ago, and at that time she was married to a jazz guitar player, Mark Di Orio.

Peter Ind (b. 1928)

Maybe the reason why I have such good memories of the time I spent with Lennie is because, in one sense, our teenage years had been extended into our twenties. The camaraderie, the excitement of expanding our musical horizons and of gaining recognition for this made those first few years very special. Though we went our own ways from time to time, there was none of what I could describe as "ego professionalism." How the scene has changed. Over the years, as jazz took a back seat and the world of rock and pop took over, it seemed essential to manifest a larger than life ego in order to keep in the limelight and keep working. In recent years I have sometimes played concerts where everyone on the stand behaved like a leader.

It is strange to look back now and see what became of this group of musicians. All of us were faced with the constant problem of how to earn a living. Jazz has, for the majority of its contributors, always been a problem of survival. Even well-known musicians have often had their times of extreme adversity. But as jazz musicians, at least partially alienated from society, trying to earn a living in such a precarious profession was never easy. Like Lennie, many of his students turned to teaching, partly out of the satisfaction it could give at times and partly out of necessity. Warne Marsh was perhaps somewhat more fortunate, getting some financial help from his family from time to time, but even for him it wasn't easy. Lee Konitz was the most successful of us and built a career recording with many small groups and always seemed to find enough work touring, etc. But Lee, having to support a large family from his early professional years, had some very difficult times in making ends meet. Sal Mosca, that extremely talented pianist, again survived precariously through a combination of teaching and working gigs. Like the others, he has not received the recognition he deserved and at the time of writing has more or less retired, though I hear he is playing again. Guitarist Billy Bauer, who has had the longest association with Lennie, is retired but still teaches and runs his publishing company, publishing the compositions of Lennie, Warne, and Don Ferrara. Don is now living and teaching in Temecula near San Diego, California.

For my part, in December 1961 I left New York and spent the following year in Europe and the UK. Returning to New York in January 1963, we then moved in June of that year to Big Sur, California. After living there with my family for three years, I returned to the UK in February 1966 and I began teaching, based initially on my studies with Lennie, and gradually expanding that understanding through experience. Still problems of financial survival continued. Within a decade I was back into recording again and formed my company, Wave Records, primarily releasing music from tapes I had previously recorded in New York. These releases featured Sal Mosca, Ronnie Ball, and Warne Marsh. I also began to release music newly recorded in the UK. In 1975/6 there was a reunion with former colleagues, initially Lee Konitz, Warne Marsh, guitarist Dave Cliff, drummer Al Levitt, and myself. This band, in various permutations, worked for the best part of a year, mainly traveling and playing European concerts, but we all went our own ways after that, apart from the reunion concert at London's Queen Elizabeth Hall in November 2002, featuring Lee, myself, and Dave Cliff. By then, neither Warne nor Al was around.

Though we were a continent apart, Lennie's concepts and philosophies were still a great influence. I found teaching in the UK challenging and in many ways very different from teaching in the USA. Some of this relates to the difficulty many UK students experience in opening up. The UK culture is quite constrained compared with that of the USA. Thus I found it not just a simple matter of teaching students how to develop the ability to play jazz, but primarily that of getting students to relax emotionally. If this is not achieved, the playing sounds artificial and unconvincing. Additionally, I found that many students wanted the quick fix, the secret, the simple clue, often coming for a few lessons expecting miraculous improvements. But of course it is not that easy. I had one student who was so emotionally blocked that I spent many hours trying to get him to sing – to make contact with the music. Eventually I succeeded to some extent. This was clearly a painful process for him. Later he joined a well-known course in jazz instruction. By that time he was ready to assimilate what was being taught on that course and made some progress. He then berated me, saying that lessons with me had been a total waste of time, implying that I had taken his money under false pretenses. What he didn't realize is that without those difficult times of studying with me, the other course would have benefited him little.

Others have found this approach more useful. I have seen, over the years, many students and it is always interesting to see how it is not always those who have the advantages or the resources that benefit the most! One recent student who really has such a good attitude and skill for playing, Jeff Cadogan, sadly has to work to support his family and can only seldom come for lessons, but he has it. Maybe some time he will be able to develop this further, but will he do it? Who knows? Others, such as Gary Crosby, who have enjoyed some success, have been very appreciative in print about my teaching.

In turn I am grateful to Lennie. Even years after my studies with him, I discovered that his concepts were still innovative and academically resisted, as the following example illustrates. In 1967, bassist Bernie Cash, a friend and former student of mine, invited me to set the curriculum for what was the very first full-time jazz study course in the UK. As often happens, such opportunities occur seemingly fortuitously. Bernie, who played frequently in a number of classical orchestras, mainly in the north of England, had met violinist Joseph Stones, who was also playing at the same engagement. Joe told Bernie he was forming a music college in Leeds and Bernie jokingly said, "How can you claim to run a well-rounded music education facility without including jazz?" Joe replied, "If I get sanction to have a jazz department, will you come and run it for me?" Sometime later, to Bernie's surprise, the offer came up for real. Bernie then approached me as a consultant – particularly to set a curriculum, and also asked if I would teach. As in those years following my studying with Lennie I had done a considerable amount of teaching, some of it institutional and some private, I felt ready to take on that responsibility. Having gained so much from my studies with Lennie and in addition added aspects that were solely my own, I welcomed the opportunity to be able to pass on some of these concepts and knowledge. Bernie was himself familiar with Lennie's music and from me he had grasped the essentials of what Lennie had taught.

Bernie Cash, I should mention, was a real motivator for jazz in the UK. He was a multi-instrumentalist, originally a trumpet player, but he then took up bass, following which he not only learned to play the sax, but also the flute and piccolo! He worked with Alan Plater to produce a jazz opera about Pres and Billie. The later years of his life were mostly spent playing with classical orchestras and it was on a tour of Germany with, I believe, the LSO, that he died suddenly of a heart attack. He had been one of those enthusiastic about Lennie and we owe it to Bernie more than to anyone that Lennie appeared at the Harrogate Festival. Surprisingly, there is no mention of him in the various UK jazz reference books.

The course commenced with great enthusiasm, both on the part of the tutors and of the students. In fact it was this tremendous enthusiasm that led to difficulties some months later. As in most music institutions, there was insufficient space for students' individual practice and materials were also in short supply. This did not dampen enthusiasm, however. We always commenced on time and students were seldom late for classes; visualize the picture of fifteen students all singing scales in four-part harmony at 8.30 in the morning in one room! It was all very different from the demure academic atmosphere of the students who attended the classical course.

These first-year students were totally committed to the course and some of them have since been very successful as jazz musicians, arrangers or players: guitarist Dave Cliff, for example, who has quietly developed a reputation as a sensitive improviser and accompanies Lee at times; as well as Trevor Vincent as an arranger, Ray Manderson the trumpet player and Gary Boyle the guitarist. One morning I sensed intuitively that this state of events would not last. Suddenly Joseph Stones opened the door while we were all practicing our scalic four-part harmony. He was obviously not at peace with himself (or with this open approach), and rather foolishly I invited him to come and join us. But with a hurried excuse he promptly left the room.

However, an issue that was increasingly of concern to me personally was that my paychecks never arrived. As in all academic institutions, there were time sheets to fill in, claim for travel and for rent. When, finally, the checks were handed out, mine was not among them. After a month or so, this caused me acute financial embarrassment. The salary was not high in any case. I was responsible for looking after my family in London, while traveling each week to Leeds (in the north of England) and paying rent to stay in the vicinity during the week. Each weekend in London I would be teaching privately and playing gigs at night. A pretty hectic schedule – one that would be beyond my stamina these days. However, I had not reckoned on the failure of the authorities to give me the paychecks that were due. I met with Joseph Stones, who assured me that this was an oversight and would be rectified. A week or so later a paycheck for me arrived – which only contained monies for about half the number of hours I had taught.

This situation reached the financial climax for me shortly after the morning that Joseph Stones came into the class. During a break I went to try again to rectify the situation. My request fell on deaf ears. I pointed out that I could no longer afford to teach there unless payment for my services were forthcoming. It then became clear that this was the excuse that Joseph Stones was looking for and he claimed that he was powerless to do anything about it. Unable to continue without been paid, I resigned from the post. Bernie (who had always been a loyal friend and was also outraged at the injustice) also resigned in protest, following which the students walked out in support of us. I returned to London and, several months later, thanks to the assistance of the legal department of the Musicians' Union, I received what had been due to me.

What I have not dwelt upon here are the innuendoes about the tuition we were giving. It soon became obvious that there were jealousies manifested by other staff (clearly the method unsettled them), and the enthusiasm of the jazz students only acted as fuel to the fire as far as other personnel were concerned. To an outsider, such jealousies may seem to be exaggerated, and hardly a valid reason for what occurred. But I include this episode because, during 2002, a British jazz magazine (*Jazz Review*) printed an interview with the person who took over after Bernie Cash and I had left. In the article, he claimed to be the founder of the jazz course at Leeds. (Incidentally, in 1967 it was considered too demeaning to include the word "jazz" in the course at Leeds, so officially it became known as "The Light Music Course.") He does mention both Bernie and me in the article, but in a demeaning way, claiming we had left Joseph Stones in the lurch and giving the impression that Bernie and I were totally irresponsible. I wrote a letter to the editor of the magazine about the errors in the article, but received no response; neither was a retraction printed. Though perhaps a small event in the history of jazz, it is interesting how true history becomes distorted or falsified in time. I also mention it because Bernie is no longer here to defend himself and I know he would have done so, vigorously.

Following the creation of Wave Records, my recording company (located first in the family home in suburban London, then eventually moving to a house I had purchased in Twickenham, south-west London), I began to concentrate more upon sound recording. By the end of the seventies, the increased activities of the recording studio led me to find premises in central London. This in turn led me to the founding of a jazz club venue in London, the Bass Clef, which opened in 1984. It ran for ten years, but with the economic depression of the nineties I lost virtually everything. I found myself, at sixty-six, without money or job and trying to find a new direction.

It is ten years since the demise of Bass Clef. It took several years to settle the financial morass I found myself in. My partner Sue has been an incredible help. There were a number of legal issues involved, which, after much bureaucratic wrangling, have now been resolved, finally all pretty much in my favor. For a number of years I found myself struggling to pay a tax claim levied against my former company Bass Clef. A letter from the UK tax authorities stated that I would be paying tax owed until I am ninety-five, after which they would compute the interest owed. Finally, after my case was taken up by Dr Vincent Cable, my local Member of Parliament, together with a stream of correspond-ence between myself, my accountant and the tax authorities, the latter relented to some degree and I was able to reach a settlement, having remortgaged my house. The way I now look at it is that if I didn't win, I didn't totally lose either. These last three years have given me much-needed time to write, to paint and of course to continue playing; 2002 was a watershed year, during which I played in the Middle East, in Jor-dan, and in Belgium. Sue and I visited Australia, when I was invited to play at the Manly Jazz Festival, with guitarist Tony Barnard and his father Bob. We also visited my sister Marjorie and husband Rod in Adelaide, and met many jazz promoters – arriving in time for the Glenelg Jazz Festival organized primarily by Bruce Hancock. I remet also former UK bassist John Aue, who now lives in Adelaide, playing, and teaching at the University of South Australia. It was heartening to find community radio stations out there that dedicate considerable amounts of time to promoting jazz and which wanted to hear about Lennie and were very interested in the forthcoming book. The presenters, such as Tony Brethrick, are completely dedicated but get little if any financial reward for their efforts, but in contrast to the UK, such promotion consider-ably increases the interest in jazz in that part of the world.

In November 2002 there was a reunion with Lee Konitz and we played a concert together at London's Queen Elizabeth Hall, which was a great success. It marked a span of fifty-two years since the first time we played together. For me it was very stimulating. Lee wrote and said how much he had enjoyed playing together too! Somewhere in the ether, I felt that Lennie was aware of this and was pleased.

To sum up the one thing I have in common with this dedicated group of musicians, who were part of Lennie's original circle: they never played the political game by switching to commercial popular music, but stayed true to their dedication to the spirit of improvised jazz. Lennie was mentor to all of us at different times of our lives and his genius and dedication to jazz improvisation affected all of us, our playing, our lives, and the routes we took. I know that Lennie also helped many of a later generation of musicians, including, incidentally, the pop musician Billy Joel.

There was a group, including pianists Connie Crothers and Liz Gorril, whom I never met but who I believe still continue to play and record. We did meet Lennie's daughter Carol, who is a drummer, and her husband, saxophonist Lennie Popkin. They are the parents of the next generation of the Tristano clan. Last year, when we were in Paris, we heard that we had just missed Lennie and Carol, who had been over playing there. But I

Wayne Marsh, Peter Ind, Lennie Tristano and Al Levitt at Manhatten Studios, August 15, 1953

Lennie Tristano, Peter Ind and Al Levitt at Manhatten Studios, August 15, 1953

cannot really write authoritatively about this later period of Lennie Tristano or about the group as their musical activities were at a time long after I had returned to the UK. Maybe one of them will complete the picture some time.

7 a reflection on lennie as I knew him – the man and musician

I could never have written a standard biography of Lennie, starting with when he was born, and detailing when he recorded, etc. This would have been far too dull and, anyway, it was not how I knew him. I wanted the reader to really have to look for Lennie in the story, to want to search him out, to find for themselves the melody in this improvised piece of writing.

But I want to pull all this together into a reflection of the man I knew and worked with at the end of this first part of the book, before looking at the technical aspects of his work.

Let's go back to the beginning. Lennie was born under the sign of Pisces on March 19, 1919, for those who want such details. He was born in Chicago of Italian parentage and was one of four brothers. I do not know for certain, but the impression I had was that the family was not rich but reasonably well off. I believe his mother was an opera singer and taught Lennie music. I never met two of Lennie's brothers and do not know whether they are still around. I knew his younger brother, Michael, a tenor saxophonist, who became a professional psychotherapist; he became my therapist for a time. I also knew a cousin, Lennie Aiello. Both seemed reasonably well off but certainly not privileged – middle American, I would say. The last time I saw Michael was in the late eighties when he visited England with his new partner and I received a surprise phone call from him and that evening he visited my club, the Bass Clef, in London. Remembering this reminds me that while the two brothers were very different personalities, they were alike in being very soft-spoken but authoritative in a quiet way. I then lost contact with Michael, but understand that not long afterwards he passed away.

Lennie had always been poorly sighted and after contracting measles in early childhood he became totally blind. Lennie told me that one day when he was about six years old his parents took him to a church where healing took place. The entire congregation prayed for the restoration of his sight – apparently to no avail, though Lennie said that somehow he could see during the brief time that they were praying for him and was able to count the number of lights on the ceiling. Later he told his parents of this and their disappointment that the prayers of the congregation were apparently ineffectual was mixed with awe at what Lennie told them about briefly being able to see. One remarkable thing about Lennie was that he always looked at you when speaking to you. Though it was obvious that his eyes were sightless, you always felt the contact of his looking at you, as though, despite his sightlessness, a powerful energy nevertheless made contact with you.

An interesting anecdote from Billy Bauer shows the intuitiveness Lennie possessed.

> Lennie, me and Bob Leininger were playing a recital hall in Philadelphia. When they opened the curtains they knocked my amplifier wire out of the socket. I guess Lennie heard my amp go dead. He put his arms over the piano and put his head where you put the music. He wouldn't play. They ran up on stage and plugged me in. That made me feel good. Lennie treated me very nicely. (Bauer 1997: 90)

Lennie was so astute in what he heard. For example, as Alyn Shipton comments: "His exceptional ear allowed him to remember and transcribe the most complex music, and he once confounded the trumpeter Sonny Berman with a part that Berman pronounced unplayable, only to be told it was one of his own solos that Tristano had written down during a broadcast" (Shipton 2001: 693).

People often marveled at his dexterity as a piano player. Because Lennie was blind, many wondered how he could find his way about the keyboard. However, it is the contours that are made by the arrangement of black and white keys that give the clue. In fact I found that many of my own keyboard students were habitually looking at the keyboard, which restricted their playing ability in many ways. This habit means that, psychologically, their sight was ruling their fingers, hindering the security the hands need to be able to express the individual's ideas fluently. In teaching I would try turning out the lights or put a cardboard cover above the keys, thus preventing the students from that bad habit of looking at their hands.

As many blind people will tell you, sighted people often treat the blind as though they are also deaf and dumb. Lennie was full of stories about such incidents. He related that during the time he was still living in Chicago, he was riding in a cab and suddenly there was a tremendous crash. Lennie was thrown forward from his seat. The cab driver got out and then engaged in a furious argument with the driver of another vehicle. After about fifteen minutes he returned, stuck his head in the window and said to Lennie, "There's been a crash!"

One of Lennie's more risky adventures, in which fortunately for us all he emerged unscathed, happened at a time when he was at a school for the blind in Chicago. While he was waiting on the curb for assistance to cross a very busy six-lane highway, someone approached him and said, "Going across?" Then, arm in arm, they both crossed. On reaching the other side, the man turned to Lennie and said, "Thank you." Neither had been aware that the other was blind!

Some of the more outrageous tales really belong to a time, as they say, "when the world was young." During his early years in Chicago, when traffic was far lighter than today, he and his friends used to go joyriding. Everyone had a "short" in those days, usually a beat-up old Chevy or Ford. Finding a quiet suburban street, they would let Lennie drive. To compensate for his blindness they would put their hands on his shoulders, saying "Turn left" or "Now turn right." Some shoulder signals were for accelerating, others for the brake, and so on. So they're all having fun with Lennie driving, when a police squad car overtakes them, red light flashing. Unable to warn Lennie in time, they hit the rear end of the police car. The cop gets out, adjusting his belt, and in fury says, "Where's your license?" Lennie says, "I don't have one, I'm blind." The cop – in disbelief and amazement: "Well, be more careful next time."

I notice also from Billy Bauer's book that Lennie's enthusiasm for driving didn't wane.

> I roomed with Jeff Morton, the drummer. We tried to play a little at night but there were complaints. Jeff sent home for his paints. We put them on the table and started to paint. He got up the next morning and looked at mine and looked at his and ripped his off the wall and said, "OK, you got the paints!" These were oil paints. The picture wasn't dry so we pinned it to the roof of the car with safety pins for the ride home. Lennie said, "Bill, I'd like that picture. I'll hang it up." The irony is, naturally, that he was blind. I thought this was odd. He asked for it several times. I never gave it to him. I guess it was also odd that he asked me for driving lessons. I did do that! (Bauer 1997: 91)

For most of us just the thought of blindness is devastating. Despite this, blind people often amaze us with their dexterity. More often than not they have such a positive attitude toward life, which can make us feel guilty should we express our own dissatisfactions. I never heard Lennie ever complain about his blindness, except about the way people treated him. He said that in the early days he had had a tiepin made with MF on it.

Unsuspecting people, not knowing what a character they were addressing, and trying to make conversation and feigning interest, would say, rather patronizingly, "What does MF stand for?" The quiet reply would be "Motherfucker" with nothing more said. A perfect way to rebuke an insincere attitude!

Often it seems that blind people are somehow compensated by having superb musical talent. This may be so, but what is most significant is the dedication with which they apply themselves to develop that talent. Lennie had worked in all ways to develop his craft. He told me that while he was playing a regular gig in Chicago and, as he put it, could "riffle off Art Tatum's solos with comparative ease," he became acquainted with a Canadian, a professional artist who came to hear him every night. Although Lennie did tell me it, I cannot recall his name. This man insisted to Lennie that he (Lennie) had not yet found himself in his music. Lennie recalled, "At first I dismissed what he was saying, but he continued to insist that I had not yet found myself in music." But this man's words stayed with him and eventually he realized that playing Art Tatum's music, though very skillful and entertaining, was not the same as developing his own skills in improvisation.

And jazz to Lennie was essentially the skill of improvising. Such a position can be very confusing to the layman and musician alike, as so much music in the world of jazz is a copy or influenced by what had originally been improvisation. Many musicians develop their musical vocabulary from studying the recordings of other musicians. This is an important step along the way, as it was for Lennie – after all, he had studied Art Tatum's recordings. But the hardest task of all is the step beyond being a good imitator of someone else's playing: that of becoming a voice in your own right. But supposing, as in Lennie's case, you had already reached the point of development where your livelihood relied on being a good imitator. It takes a brave person to go beyond that point, to learn to find your own voice. This can often mean losing work, the kind of employment where you were expected to play in the style of an accepted idiom. But Lennie certainly regarded those meetings with that Canadian artist as very significant. I am sure that, in turn, this helped to make him the outstanding teacher he was.

Lennie was always disarmingly direct. One could never take offense at his directness. He was always so gentle, so charming and so quietly spoken that his directness could be unnerving, especially since he was blind. A bass player friend of mine related how he had agreed to take a neighbor's young son to study with Lennie. On meeting him, Lennie mistook who was coming for the lesson. Thinking that it was the bass player, Lennie said to him, "Do you listen to Bird?" (He always encouraged his students to study Bird's recordings.) Though all jazz musicians paid lip service to Bird, many were secretly in awe of his music and so did not really absorb it. In response to Lennie's question, the bass player affirmed that he did listen to Bird. Lennie replied, "But I can tell from your answer that you don't." His perceptiveness could really catch you out and, in some ways, that is why people found him daunting.

His openness often affected people as though their inmost motives were being questioned or exposed. I know that in later life Lennie tried to curb this directness. He told me he wanted people to feel at ease with him – and not relate to him as though he were some sort of jazz guru, as he felt others had portrayed him. The difficulty was that it was more than anything his lack of guile that made some people feel uneasy. Many of us quite unconsciously develop a persona to face the world. When meeting Lennie for the first time, many people would become aware (perhaps for the first time in their lives) that their persona was a front, a cover-up. They could go in one of two directions: either strongly relate to Lennie or become defensive and dismissive, even rejecting. (This is well described in psychoanalysis as positive and negative transference of feelings.)

But as great a jazz musician as he was, Lennie never promoted himself. He lived relatively quietly, teaching, playing, and occasionally doing concerts or resident gigs, increasingly without the recognition he deserved. This was the man I knew. It was clear that popularity was not merely the result of society liking something. It was much more complex than that. On the one hand popularity depended upon promotion, which in turn meant developing ties with those that promote and launch new creative endeavors. It also, and more importantly, depends on peer group acceptance. Lennie was, in his way, a pioneer and he would not/could not play the game.

He was always his own man no matter what, and he admired this in other people (such as Reich). It was typical that at a time when due recognition was seldom given to blacks, it had been Lennie who was their chief advocate, pointing out that it was predominantly black musicians who had been the greatest creative influences in jazz, especially in relation to improvisation – Louis Armstrong, Lester Young, Charlie Christian, Charlie Parker, and Roy Eldridge – and he promoted them as people to learn from.

Lennie also saw the crucial importance of teaching at a time when the general view was that jazz could not be taught (one either had the talent or not). This, plus Lennie's disarming outspokenness, unfortunately did much to set him apart from the mainstream of jazz. In the main, jazz critics avoided too strong criticism of his music, especially when Lennie was being lauded, with recognition in the late forties from the magazine polls, including being voted in 1949 as best leader, best arranger, best piano player, and best small band leader. But often they appeared puzzled or confused about what he was doing. Rather than directly show this, his students and associates seemed to be the target for negative criticism or at best low-key praise about the kind of music they were playing. In 1955 when Lee and Warne recorded the album for Atlantic Records and one of the tunes was Lennie's composition, "Two not One," in which the first note of Lennie's line commenced on the second beat of the bar. This confused many listeners and even some critics, who judged the music as though the musicians had started in the wrong place. Another track on that album was Charlie Parker's "Donna Lee." Bird's line consists of two sixteen-bar sequences. On the second section (the seventeenth bar) Lee and Warne played the last section one beat apart from each other and then resolved it neatly in the last four bars. An incredible feat of musicianship – imagine playing the same tune at the same time in this way! The result, when this album was released, was that many critics were convinced that they had lost their place, as though they were stumbling over each other! Perhaps in the future it would be wise to open an academy specifically for the education of jazz critics! Those critics who really are clued up would be exempt – and they know who they are, of course!

As I see it, it was Lennie who was the first to comprehend what was needed to convey how to play jazz. Even if Lennie's recordings have not taken pride of place in our jazz collections, I feel we owe him this recognition: that he was the first to understand what was needed and he spent a good part of his life sharing this with others.

He had great strength of character. When he realized many years ago, way before America became aware of its unique artform, that he would never be able to earn a living from playing the way he wanted to, increasingly he concentrated upon teaching – taking gigs only when conditions were favorable. He seemed very aware of the negative reactions expressed about his playing; Lennie has related how he first recorded the two free-form sides for Capitol Records:

> During our Capitol recording session in May 1949 some significant things happened. After we did the conventional part of the date, we did the two new sides, "Intuition" and "Digression." As soon as we began playing, the engineer threw up his hands and left his machine. The A & R man and the management thought I was such an idiot that they refused to pay me for the sides and release them. Free-form means playing

without a fixed chord progression, without a time signature, without a specified tempo. I had been working with my men in this context for several years so that the music that resulted was not haphazard or hit and miss. Several months after that Capitol date, Symphony Sid, who was a prominent disk jockey during that period, managed to grab a copy of those two free-form sides. He played them three or four times a week on his nightly show over a period of several years. Through that, Capitol Records received enough requests for those two sides to warrant releasing them. And, of course, they did pay me for them. In view of the fact that fifteen years later a main part of the jazz scene turned into free-form, I think this incident is very significant. These two sides were completely spontaneously improvised. A lot of people who heard them thought they were compositions. To my knowledge Miles Davis is the only noted musician who acknowledged in print the real nature of the music on those sides. (Bauer 1997: 94)

Lennie was such an innovator. Those two sides were the very first free-form improvisation ever made. When, ten years later, Ornette Coleman made his free-form recordings, these were lauded as original and as great art. Everyone had somehow forgotten that Lennie had been the first. Moreover, those two three-minute tracks he made in 1949 evince so much more creativity in that form than later free-form records, which to my ears at least mostly sound very self-indulgent. But "free-form" – music played without a preconceived structure – can be played by just about anyone who has rudimentary playing ability. I see comparisons between free-form and abstract painting. Although some abstract painting has been groundbreaking, it has unfortunately left the door open for less talented artists, or those who are unwilling to devote sufficient time and energy to develop their craft. Similarly with so-called free-form jazz: some musicians can hoodwink people about their limited skills. On the other hand, to create worthwhile music – without a preconception of structure – requires real musical skill and the ability to empathize with what the other musicians are playing. But little free-form music has the latter quality. So much so that free-form often arouses suspicion among many professional jazzmen. Altoist Peter Cook jokingly said that if anyone tells you they like free-form jazz, never trust anything they say.

Lennie was always striving for perfection. I feel that in this respect he was sometimes his own worst enemy. His perception of the merit of other players' recordings was always spot on. Yet I believe he rejected some of his own best playing, maybe because of a minor fault that others would hardly be aware of. Almost all of the great recorded solos in jazz are imperfect to some degree. I know the difficulty from my own recordings. A slight hesitation or error can magnify itself in the mind out of all proportion to the overall solo. I just wish that Lennie, having striven so hard to achieve what he did, had recorded more, perfect or not.

But there was one particular recording that Lennie detested. A forty-five r.p.m. disk entitled "A Knight in the Village" had been released under the leadership of bassist Chubby Jackson. This was a bootleg recording, for which no one apparently got paid. I believe this occurred shortly after Lennie had moved from Chicago to New York. It had been just a routine gig somewhere in Greenwich Village. Someone had walked in with a portable recorder and subsequently released a disk of the performance. Lennie took the person to court and he lost the case. According to Lennie, the judge ruled against him because the record producer claimed that the bandleader had said it would be OK. Then, as now, justice is unpredictable and elusive.

Lennie had strong ideas about recording. He felt that, with the advent of the LP and the extended playing time available, many musicians were being careless – if it didn't happen on the first chorus it might happen on the second or third. With 78 r.p.m. recordings the challenge resided in the confined time allowed – to produce one's very best efforts. In contrast, with LPs there developed a more *laissez faire* attitude toward recordings. But that certainly was not the case concerning his LP *Tristano*. Lennie used this opportunity to show what new directions there could be, opening with the revolutionary and startling "Line Up" in which Lennie had overdubbed his improvisation upon one of the tracks that Jeff Morton and I had made for him.

Although Lennie had regularly recorded in his E 32nd Street studio, very little of this music was released at the time. Following the *Tristano* album, nothing further appeared until 1962, when Atlantic Records released a second album of Lennie's music. Titled *The Real Tristano*, it is a *tour de force* of solo jazz piano. One track, "C Minor Complex," is to me a majestic statement of all Lennie stood for. To this day it reaches beyond any other solo piano recording. Ironically, using the same basic sequence as the "East 32nd St" track (the one that Jeff Morton and I had recorded the rhythm track for), it needed no rhythm section. The incredibly strong and creative left-hand walking bass gave complete strength and authority to an unbelievable right-hand improvisation. Recently the two albums *Tristano* and *The Real Tristano* were reissued as one CD on Atlantic/Warner, but for some obscure reason – presumably the decision of some unenlightened A&R man – the supreme track "C Minor Complex" was left out. Perhaps it was just too much for him. However, Mosaic Records have released a boxed set that does include this masterpiece.

It has occurred to me that no one has commented on Lennie's musical development. There is a huge range of development from the early forties trio recordings with Billy Bauer, to the time in 1962 when *The Real Tristano* was released. In his early recordings it is apparent that Lennie's ambition was to extend harmonies beyond what was generally accepted at that time. I still have a number of classical albums featuring the work of Hindemith, Schoenberg etc. that Lennie gave me. I know that his study of these was part of his exploration of harmonic extension and innovation. But already by 1949 he was exploring rhythmic possibilities in jazz. His sextet recordings such as "Wow" and "Crosscurrent" reflect the beginnings of this new direction.

By the early fifties Lennie had become fascinated by the possibilities of time displacement, something that Bird had already developed. Bird was not the first, Lester Young having recorded solos evidencing that ability, for instance "Taxi War Dance." But Lennie developed this beyond Pres and beyond Bird. Lennie would take, say, a seven eighth-note phrase, repeated a number of times, so that it would spill over the bar lines, without him losing his place in the harmonic flow of the piece. Understandably this could be hard on rhythm sections, unless the rhythm section members had learned to hear this for themselves. It became problematic for Lennie to find players who could sustain a relaxed swing in such circumstances. Lennie then received unjust criticism from other jazz musicians, that he couldn't swing. The combination of accompanying rhythm sections tightening up due to Lennie's playing a long line of such unusual rhythmic complexity was simply misunderstood by many listeners as Lennie being unable to swing. One can even hear something of this in the Atlantic recording *Tristano* on the live tracks made at the Confucius restaurant. The rhythm section, Art Taylor and Gene Ramey, begins to tighten up during many of Lennie's solos in the effort to maintain time.

Jazz was not overshadowed in those days by pop music, but was still very much music of the underprivileged and was culturally unappreciated. Though many affluent Americans had a high regard for the music, it was still in left field as far as mainstream America was concerned. What was so striking about Lennie was his complete conviction as to the artistic merit of jazz, together with his admiration and high regard for those musicians who had achieved greatness. He expressed the kind of dedication to the music that was normally expected for the classical musical idiom.

"Tristano stressed that jazz is not an inferior music and that jazz musicians are expected to have greater command of their instruments than classical players" (McKinney 1978). But there was one important difference: Lennie lacked the cultural snobbery that is so often associated with the classical music world. Lennie was both serious and approachable.

I believe too that Lennie had something in common with many other great jazz musicians. This elusive something – directness, an immediate contact with music and with people – means that they cut through a lot of the nonsense that can surround jazz. There is a tale of a drummer, trying to be "the man," asking Lester Young, "When was the last time we played together, Lester?" Lester replied, "Tonight." That's what I mean by something! It is the insight and sureness to cut through the bullshit and be your own person. I also think that that was what many of those older jazz musicians saw and respected in Lennie, as did Miles Davis, Charles Mingus, Max Roach, and Roy Haynes. His openness and directness were rare qualities.

Later, greater competition and struggling for work, categorization of what was or was not jazz, self-promotion, the downgrading of others and commercial pressure for what was new or the latest thing in jazz all had their effects on Lennie. Peer group reactions also played their part, and Lennie's music and that of those associated with him became labeled as "cool," i.e. without emotional intensity. Unfortunately, at least some of this stuck. Lee Konitz, went out there and played hot. Lee has succeeded in reaching and maintaining a prominent position in the jazz world despite being tagged cool. As Lee once joked to me, "I could roast in hell and I would still be cool."

Lennie Tristano's strength was that he remained clear, throughout all of the changes in jazz, all of the debates about what jazz is or is not and all the debates about who is or is not where it's at. Lennie listened to people – he listened to what they said, how they said it and what they played. What remained paramount to Lennie was the creative quality of the musician, not someone's race, or lifestyle, or whether they had a narcotics habit or not. Many revered Lennie for his forthright ways, but inadvertently he made many enemies. In those days, in the forties and the fifties, he had considerable influence. Gradually, almost imperceptibly, his influence waned. As I saw it, jazz became more stylized. Lennie was a champion of improvisation and was less concerned with stylistic development. He pointed out that it is a matter of developing the ability to allow your fingers to express the music that "is in your mind – the music is there in your head." And when you listen to a great jazz solo, you re-experience someone in the act of expressing great beauty. Lennie was clear about making the distinction between emotion and feeling. He said he was not interested in expressing raw emotion – if he wanted that he could visit any state hospital. The core of the music for him was playing with feeling.

Ira Gitler, interviewing Lennie in 1964, asked what Lennie thought of John Coltrane, Sonny Rollins, and Miles Davis. Tristano answered, "All emotion, no feeling." "How do you distinguish between the two?" "Well, say I believe that there is no real hysteria or hostility in jazz, their stuff is the expression of the ego. I want jazz to flow out of the id. Putting it another way, real jazz is what you can play before you are all screwed up; the other happens after you're screwed up" (Gitler 1966: 243).

As a student I always marveled at his ability to conceptualize and analyze what was needed in order to develop as a jazz musician. A half-century later, much of this appears obvious. It was awesome for us – as twenty-one-year-old budding jazz musicians – to meet someone who not only was a great creative jazz musician but who also understood intellectually how to approach the music and develop one's skills. Gradually, with the passing years, my appreciation of Lennie increased, as he became for me less of a mentor and more of a friend, someone with whom it was possible to discuss the most interesting and far-out subjects, without being regarded as a "nutter" or as "too serious."

For me personally Lennie's legacy is two-fold. For all of us, especially those who played with him at that time, Lennie's legacy is what he added technically to the jazz vocabulary and his vision of jazz as a serious musical craft. I want to look at this in the second part of the book and focus on a technical consideration of his legacy. But for me personally there is another legacy left by Lennie: seeing what happened to him has made me reflect more broadly over the years on jazz; how some are lauded and others, more deserving, are not. So in Parts II and III I want to reconsider Lennie's legacy. To do this requires a consideration of how and why jazz became so commercial. But, linked to this, it also requires a review of what people said about Lennie and how and why this has been welded into a set of myths that do not bear close examination.

Part II

Lennie: A More Technical Consideration of Jazz Improvisation and His Legacy

8 what do we mean by jazz?

So far we have looked at what was happening in New York, mainly in the forties and fifties. To discuss why Lennie's contribution was unique we need to talk more about jazz, about all its complexities, and especially what it does and doesn't mean. I want briefly to discuss this as a backdrop for an evaluation of why Lennie's music constitutes such a special contribution to jazz.

When I recently attended the Denver Jazz Film Festival, there was a discussion about whether jazz is a purely American artform. I expressed the commonly held view: that it originated in the United States but that it has now spread worldwide. Today the concept "jazz" embraces many musical styles of great diversity (from Latin America to South Africa to Eastern Europe), which would have been unthinkable fifty years ago when Lennie and his music were first recognized. The wide range of music that now comes under the umbrella of jazz often leads to arguments as to what is true jazz and what is jazz-influenced music.

There was also a heated debate at the festival about whether jazz is solely the music of black people. More particularly, there was the claim that black people created it, owned it, and that whites have "usurped it." What seemed strange to me is that those making the claim seemed unaware that for many younger black people jazz is not where "it is at" at all. The focus has moved on to areas such as "rap," which, as far as music is concerned, have extremely tenuous connections with jazz.

There is an oft-expressed view that the most recent contributions to jazz are superior to what has gone before, as though the earlier music were merely an unsophisticated forerunner of today's jazz creativity. To gain a better perspective I often compare the development and evolution of jazz with that of classical music. The evaluation of classical music is constantly changing with our changing culture. We do not now consider J. S. Bach a lesser musician simply because he preceded Beethoven and Mozart. Yet, at one time, this was a commonly held belief.

In evaluating any artform we are inevitably swayed by what moves us most. There is nothing wrong in this, of course. However lyrical we may wax about a particular painter, composer or jazz artist, those we try to convince may remain totally unmoved. We may find it hard to accept that something that appears so obviously beautiful to our senses is not equally obvious to everyone. We may proselytize until we are blue in the face, without convincing anyone of our views. In fact such attempts may only further alienate people. When our views are thus rejected we may begin to question our own perception – why is it that something that moves us so greatly leaves others cold? This can be, at least, partly due to the fact that each new generation comes into the world with a different agenda. Such is the pace of today's world that five years sees shifts in outlook that a century ago would have taken twenty-five years. But the most crucial factor concerning appreciation of any artistic endeavor is just how open a person is when confronted with a particular form of creativity? And there are so many kinds of openness. Someone may be open to impressionist paintings, for example, yet be totally unmoved by the music of Charlie Parker. Or vice versa.

This can be a stumbling block when teaching. Lennie had firm opinions on who were the greatest jazz musicians, and while teaching would insist that his students study the recordings of those greats. In principle that is fine, but I believe it was also the power of Lennie's personality that overcame many students' hesitation in viewing things likewise. This can have an unwanted side effect on the student: failing to use independent appraisal of other jazz. I have a special admiration for Bird in this respect, because Bird enjoyed all kinds of music without having to see it as the greatest. Different generations react differently and if a student secretly admired Elvis Presley's music or that of the Beatles but felt duty bound to study Lester Young instead, it is doubtful that he/she would actually lock on to the spirit of Lester's music, even if learning Lester's solos note for note.

Among the varieties of popular music, the music generally played in clubs, venues, and on TV and radio (jazz these days appears to occupy the rearguard), it is seldom realized that there is a hierarchy in music. To point this out can be very controversial, particularly to someone (oddly enough) who may be extremely sophisticated in other ways. Let's give an analogy. Supposing you are a crossword puzzle fanatic. You may have been drawn to crossword puzzles as a kid. You would have learned to solve simple puzzles. After a while these would seem old hat – too simple – so you would look for more challenging puzzles. You would perhaps eventually discover cryptic crossword puzzles and then these may have the fascination for you that children's puzzles had when you were a kid. Just as there is a hierarchy of complexity (and wit) in crossword puzzles, so there is in jazz.

Additionally, jazz can express longing, frustration, humor, cleverness, sensuality, sadness. Often a person locks into jazz apparently accidentally. I remember someone playing me some music that was close to their heart; I immediately followed this by a Charlie Parker recording. Suddenly the penny dropped and the person "heard" Charlie Parker for the first time. The openness induced by the first piece enabled the person to "open up" to the Charlie Parker track.

But for many, jazz means little more than a kind of sound. As our technology has enabled high-quality sound reproduction to be heard in every home, in every restaurant or public place, music has increasingly become a background for all our activities. Music sets our mood. To counter stress we now have smooth classics, or smooth jazz. While we wait on a telephone extension we may be bombarded with the incessant beat of pop music, or somewhat more rarely, the sedation of eighteenth-century dance music. In the current milieu, jazz is seldom listened to; it is merely "heard." Consequently, few realize the wealth of musical experience inherent in good jazz, and few are able to sort out the wheat from the chaff. Much of what comes under the umbrella of jazz is superficial, some seems complicated or confused, or, to my ears, at least downright ugly, though some is sublime.

What I really want to stress is that, first of all, you really have to find your own way in jazz and not be frightened to follow your instincts, bearing in mind that as you develop your awareness your tastes may change as new subtleties in the music become apparent. But if we habitually treat music as mere background to our other activities, we may miss out on the deeper pleasures that jazz offers. To paraphrase Goethe: "What is it that is hardest to hear, that which lies before our very ears."

Note that so far I have refrained from using specific examples in discussing jazz. I wanted to focus first on listening rather than defining or categorizing. Anyone in jazz will tell you what in their opinion is the best jazz. Jazz is possibly second only to politics or religion in its ability to arouse fierce passions. I want to encourage unbiased listening and appraisal of jazz and to place Lennie Tristano's music in context, both temporal and artistic, so you can judge for yourself.

Only by going back to the beginning and looking at how it all evolved can we understand where jazz is now and where Lennie fits in. Few will disagree that when Africans were transported to America, they brought with them a culture far removed from the essentially European culture that had already taken hold in North America. There were already many differences between the emerging American culture and that of the various European cultures the émigrés had left behind. Nevertheless the striving for religious and political freedom that drove many Europeans to flee Europe and embrace the New World still resulted in a culture with a largely European framework.

It is hardly surprising that the two cultures, African and European, clashed head on. Africans were forcibly transported to the New World as slaves and vassals – and inevitably have struggled over the past two centuries to achieve some kind of emancipation and dignity from conditions of slavery and servitude. One of the less violent aspects of this striving has been the development of music, known to us as jazz. It may seem platitudinous to state that African Americans brought to the music a certain emotional directness, untouched by the emotionally repressed European cultural background. From an orthodox European outlook, African culture was seen as louche, immoral and as a threat to civilization. But for many Europeans, who longed for the kind of freedom that was proscribed by the European cultural background, there was also a fascination and even envy of black culture.

Today, many of those differences are blurred. The effect of the merging of cultures (and it should be borne in mind that this merging involved not merely the popular concept of black and white cultures but of a variety of differing European, Latin American, Middle Eastern, Oriental and Jewish cultures, as well as other cultures from all over the globe), has been a broadening and loosening of the North American jazz culture, with increasing sophistication of all ethnic groups, as far as their interest in jazz is concerned.

It is a generally accepted viewpoint that the music developed first of all in the marching bands and speakeasies, presumably around the early part of the 1900s. Books such as Chris Goddard's *Jazz Away from Home* are enlightening in that respect. The musical medium of those days was the popular song. (It is still very much the same today, though we now have a jazz heritage of almost a century to draw from.) The tradition of jazz developed to a great degree (despite the comparative lack of musical education in those early days) simply through the practical experience of playing and of listening to recordings.

Classical musical training (which few jazz musicians experienced) consisted mainly of learning how to become an artisan, not a creative musician: being able to play as directed by the conductor to a set and prescribed piece of music. In contrast, audiences for popular music expected musicians to add energy and interest to the tune. The demand for popular music led to a typical instrumentation of trumpet, which would play the lead, or melody, of the popular song; a banjo, which would punch out a rhythmic chordal accompaniment; a sousaphone, which would play the equivalent of "figured bass"; and a clarinet, which would weave a descant harmony around the trumpet melody. These working musicians were forced to use their ears and could not rely solely on being artisans, but had to become creative musicians. To be effective musicians they had to learn to "know" the melody and the harmony, not merely on an intellectual level, but to become totally immersed in the tune. In the early days the tunes were comparatively unsophisticated, making fewer demands on the musician than in later years. It is partly for that reason that the early music created in New Orleans and Chicago is still heard as jolly and easy to listen to. That is not to say it isn't interesting but, being less complex, is therefore easier on the ear (and the brain!)

As the musicians developed their improvising abilities, they began to experience a new freedom: that of taking a "chorus" and creating their own improvisations, while the others accompanied them. Then the typical playing format became standardized as a first chorus, in which the melody was clearly stated, followed by several choruses of improvisations and then a final chorus where the melody was again clearly stated. That became the essence of jazz and, although jazz in the New York clubs was in continual development, one could still hear this form in the music of the forties and fifties. Indeed, despite increasing sophistication, it still plays a major part in today's jazz.

During my time as a jazz musician in New York, I was fortunate enough to play alongside some of the older musicians who had known those days in New Orleans. This illustrates the rapidity with which jazz evolved; it was possible to gig alongside Buster Bailey, who was one of the early jazz musicians, and also to be playing alongside musicians, such as Lennie Tristano and Lee Konitz, who were musically worlds apart yet similarly contributing in that jazz era of the fifties.

However, in the early days of improvisation, it was very much extemporizing around the melody. By the twenties, Louis Armstrong realized that by weaving an improvisation on the chord changes one could disregard the melody and create entirely new music. As musicians developed self-confidence in their improvisation they became less dependent on the original melody and could then base their improvisation upon the harmonic pattern alone. The true art of improvisation became not merely arpeggiating on the chord structure (i.e. playing a series of individual notes on a chord) but creating a new melody based on the structure. As the music became more complex, and especially with the challenge of the "jam session" in which musicians strove to outplay one another, there came the temptation to play faster and with greater intricacy than their fellow jazzmen. Sometimes this resulted in mere musical gymnastics, but the greatest music was created by those who were not content with trying to outplay their fellow musicians, but were also striving to create meaningful and innovative music.

Thus the greatest jazz soloists were those who created the most beautiful and moving solos. From the twenties through to the early fifties, there developed a hierarchy based almost entirely on musical merit. If a musician developed a commercial reputation in addition to a musical reputation, so much the better. But it was first and foremost the musical hierarchy that counted, especially among the black community. But then, as now, it was not always the greatest musicians who reaped the most success. It helped even then to have a good manager. Outstanding was Louis Armstrong, who found in Joe Glaser (MCA) a manager who promoted him to the full.

But most of those whose reputation was based on musical merit did it the hard way, through the acknowledgment of jazz aficionados and musicians who heard their playing. Those such as trumpeter Roy Eldridge, tenor saxophonist Lester Young, and guitarist Charlie Christian, established their reputations first as sidemen with bandleaders such as drummer Gene Krupa and clarinettists Artie Shaw and Benny Goodman. It is incredible to think that guitarist Charlie Christian died of tuberculosis at twenty-five years of age, and Jimmy Blanton, arguably the first great modern jazz bass player, at twenty-three. Even by their early ages, their incredible musical skills were widely acknowledged. Both were outstanding in their musicianship and left an indelible influence on the music, despite the fact that they were never bandleaders. Clearly being black was a tremendous social disadvantage during those early days, so respect for their music was even more hard won. This was way before the pendulum swung the other way, toward the view that it was only black musicians who held the key to greatness in jazz.

From these early days of big bands that gave short solos to featured musicians, came the smaller bands which gave greater freedom to each of the musicians to do solos and show what improvisation was possible with each of their instruments. Vocalists fronting such smaller bands also had greater scope for improvisation, as against the big bands, where they would have featured songs, often slow romantic ones for dancing to, and then sit on the side. Since then there has been a greater focus on some of the musicians in the band, the front-line musicians such as saxophone, trumpet, and piano. The bass and drums have generally been pushed into a supporting role, maybe with the odd improvisation slot. It took a huge personality such as Mingus to refuse such a sideman position. Now we have a cult of the personality, where only the front-line player is the commercial draw and really the only one with scope to improvise or perform solo spots.

But through all of these changes, the format of melody, improvisation and solos, then a restatement of the melody, is still applicable to much jazz even today.

Nowadays, for the majority of people – including musicians, critics and jazz enthusiasts – this jazz umbrella shelters many, many styles of music, ranging from the early New Orleans ragtime, the hot music of the twenties, the so-called Chicago era, swing music, big-band music, bebop, cool, West Coast, Latin, Township music, smooth, free-form, vocalists such as Frank Sinatra, Billie Holiday, Ella Fitzgerald etc., blues, acid, world music, even rap. Such a wide spectrum. What (if anything) links such wide-ranging aspects of music? And how can people new to jazz understand what jazz is, or maybe what is not jazz?

You would think it would be, perhaps, fairly easy to distinguish jazz from classical music, yet what of Jacques Loussier's renditions of Bach, or Bud Powell playing C. P. E. Bach? Or the various efforts to jazz the classics? You could perhaps point out that classical music is arranged and played formally. But what then of the Modern Jazz Quartet, or much big-band music? Much of this is formal. One could then point out that even in the most formal jazz, there are improvisatory breaks. However at least some classical music has counterparts to this (in recitative for example). The boundary between jazz and classical is not as clear as you would first think.

Perhaps we can get closer to a finer distinction if we consider the musicians themselves. Many, perhaps the majority of classical musicians, owe their reputation and livelihood to the fact that they are artisans or interpreters of the music. So is it a question of interpretation of the music that distinguishes jazz? In jazz there is that sense of abandon, which comes across strongly in the tone and inflection of the playing. But what about jazz vocalists and musicians who have honed their skills to provide easy-listening concerts? Are they still creating jazz? With virtually a century of development, what may be thought of as abandon may only after all be mannerism. This is a different form of expression than classical, but perhaps just as mannered as the performance of an often-played Beethoven symphony. Can this still be thought of as jazz?

So what, then, distinguishes jazz? Personally, I have always regarded jazz in a specific sense, as being about improvisation. Improvisation can be likened to the seed from which jazz germinates. It is the improvisatory nature of jazz that has led to the development of styles. There is a subtle difference between improvised jazz that has led to a development of a style, and the acceptance of a style and the ability to play in that style. (People often confuse style with improvised jazz.) Playing in an accepted style does not invariably mean that the player is improvising. Nor can you say that someone with his or her own style is not also a tremendous improviser. Guitarist Martin Taylor, for example, is an exemplary player, and has developed a style of his own. To those who follow his playing, his music is immediately recognizable. Yet, as Martin freely admits, not all of his music is improvised. While this makes sense for one who frequently and mainly performs these days as a solo artist, it does not detract from his prowess. I would not hesitate in describing him as a superb jazz musician, simply because he has such incredible expertise and skill that he can improvise effortlessly. Yet a preconceived and arranged performance would not come under the banner of jazz improvisation for me. Similarly Bud Powell's rendition of Solfigietto (which I heard one night at Birdland), for example, was not jazz improvisation but a classical piece played in Bud's inimitable jazz style. Lee Konitz and Warne Marsh played a couple of J. S. Bach's Two Part Inventions, yet these too were played in their individualistic jazz approach.

All this highlights the confusion that has arisen over definitions of jazz, jazz improvisation and the various styles that have developed from jazz improvisation. But it is clear that Lennie Tristano was one of the greatest improvisers.

Although a number of great improvisers are household names to jazz fans, improvisation is not necessarily seen as center stage. Jazz styles seem to remain at the focus of jazz; even the majority of innovators are innovators of style rather than of improvisation. Louis Armstrong is better known for his vocalizing and stage personality than for his creative soloing on the trumpet, which was formidable; in the early days, he was highly respected among musicians for that skill. Lester Young was better known for his mannerisms than for the merit of his great solos, one of which ("Lady Be Good") was his first ever recording! Some musicians, for example Duke Ellington and Count Basie, although household names in jazz, are known mainly because of their bands.

Coming to the USA for the first time, I was completely naïve as far as the history of jazz was concerned and unaware of who had contributed what to the music. It was jazz music that I was drawn to. This was music that I liked, uncluttered by all the snobbery and fuss associated with classical music. Above all, I was fascinated by the music of the Lennie Tristano Sextet, which was clearly attracting wide appreciation.

This was the jazz music of the day, and was recognized by the jazz public in polls. This is not to affirm or deny the real value of Lennie

Tristano's contribution to jazz, but to show that at one time this music was seen as creative jazz. As we all know, polls and popularity are fickle signs – not always indications of lasting worth. But in Lennie's case, his focus was on improvisation, while increasingly the popular focus became one of jazz style and not improvisation. So let us take a closer look at what we mean by improvisation.

9 appreciating jazz improvisation

As for Lennie, the essence of jazz for me is improvisation.

When most musicians study jazz, they look to emulate other musicians. Once they begin to play similarly, they feel they have arrived. But this is only a first step toward genuine creativity. Then comes the real task of making your own music and finding your own voice as an improviser. Many only reach that first stage of mastering the jazz idiom and seem satisfied with being stylists in the image of someone else. Who wants to be a clone? The difference is between learning the instrument as an imitator and mastering the means of opening up to a limitless range of creative possibilities.

Elements of improvisation surface in gypsy music, in Indian ragas, in Near Eastern music and many kinds of folk music, but jazz improvisation stands in a class by itself. This fact in no way denigrates the improvisatory factors of other forms of music. Great jazz improvisation occurs as an immediate inspiration. Quite simply, the musician, playing on standard tunes and knowing the shape of the music from the original melody, then moves from there in various directions, but with such musical skill and understanding that he or she would be completely able to return at any one moment back to the melody with ease. It is like a vast array of patterns, shapes and colors that are spontaneously expressed around a central core that is not even stated. Though it is possible to learn to run through the chord changes and improvise to a certain degree, it is the excitement of the music and stimulation from other musicians, particularly rhythm sections, that urge the jazz soloist to the greatest heights. In a concert the audience may pick up on the enthusiasm, but generally very few really appreciate or understand the nuances of a solo.

A great solo includes not merely the basic harmonic structure of the music, but a departure from it – say playing a phrase temporarily in another key and then resolving it, like a trapeze artist taking a daring leap. Similarly a phrase may be displaced from its expected position within the bar lines, only to resolve neatly and unexpectedly – all without interrupting the basic pulse. Sometimes a melody from another source may become part of a solo – especially notable if the melody is of another well-known tune and occurs in an unexpected part of the solo. Did you ever hear a jazz solo and suddenly hear an interpolation of another well-known tune without an interruption of the musical flow? It is related that Charlie Parker, when playing at a ball, would inject the phrase "a pretty girl is like a melody" whenever a particularly attractive lady would dance by, without any break in his harmonic flow. But such aspects of creative jazz cannot be appreciated if the listener treats it merely as background music.

During the late forties and early fifties, in America at least, jazz was listened to and not regarded solely as background music and it was easier in those days to appreciate what was happening, even if for no other reason than that there was not the plethora of recordings that exists today. Now so many recordings are made that it is impossible to listen to everything. The most we can do is to sample tracks from here and there. The music that is successful today is almost entirely that which has been promoted by major record companies. Marketing thus becomes more important than talent. And improvising – which was the essence of those earlier jazz recordings – is less appreciated, less in demand in today's world. But thanks to reissues we can go back and immerse ourselves in some of those great moments of earlier years.

In pointing this out I have no wish to denigrate today's creativity in jazz. It is just that the emphasis has changed: improvisation is being looked upon more as decoration than as the core of the music.

One can only guess at what heights were achieved in some of the jam sessions of earlier years, where there was no studio environment to inhibit creativity. As many jazz musicians will testify, the very act of switching on the recorder seems to dampen the vibe. It almost seems as though jazz was never meant to be recorded. In spite of this, some great moments have occurred and have been preserved on tape and sometimes even on film. A personal favorite is the wonderful bass duo of Ron Carter and Christian McBride at the end of Robert Altman's film *Kansas City*.

Enough has been preserved, anyway, to give today's enthusiast some glimpses into a glorious musical past. The black writer Leroi Jones (Amiri Baraka) complained that, as he saw it, jazz was demeaned by the late fifties as it was purloined by white musicians and was, as a result, losing its meaning. Many people viewed this merely as racial prejudice – an attempt by a black writer to claim jazz as the sole creation and prerogative of black people. That may be, but as I see it, there is another element of concern here. The innovation and excitement of jazz as a one-off creative experience has been almost lost today. Leroi Jones sees it as the fault of white musicians; I would see it as a more complicated process.

Over the years – from the very beginning of jazz – a musical vocabulary was built up from musicians listening to each other and copying each other's ideas, whether they were black, white, East European, etc. The trumpeter Freddie Keppard refrained from recording for that very reason. He believed that by not recording he would retain an edge over others, as they would be unable to imitate his music. But the tide of improvisation rolled on regardless. In fact it is arguably due to the fact that sound recording became available during the twentieth century that jazz developed as it has. An essential element of jazz lies in the nuances of phrasing, and the many subtle emphases of accent cannot be written down as musical notation. The marvel (which today we take for granted) is that by listening to a historic recording, we hear not just the notes but the subtleties of inflection and phrasing which give meaning to the music, in a way that would be impossible otherwise and which were created only at that moment. Such nuances in an original recording of jazz improvisation can be copied and are often copied – not as inspiration but as mannerisms. Such musical imitation replaces the blood, sweat, and tears of the originators. Recently a young jazz musician transcribed one of my solos and got his scholarship for that. I wish him luck, but at the time I couldn't even get a gig!

But even the originators relied on the vocabulary of their predecessors for their own explorations. In fact every jazz musician does so. In this way a musical vocabulary developed from those early days of marching and speakeasy bands. Improvisation has developed from copying and influences from copying, which in turn develop into styles.

From such development came not only the great instrumental soloists, but also the development of big-band music. For jazz phrasing became even more exciting when a brass or sax section played it in unison or in harmony. Riffing became a particular improvisation aspect of big bands. This was when a section played a repetitive phrase across the harmony that moved underneath. Each phrase, though identical to the previous one, would convey a different connotation as the underlying harmony changes, for example in Basie's number "One O'Clock Jump." Later, riffing sometimes also made use of phrases that rolled across the bar lines, such as a 3/4 phrase, superimposed upon the basic 4/4 bar line.

Complaints that jazz was demeaned because other musicians purloined their ideas have to be seen in context, a context where jazz musicians learn and develop from previous musicians, whoever they are. The important thing is that they use this to develop their own vocabulary.

There is also the factor of the intensity of the playing that is part and parcel of creativity. Although recordings do enable a musician to emulate the great originators, the crucial question remains: do those who emulate go further and find their own voice or merely use the inspiration of others' recordings as a means of carving a niche for themselves? Those who emulate often make the music more accessible, and it can happen that the emulators become more popular than the originators who have influenced them. But once a concept (be it a particular phrase or solo) has entered the domain of recording it becomes common property and it is easier for followers to copy, credit going to the popularizer, not necessarily the original creator!

Although jazz education helps to develop awareness and facility in playing jazz, it is often rightly criticized as merely producing clones. It is but a short step from the original creativity to the facile wallpaper of smooth jazz. Granted that Leroi Jones has a point in regard to the popularizing of jazz, but trying to claim the music as belonging solely to black people – this is, unfortunately, racist, and not borne out by the actual development of the music. As Lennie pointed out (and he was promoting black talent at a time when black musicians' contributions to music were largely overlooked), "No one has an edge over music!" Was John Coltrane to be accused of purloining the music of *The Sound of Music* or the Count Basie band criticized for recording Ray Noble's "Cherokee"?

Leroi Jones's comments bring us back again to the knotty question of what is jazz? It is a word that covers a wide variety of concepts. It is a racy, snazzy word – even used as a name for a man's perfume. For some, the key defining factor is race; for me, the key defining factor is musical ability. Thus far I have used the concept of jazz to mean improvisation that stemmed from the original extemporization of the early marching and speakeasy bands. It is relatively easy to see the same essential threads from those early days at the beginning of the twentieth century right through to the early fifties. From that viewpoint the essence of jazz lies in improvisation on a theme.

So let's look a little more at this issue of themes (or jazz standards, as they are called). Generally, those themes were based on popular songs of the time and of course the ever creative potential of the blues. Though there were variants on the blues, the blues themes were usually of twelve-bar sequences, consisting of three groups of four bars. The first four bars stated the harmonic theme, the second were a variation and the final four bars brought the theme to a conclusion. Popular songs also provided the basic material for improvisation. During the twenties, thirties, forties and fifties, these usually had very basic thematic structures. A typical song of thirty-two bars would have a structure of A, A, B, A, each section being of eight bars. The first theme would be repeated, followed by a bridge section (B), which would effectively join the original themes together. For simplicity, let's take the folk tune, "Pop Goes the Weasel." Sing the first phrase, then see how it repeats (but not quite identically), then the third phase repeats exactly like the first, but the fourth phrase is different and brings the first part of this nursery rhyme to a close. We could describe this as A, B, A and the final stanza as C. An essential discipline for an improvising musician is to develop the instinct for such thematic sections, without the need for counting or being consciously focused on each section. (Beginners may have mentally to keep count throughout their playing, but try it!) To the extent that this became instinctive it would allow the improviser to become more creative. Such is the development of the music today that the ability instinctively to feel a section of eight or twelve bars is virtually taken for granted.

That such instincts had originally to be learned will come as something of a surprise to many present-day jazz musicians, who often view this as a natural skill. The real challenge then was to create essentially new music from relatively basic themes, of previous or current popular songs. In addition to the blues themes, one or two harmonic themes of thirty-two-bar duration became as popular as blues themes themselves. The first and foremost of these was based on George Gershwin's "I Got Rhythm." The sequence was originally one of thirty-four bars, two A sections of eight bars each, a bridge section B followed by an extended A section of ten bars. For ease and convenience of improvising the last A section was usually shortened to eight bars. This thirty-two-bar harmonic sequence was subsequently used as a common sequence for improvisation, often commencing with a line or "head" specially written as a jazz composition. Charlie Parker's "Anthropology" was a line written to fit this Gershwin standard. It also had the practical advantage that publishing rights went to Charlie Parker. Melody is the basis from which a tune is copyrighted and no one has succeeded in copyrighting a harmonic sequence. The other thirty-two-bar sequence that proved enduringly popular as a harmonic theme was the chord structure of "Honeysuckle Rose" (a tune written by Thomas "Fats" Waller). Charlie Parker used this harmonic theme as the basis for his tune "Scrapple from the Apple."

Lennie Tristano also wrote a number of "lines," as he called them, based upon the harmonic structures of well-known standards. The line entitled "317 East 32nd Street" was based upon the structure of Johnny Green's "Out of Nowhere." In this Lennie changed some of the original harmony to accommodate the line he had written, but the improvisation that followed was based entirely upon the harmony of "Out of Nowhere." Lennie's line "April" was similarly based upon the harmony of "I'll Remember April," "Lennie's Pennies" was based upon the sequence of "Pennies from Heaven" – except that, whereas "Pennies from Heaven" is written in the major mode, Lennie changed the sequence to a minor mode. You can see that with the passing years the music became more sophisticated. But the thread that linked the earliest jazz was still there even in the bebop years of the late forties and fifties. The essence was improvisation upon a standard harmonic theme.

As pointed out in Chapter 7, the first real break with that tradition came with a 1949 recording of Lennie's released by Capitol Records as a 78 r.p.m. disk. Those two tracks, entitled "Intuition" and "Digression," heralded the start of what became known as free-form jazz. As with many of Lennie's recordings, the critics were somewhat nonplussed by what he was creating. It was almost ten years before other musicians attempted similar free-form creativity. In 1958 Lee Konitz recorded some free-form music, while he was contracted to Verve. The personnel were Lee (alto sax), Don Ferrara (trumpet), Sal Mosca (piano), Ed Levinson (drums) and myself on bass. I recall how the music just seemed to unfold, and we were all quite excited about it. The remainder of the music for the proposed album was based upon well-known standards. In the event Verve did not release the music. The masters were lodged at the MGM Hollywood studios and were either damaged or destroyed in a subsequent fire. I have since heard that only the labeling was damaged and that the tapes remain intact. To my knowledge, they have not been released to date. But as I discussed in Chapter 7, the following year (1959), Ornette Coleman and his group recorded an album of free-form music and this time the genre was duly recognized and commercially exploited. By then Lennie's free-form recordings had been overlooked, and Ornette is thus erroneously credited as being the originator of free-form jazz. It is interesting to compare these two aspects of free-form improvisation, that of Lennie Tristano's group recorded in 1949 and that of Ornette recorded a decade later. I know also that Lee Konitz was disappointed that his "free-form" music was not released, while a year later the free-form music of Ornette's was released to considerable acclaim.

One of the criticisms leveled at so called "free-form jazz" is that it is undisciplined. To some ears the music sounds cacophonic. Whether this is so or not has little to do with free-form but everything to do with the improvisational skills of the musician. Poor musical ability can be covered up under chaotic noise. Free-form can sound abrasive, but it was apparent on Lennie's recordings that the musicians were listening to each other. As each picked up his own free-form theme the others backed him with sympathetic and harmonious accompaniment. Today much of the subsequent free-form music seldom gives the impression that the musicians really listen to each other. (Mind you, it amazes me anyway when I see jazz musicians wander off, go for a cigarette or talk to other musicians etc. during a colleague's solo.) Much free-form recording is more like a free-for-all (which results in freedom for none). A commonly expressed doubt regarding the validity of some musicians' free-form efforts is that many remain unconvinced of these musicians' ability to play on changes. Are they therefore copping out, pretending that theirs is the music of the future before having achieved even the basic mastery of playing on changes? You see it in other disciplines as well. Look at the early works of Matisse, Picasso, and Dali. They could paint in the style of the great masters – they had mastered the idiom. But they had subsequently gone beyond that to find their own "voice," in the knowledge that they understood the full range of skills. Could free-form musicians do the same? My personal belief is that an essential precursor to creating valid free-form music is first to develop the mastery of improvisation on harmonic changes. It is interesting to quote the great trumpeter Roy Eldridge concerning Ornette Coleman:

> I listened to him all kinds of way. I listened to him high and I listened to him cold sober. I even played with him. I think he's jiving, baby. He's putting everybody on. They start with a nice lead-off figure, but then they go off into outer space. They disregard the chords and they play odd numbers of bars. I can't follow them. (Hentoff 1976: 218)

From my own experience I can say that it's not easy to create something worthwhile as free-form music. On the other hand, it's easy just to play anything without regard to what other musicians are playing around you. But such efforts lack discipline and rarely produce anything worthwhile. It is puzzling when random playing becomes accepted as valid. However, in an age such as ours, when many people are fractious and ill at ease with themselves, I suspect that for many, there's a ready identification with undisciplined free-form. As though salvation can be reached through chaos. Perhaps it can, but I remain unconvinced. I am not a believer in shock therapy.

Clearly the debate about jazz improvisation is complex, problematic and often muddled. How it is defined depends upon the perspective taken. From the early twentieth century jazz evolved through several styles following the early New Orleans-type jazz (New Orleans being traditionally regarded as the birthplace of jazz), but surprisingly, the basic approach to jazz remained virtually the same. That is: a melodic instrument, usually saxophone or trumpet, playing the theme, piano or guitar playing the harmonic accompaniment, string bass playing the figured bass and drums boosting the rhythm. Though instrumentation changed over the years, this basic structural approach remained. It is true that the music became more sophisticated, the tunes sometimes more complex, but the simple blues structure remained as a fundamental aspect of jazz. This was also true of Lennie Tristano's playing. Even his then radically new and different 1949 sextet recordings were still based on the standard format. By then, however, the original melodies had been replaced by new themes – while the harmonic structure of the original standard had been retained. Lennie did not set the precedent in this concept, which was already being exploited by the beboppers. The jazz standard "Whispering," for example, was transformed into "Groovin' High" – an early bebop tune. What they had in common was the harmonic structure.

As jazz was developing, musicians might enjoy the challenge of playing on a particular harmonic sequence, but would begin to feel that the original melody lacked the kind of excitement they were looking for. Then they would compose a theme that exemplified the new idiom that they were beginning to develop. A good "line" – the name given to a new theme built on standard changes – would give a kick to the soloist, challenging him or her to a higher creative level.

Now the concept of jazz has expanded to include far wider horizons, improvisation having lost its primacy. Improvisation today has become filler, an interlude within the many different kinds of music that are today considered jazz or at least jazz-oriented.

The greatest improvisation occurs when, having mastered the idiom, the excitement of musical ambience, often generated by an inspired rhythm section, leads the soloist to excel him- or herself. On such occasions it is like being touched by the gods! I am reminded that the word enthusiasm comes from the Greek *En Theos* – from god.

10 the technical base of jazz and lennie's approach

I have already spoken at some length about Lennie's teaching approach (in Chapter 2), but I want to describe what I learned from him in more technical detail. Genuine improvisation demands great technical and musical skills. This chapter will be more interesting to those with some musical knowledge, but I hope it will help others see the technical complexity underlying jazz.

I have emphasized that his was a revolutionary approach at that time. But what is also crucial is that his teaching had been partly based on classical training. This combination was unique; that was what was so different about Lennie. Lennie's approach was more than just combining different techniques.

Teaching jazz is not merely about conveying intellectual knowledge. To be a good teacher you need also to be a psychologist. Effectively, rapport has to be developed with the student. Success is as much about having an instinct about what a particular student needs. This, at the time I knew him, was what Lennie had. In his book *An Unsung Cat* about Warne Marsh, Safford Chamberlain states that, according to psychiatrist Steve Silverman, Lennie was a "born analyst." Although another student, who subsequently became a psychoanalyst, attended two of the Saturday-night jam sessions and found them "very peculiar experiences." As often, the studio lights would be dimmed – which actually increases musicians' awareness of the music. In between playing we would often talk. This student saw these talks as Lennie giving advice about everyday problems and felt a "messianic," mind-control quality in Lennie.

Certainly, many of us were influenced by Wilhelm Reich and other psychologists' writings, and Lennie was not alone in believing that by striving to become freer from repression our ability to be creative would be enhanced. Though Lennie's understanding of psychoanalysis and the deeper revolutionary concepts developed by Reich came from books, that should not detract from the fact that Lennie understood them, and experienced those concepts as real. Contrast this with the academic reality, where students have to study books primarily to give the "expected" answers during exams – and from such tests come the sought-after academic credentials.

From Safford's description, I cannot recall who that embryonic young psychologist and Tristano fan was – but I wonder if Lennie triggered his choice of the psychoanalytic profession. If so, was that choice influenced (albeit subconsciously) by a desire to emulate and replace Lennie as a father figure? Certainly Lennie was a dominant figure. I have no quarrel with that. I learned much from him and certainly had no desire to emulate him, but through him I became a better musician and Lennie helped me to strengthen my convictions about music and life experiences.

As an aside from this, I feel I have gained strength from knowing those who have stuck to their convictions. Even now, after Lennie's death, I feel the strength of his convictions as a support, especially in these days of loucheness and unmitigated commercialism. I think of jazzman Roy Eldridge similarly: he had moral fiber that is rare in these days. Though I never met Reich, I feel the same way about him: as though his courage, set against the sleaze of the modern world, is always a support – even long after his demise.

But back to the issue of teaching and psychology. As in other psychoanalytic situations, the student can know all the answers yet he or she doesn't necessarily develop the ability to play jazz. Though an intellectual approach may work fine with a naturally talented student, there are those who feel bewildered about jazz. The fact that they decide to study the subject indicates an interest at least, but their motives may be mixed. Sometimes it is simply a lack of confidence. If someone feels like a novice and then is expected to stand up in front of an audience (or even the other musicians) and do his/her own thing, the fear of ridicule can make the student dry up completely. The classical musician may be competent in his/her own field, but in jazz there are no props. There's no written music to be played, just an empty space to be filled by your own musical creativity. Such a situation can be extremely daunting. As Lennie used to do, so now it has become standard practice to organize students to play together, ideally to group together those of comparable ability. It is also necessary to counsel the students not to be critical of others, just as they would not want others to express negativity over their own efforts. All of these psychological considerations seemed to me to be an instinctive part of Lennie's approach and something that I have developed in my own teaching.

What also sets Lennie's teaching apart was the understanding he had of the underlying reasons why a particular study was necessary. Considering scales for example – here was nothing new – scales were traditionally part of classical training. But with Lennie, the reasons why and the emphasis he gave marked a great shift in understanding. In classical circles it had become habitual to teach scales as though in so doing the aim was to develop technique. Lennie would request his students to play at a slow enough tempo to bring them into complete contact with music: scales as music, not merely as technique. Though some scales are technically more difficult to master than others, much of the anticipated difficulty stems from musical notation, which is visually offputting. As a result, many musicians never overcome their phobias of certain keys. Often musicians groan when a singer wants them to play in an unusual key. Though achieving mastery over scales is a first step, it is an extremely important one, as it is from the scales that harmonic knowledge is developed. From a jazzman's viewpoint it becomes necessary to become totally familiar with the flow of harmony. It is not merely a matter of mastering chords but developing an instinct for the flow of harmony.

To this end, when you have mastered the scales, it then becomes essential to practice them in a particular order. Confusion regarding the order of scales often occurs. Some people consider this to be the "cycle of fifths," others the "cycle of fourths." Neither of these describes the concept accurately. Does this mean taking the fourths or fifths in an ascending or in descending manner?

So, if this direction of practice is not clarified, the student may spend a lot of time to little advantage. It is necessary therefore to clear up this anomaly. The scales should be played in the order of ascending fourths. Most students presume that you can develop a flow of harmony only through playing chords. So let's try a little experiment. Play a scale of C major (one octave will do) CDEFGABC and then down again CBAGFEDC. Having done that, the ear will recognize that our key center in this instance is C. C becomes the doh of the scale. With the memory of that scale, one will relate C to doh no matter what. Play any other note in proximity to the C and it will sound as though it is in tension. Follow it with the C again and the ear will recognize that the tension has been resolved. To recap, playing a scale up and down will give the ear a reference point. The commencement and finishing note of the scale (in this case C) will tell the ear C is doh.

Having done that, now play the first four notes of the C scale – but with a long pause on the third note (E), then play the F after this pause, and on account of the pause the ear will now recognize F as the new doh. By pausing on the third note (the E) the ear has grown impatient of the wait and now settles for the F as a resolution of the tension. This is a fundamental aspect of melody, and we see that we have moved the musical tension just as convincingly as if we had used harmony to achieve the same ends. Having reached the F by this little sleight of ear, now play the F scale. Upon completion, play in similar manner the first four notes of the F scale with a long pause on the third note. The tension then leads us to play the B flat (which is the fourth note of the F scale). In turn the B flat becomes the starting point of the new key, and in this manner we can proceed through all of the keys in the same order of ascending fourths. Persuading students to understand this very basic set of patterns is crucial when teaching them, and yet many musicians and teachers fail to understand the significance of playing scales in that order.

The reason for practicing them this way is that it subconsciously instills in the student the prime order of harmonic flow. It also conveys the fact that the fourth note of the major scale is only one semitone (a half step). This becomes apparent from the key of F onwards, as the fourth note is (on the piano keyboard) represented as a black note. Proceeding through the keys until all the black notes are used, we come to G flat, which then employs the white note B as though it were a flat. (Technically in this key it is written and referred to as C flat.) When we continue we are then in the sharp keys, and on the fourth note of the sharp we take away a sharp, making it a natural. Thus we achieve the same result as when in the flat keys we make the fourth note a flat. We need to become so familiar with the keys in this order that we are then beginning to develop an instinct for harmonic flow. All of the great jazz musicians will have spent time on this; it was the foundation of Bird's exploration of harmony in unusual ways. This instinct is further developed by playing thirds (diatonically) in each key, followed by diatonic triads, sevenths, and elevenths etc. Each level of practice needs to be thoroughly absorbed before proceeding to the next. For example, if one proceeds to the diatonic thirds on the scales, without having first become thoroughly familiar with the scales themselves, the task of thirds on scales becomes inordinately difficult. And then if the thirds have not been properly absorbed, attempting triads on the scales may again cause undue difficulty. Should any particular level of this approach seem too difficult, it is a sure sign that the previous level has not yet been sufficiently absorbed.

Lennie would have his students develop this in the major and harmonic minor keys and also recommended a similar approach to the melodic minor scale. However, he used a fixed form (the ascending form of the melodic minor scale). This scale – as taught in the classical world – has a different configuration descending and ascending. But a fixed form was necessary in order to be able to build harmonic patterns (thirds, triads, sevenths, elevenths etc. upon a scale pattern).

Lennie (justifiably in my view) had little patience with such exercises as scales in contrary motion or with a scale such as the melodic minor – which has one ascending form and another form descending. As he viewed it, it tended to intellectualize the music rather than bring the student into real contact. Lennie's criticism was that the conventional classical training taught students to be artisans rather than encouraging creativity. You could not get far into jazz if your study was on a merely intellectual level. Much of this has been realized during the intervening fifty years, but such emphasis was new in those days of the forties and fifties. Lennie's teaching was ahead of its time; it demanded total thoroughness by jazz students.

One apparent advantage of Lennie being blind was that he did not have to concern himself with the complexities of written music. Academic teaching, proceeding mainly from the written page, grew unnecessarily difficult due to the complexity of written notation. The concentration and energy needed to come to grips with this distracted from the contact with the sound of the music itself. If creativity does, as many maintain, stem from the right side of the brain, the complexities of written notation would tend to put the emphasis on the left hemisphere and block the emotion and feeling for music itself. Lennie concerned himself little with how one developed the technique to play the bass, for example; his concern was how convincing you sounded and how you produced music that came alive, even in the simplest of exercises.

He helped me to realize that the essence of jazz is a living force in music, something that has come to the fore during this past half century. It was this emphasis on music as a vivid reality – to be expressed even in the playing of simple scales. Thus, the study of scales, not as mere exercises but as music, led to learning thirds, triads, and arpeggios built on each degree of the scale. Arpeggios played with musical feeling developed the longed-for instinct to hear the music as harmonic flow, and not just an unconnected series of notes. Today such concepts may seem pretty obvious, but were as revolutionary as they were simple a half century earlier.

Other aspects of his teaching were learning melodies and then learning the "changes" (i.e. harmonic sequences) underlying those melodies. This also led to learning jazz solos from records. As I said earlier, he would advocate that his students learn famous jazz solos. Lester Young (known affectionately as Pres) was respected by Lennie, not because of Lester's fame (in fact at the time Lester's fame had not then reached its zenith – though Lester's greatest playing had already peaked). It was because Lester had, in his time, taken the nuances of improvisation further than anyone else on his instrument. Though Lester had influenced such younger players as Stan Getz and Zoot Sims, there were certain subtleties in his playing that neither Stan nor Zoot appeared to realize. If players themselves were unable to reach or understand certain subtleties, how can we expect critics or the jazz public really to appreciate the depths of the music? Without that appreciation, the music cannot be fully understood. In our culture, sadly, that means a product that cannot be easily sold. And we seem to have reached the point whereby music is judged solely by its saleability.

One of the aspects of Lester Young's subtlety was that of displacement of a phrase or phrases against the underlying time. All of Lester's recordings were based upon tunes or motifs in common or 4/4 time. In fact, most of jazz even to this day is still based upon standard motifs and played in 4/4 time. This is not to dismiss jazz played in other time signatures. But using the basic 4/4 time, Lester displaced phrases and played a kind of hide and seek – without ever losing his place in regard to the underlying time signature. One can find examples of this in other recordings, but Lester was one of the first and greatest exponents of such abilities. Unfortunately, to explain such a process is somewhat analogous to analyzing a joke – in doing so the humor and point of it somehow get lost. Bird also was a master in this respect, building lines that literally played with the basic time signature yet never losing his place. Sometimes, when following a particular idea (especially one that uses a rhythm other than the basic rhythm), the idea itself is dropped because of a player's inability to take it to its logical conclusion for fear of losing the basic time and losing the underlying chord sequence. Have you ever been listening to a jazz solo that seems to be getting exciting and different and then, suddenly, you can't follow where it is going?

Lennie Tristano, understanding as he did the jazz legacy of Pres and Bird, built upon those aspects that were embodied in their music. Extension of harmony beyond the octave was not new, but the concept of soloing on the upper harmonies (i.e. beyond the seventh of the chord) and leaving the rhythm section to outline the basic harmony did go beyond what had been achieved before bebop. Substitute harmony had been used before, but not in such a developed way as in bebop. Soon it became the practice to use substitute harmony to a degree not before thought of as possible. Bird developed this to a fine art. Lennie did too. One notable example of harmonic substitution is found on Lennie's Atlantic recording *Tristano*. On the track "All the Things You Are," recorded with Lee Konitz at the Confucius Restaurant in New York City in 1955, Lee takes the first solo and then Lennie commences his solo on the second beat of the second bar. The original chord to the first bar is an F minor seventh. But Lennie's eighth-note phrase (starting on the second beat) commences with an A concert, down to F sharp, down to D natural and B natural, resolving neatly into the following chord of B flat minor seventh. The B minor seventh chord (played from the top down – indicating that Lennie did not know his harmony merely from the chordal root positions alone), though resolving perfectly with the succeeding chord of B flat minor seventh, comes as such a surprise. For the normal flow of harmony would commence with an F minor seventh chord. The five-beat pause gives an effect of expectancy, and when Lennie comes in on the strong A natural, it conveys such an air of surprise – as though lifting the expected harmony right out of its seat.

Most expressions of substitute harmony at least commence with the original chordal harmony before taking the listener to substitute harmonies. But to keep the listener waiting and then jumping in (from left field as it were) was taking improvisation beyond the usual bebop concepts. It was not only Lennie's ability to create such an unusual and surprising start to his solo, but the ability to continue with that strength of improvisation throughout the solo. Little wonder then that not everyone latched on to what he was doing, but those who did became fascinated with his exceptional jazz creativity.

What also sets Lennie's music apart is the incredible and exciting displacement of phrasing, of "telling a story," which reached new heights in bebop and even more so in the developments of Lennie's music and that of those he influenced. Over the following years Warne Marsh developed this aspect of displacement, unsurpassed by other saxophonists to this day.

In addition to studying solos, there was also the question of learning tunes. In those early days there were no cassette players, tape recorders were comparatively rare and record players were nowhere near as good or sophisticated as today. Sometimes, in order to learn the intricate parts of some solos, we would slow the record player down from 33 r.p.m. to 16 (provided we had a machine capable of that speed change). Later this became easier with tape recording, as most had two speeds (today computer software is available to do this). Recording something at the fast speed and playing it back at the slow speed would make it easier to "get into the corners of the music," so to speak. A similar approach also applied to learning standard melodies.

So with Lennie we would learn to sing the melodies of jazz standards before learning to play them, then learn to play them through the keys. It was a more formidable task to learn to play someone's jazz solo through all the keys. It was very tough in the early days, but as our familiarity with the music developed, such tasks were not as difficult as expected. But the essence was always learning the music through singing, which led to quick development of the ear and hence to jazz playing. Using a tape recorder, we could also play a melody with a metronome in the background to keep the tempo and then, on playback, play the chord changes in arpeggio form to help us grasp the underlying harmony. Only after considerable work on these tasks did the student feel confident to branch out with his own attempts at improvisation. The work on scales and the exercises built on the scales gave the basic groundwork. Learning tunes and putting arpeggio harmonic patterns to those tunes gave an insight into composition and learning jazz solos helped to develop the concept of a jazz vocabulary. Also, learning some of the earlier recorded jazz solos helped to develop an understanding of how jazz had evolved from its comparatively simple beginnings. This, then, was the basis of Lennie's teaching technique; it required considerable patience and hard work, but led to mastery of the idiom.

Just as Lennie analyzed what was needed to develop the harmonic and melodic instincts as a prerequisite for playing jazz, he also analyzed what to do in order to develop rhythmic freedom. These concepts were not just for the benefit of drummers or percussionists, but were applicable to all of us who studied with him. Just as in the other aspects of his teaching, the approach would be simple but thorough.

For example, he would have us practice simple rhythms such as beating one with one hand and two with the other, i.e. the left and right hand both beating one and the right hand only beating two. Very simple and very straightforward. Then change the order: the right hand taking both beats and the left hand beating the second one only. This then led to beating similarly with the feet. As with the hands then with the feet, then feet versus hands. Though the basic time is simple, it is not always that easy to do the different permutations of hands and feet. Having mastered this, we then did similar exercises of two against three, followed by three against four, four against five, three against five, and so on. As is the case with the development of patterns based on the scales, it is wisest to become thoroughly familiar with the simpler rhythms before attempting the more complex ones. Then you can build rhythmic independence even further, to the point that each limb is beating a different rhythm. I remember the drummer, Al Levitt, arriving at Lennie's studio on E 32nd Street one rainy evening, and Al, all excited, said, "I just got off the cross-town bus and his wipers were going four against five – and he didn't even know it!"

Listen to the rhythmic complexity expressed in Lennie's recording entitled "Turkish Mambo" with even more subtle effects expressed in tracks like "Lineup" and "East 32nd Street." One of Lennie's difficulties with rhythm sections was simply trying to get them to relax behind the complexity of his lines. Amazingly, Lennie was wrongly criticized in those early days for being unable to keep good time. I remember one drummer being so confused in this regard that when Lennie was playing a 7/8 phrase across the bar lines, the drummer tried to cram an entire bar of 4/4 into those seven eighth notes. Of course the excitement of that kind of phrasing was that it recurred an eighth note earlier each bar and would eventually fall back to being on beat one again, if the phrase was continued for long enough. The effect was like playing tag with the rhythm section. Being part of the rhythm section, you had to hold your own. Bird had something of that quality about him too, which often made inexperienced rhythm sections tighten up. But once a rhythm section tightens up, all is lost – there's no more swing. Lennie was often thought to be too demanding; in fact this was only because the rhythm sections had not comprehended his level of rhythmic development.

To be able to play in that rhythmically exciting way, Lennie also needed rhythm sections to play an even pulse. If a rhythm section played even a trace of syncopated rhythm it cut across the accented rhythm that characterized Lennie's improvising. It is on that account that I was able to recognize (as discussed in Chapter 5) so clearly the Charlie Parker track that originally had Lennie playing on it, but was then used (minus Lennie) for the movie *Bird*. No one but Lennie set those even but swinging tempos.

There is another aspect of the impact of rhythm on melodic improvisation. It is seldom realized that a simple melody conveys rhythm. Here is a simple exercise. Play arpeggios of seventh chords built on a major scale. For simplicity let's use the scale of C. The exercise then is (ascending): CEGB, DFAC, EGBD, FACE, GBDF, ACEG, BDFA, CEGB.

Then descend as follows: BGEC, AFDB, GECA, FDBG, ECAF, DBGE, CAFD, BGEC.

Take note then that this creates a melodic rhythm of four. If we then superimpose a rhythmic accent of three on this melodic pattern we will create a simple "moiré"-type pattern analogous to the birefringence patterns (like the musical equivalent of the moiré patterns that Bridget Riley painted) that occur in optics. I will use capital letters to denote the rhythmic accents. Our exercise thus proceeds as follows: CegBdfAceG-bdFacEgb, Dfa, Ceg and then descending Bge, etc.

Further rhythmic freedom can be reached by practicing melodic exercises built on scale patterns and superimposing other rhythmic patterns, such as 5/8 (3 plus 2) or (2 plus 3), 7/8 (4 plus 3) or (3 plus 4). Combining melodic rhythms in the Turkish mambo track (just mentioned) – 5/8, 7/8 and 12/8 – meant that it sounded peculiarly Middle Eastern. How-ever, using a 5/8 pattern consisting of three eighth notes followed by an eighth-note triplet, meant that the combination of these rhythms only recombines after 105 bars and makes the rhythm appear to float across the entire piece. The musical effect was like ripples on a pool on which Lennie further superimposed a kind of bluesy Middle Eastern improvisa-tion. It is a good illustration of Lennie's analytic awareness and under-standing of the melodic use that can be made of rhythm.

In their soloing, Bird and Pres expressed some aspects of such rhyth-mic complexity. In Pres's case this might have something to do with the fact that he was also a drummer. But Lennie realized that by deliberately practicing such exercise patterns, eventually this aspect of music would be instinctively absorbed and would express itself in improvisation. Such possibilities of development fascinated many of his students and one can hear that influence in many of their recordings. It enabled his students and associates to play rhythmic phrases across the bar lines without get-ting lost or having to relinquish an idea for fear of becoming confused. There is a specific kind of anxiety when an idea takes hold but wanders outside of the normal musical safety of accepted phrasing. Sometimes this happens anyway, and we would kid each other with a pun on the standard tune "You Don't Know What Love Is" by saying, "You don't know where one is."

Are there precedents for what Lennie was doing in regard to time displacement? Lester Young's solo on "Taxi War Dance" comes to mind; another example is Bird's solo on "Warming up a Riff." Time displace-ment is more obvious and more exciting in jazz because there is a strong underlying pulse – which sets the rhythm. But this is not only an aspect of jazz. Let us turn for a moment to classical music. The most frequently played example of time displacement is the first movement of Beethoven's Fifth Symphony. The music commences on the second beat of the bar. But whereas in jazz the pulse is already established, in Beethoven's Fifth Symphony the beat comes in cold as it were. The orchestra has no guide as to tempo apart from the memory of previous performances. To my ear most recordings of Beethoven's Fifth Symphony do not establish the reality of the first beat of silence. Only when the phrase is repeated the second time do we get the point – that Beethoven was playing a game. Shss! – Ba *Ba* Ba *Baa*, *Shss!* – Ba Ba Ba *Baa*. In jazz, with such a firmly established beat such a nuance would be obvious. However the man-ner in which Beethoven's Fifth is approached, with no tempo established by the conductor, means that the first phrase sounds arbitrary. Only in the second phrase does the "game" become apparent. In Lennie's composition the "line" "Two Not One" is of course implied in the title. As is customary in jazz, the beat is first established – usually by snapping the fingers on the second and fourth beat for a couple of bars – so that when the players come in they all feel the beat and the "game" of starting on the second beat is clear. Lennie's composition "Two Not One" was often misconstrued by listeners, as though Lennie could not keep accurate time. Many jazz listeners (including, oddly enough, some jazz critics) do not appreciate the nuances of the music. When Pres or Bird accented the time in unusual ways such nuances would not be remarked upon. Lennie, however, was frequently regarded as a maverick; the subtleties of his playing were often misunderstood.

From Lennie's own words, it was clear that to him jazz was first and foremost improvisation. He was so firmly fixed in that belief that he said, "I don't compose, I play what comes to me as it happens." That may be true of his improvising. I believe, however, that he was also pointing out that many jazz musicians don't improvise in that sense. Having already established a framework for their playing, genuine improvisation often plays only a small part. Lennie's credo was to reach the point where there was no preconceived melody or line, only the moment (the "now"), during which anything could happen. This was based on deep understanding of the structure and rhythms of music and solid musical skills, not just self-indulgent sprawls of notes. Only the underlying flow of harmony would be the guide and the challenge with which to create something new. He realized that the greatness in Bird's playing and also of Pres's playing was the incredible spontaneity and complete skill in their music. It was this that Lennie strived for and achieved in those few recordings that he left to us. In those remarkable recordings made in 1949, two tracks, "Intuition" and "Digression," even dispensed with a set harmonic sequence, and the discipline with which the musicians approached this free-form creativity has never, even to this day, been surpassed. It is tragic that such inspired recordings have been overlooked and that credit has instead been given to (to my ears) more superficial improvisers, who attempted such an approach ten years later.

But focusing on his belief in improvisation, it is easy to overlook the fact that Lennie was also a master of jazz composition. His compositions are few in number, yet in many ways they are developments beyond anything in jazz composition before or since. Nevertheless they are traditional in the sense that they are melodies created upon well-known sequences. The possible exception is "Lennie's Pennies" (discussed in Chapter 9).

Studying with Lennie enabled me to develop unusual skills as a bass player, even though he wasn't a bass player himself. In the early days (prior to the late fifties) almost all bass playing was acoustic. In addition, most strings were gut or wire-wound gut. String breakages were common and the temptation was to have a higher action (that is a greater distance between the string and the fingerboard). This was to make yourself heard against such things as loud drumming and noisy audiences.

The fifties saw great improvement and development of strings – nylon, wire-wound nylon, and then steel-wound strings. There were early problems with steel strings because of the additional tension and subsequent strain this put on the instrument itself. There was also the added problem of the strain on the fingers. In trying to overcome these problems you had to develop very strong wrists. Bass player Vinnie Burke even resorted to taking day jobs – laboring on a building site – to help strengthen his wrists. The physical difficulties of playing bass with jazz groups adversely affected technique and is perhaps the main reason why bass playing in those early years sounded relatively unsophisticated. Until the fifties most groups wanted the bass to play good swinging time and expected little more than that. Bass players tended to form little cliques – discussing their problems, how to develop a good sound, how to develop soloing ability. Most of these problems stemmed from the physical difficulties of bass playing.

From the late fifties the improvements in the quality of strings, and the availability of bass amplifiers, enabled bass players to develop a technique not reliant upon muscle strength alone. There is a tremendous difference in sound quality when an acoustic double bass is played gently from when it is played to try to get the maximum sound acoustically. This is especially true of pizzicato bass – pizzicato being the traditional way of playing jazz bass since the very early days of ragtime. With the advent of good bass amplification it became possible to play gently within a jazz group and yet still be heard adequately. This made an enormous difference to the bass player's role in jazz.

There had been some remarkable early recordings of jazz bass solos; Israel Crosby is perhaps the earliest example in his recordings with Edmond Hall on "Profoundly Blue." Then, most notably, there are the recordings of Jimmy Blanton with Duke Ellington: "Body and Soul," "Mr. JB Blues," "Pitter Panther Patter," and "Sophisticated Lady." These set the standard for great jazz bass improvisation and even today, with all the instrumental improvements and the technical developments of bass playing, Jimmy Blanton's few recordings still remain in a class of their own. Within a year or so a later bass player with Lionel Hampton

– Charles Mingus – recorded "Mingus Fingers" and as I mentioned earlier (Chapter 1) that particular solo inspired me in the early days while I was playing as a teenager in London. Following that came the playing of Ray Brown – a recording of his "One Bass Hit" also became a favorite among bass players generally.

Up until the mid-forties, bass players – playing "time" (that is four in a bar) – generally played more percussively, in trying to cut through the ambient sounds of the band (and sometimes a noisy audience). But with Ray Brown there came an emphasis on playing as legato as possible, while still playing four notes to a bar. The concept was to make each note as long as possible, releasing it only when the next note was sounded. This gave an immediate sense of excitement and pulse, much more so than the earlier percussive playing. For me it is Ray Brown's playing that has influenced me more than anyone's. Ray was the first to develop the sound of what is now recognized as modern jazz bass playing. Lennie was quick to realize this and encouraged me to develop more of a legato sound.

Then there was Oscar Pettiford, who perhaps more than anyone played very melodic solos. It is perhaps unsurprising that as jazz bass playing became technically easier, due to improvement in strings and with bass amplification, the earlier need for high actions was no longer paramount and technique began to become evident as a feature in itself. It is not difficult to play fast on a double bass if one plays notes that fall under the fingers. Lennie's insistence that one learned to give priority to the music and not the fingers meant the fingers must not rule the head. The challenge was to enable the fingers to express the music that comes from within. Bassist Red Mitchell also studied with Lennie, and even in the early days I could hear that approach in Red's playing.

It was but one step from the legato playing of Ray Brown to the development of a technique in which the left hand stops the note without the right hand actually plucking it. To illustrate: supposing we play a scale of B♭. We finger the first note (first finger on the string) and pluck it with the right hand. We then play the C with the left hand (fourth finger on the string) by bringing the fourth finger down sharply on the string, the note sounds (though faintly) without the right hand plucking it. It then sounds as though "ghosted." Then play the open D on the D string, followed by "ghosting" the fourth note – by bringing the first finger down sharply on the E flat. The fifth note of the scale is sounded by the fourth finger stopping the note (F) on the D string and plucking it at the same time. The sixth note of the scale (the open G) is just ghosted, and the second finger then placed on the A (which is also plucked) and the final note (B♭) is again ghosted by just bringing the fourth finger down sharply – but not plucking it. A fairly straightforward exercise – but practicing in this manner enables you to develop independence between the left hand (which creates the position on the string) and the right hand, which actually sounds the notes. Development of this technique, which is a great asset in soloing, leads you to begin to regard the right hand that plucks the note as more in the nature of a bow. The left hand does most of the work while the right hand, in plucking the string, just lends emphasis to certain notes. When a musician has mastered this technique by plucking every other note, then it can be developed further by plucking every third note. This technique became practical only with the advent of better strings and at least some amplification. Later this technique can be extended still further by mixing it up, say in groups of twos and threes. It is in many ways similar to that used by modern-day electric guitarists. Lennie had me practicing such technique in 1951, years before amplification became generally available. Always the emphasis was on allowing the fingers to follow the musical flow and never allowing the fingers to dictate what they might have wanted, simply because it sounded flashy.

Studying with Lennie, and practicing according to our own particular talents, almost without realizing it, we set ourselves apart or were set apart from what has become the mainstream of jazz. This gave rise, on the one hand, to increased determination to develop further and, on the other, to the frustration and disappointment of being, to an extent, alienated from the mainstream. I don't want to convey the impression that we totally divorced ourselves from mainstream jazz development. I suppose, deep down, we all hoped that as our playing abilities developed, this would have a greater and more obvious impact upon jazz. In fact it has had an impact, but the effect is somewhat analogous to what happened in other fields of endeavor, for instance to Velikovsky in the fields of geology, astronomy and archeology, or to Reich in psychology and biophysics. The influence eventually made itself felt in jazz improvisation, but without recognition of its roots and without recognition of Lennie as the originator.

Lennie Tristano and Peter Ind at Manhatten Studios, August 15, 1953

Lennie Tristano, Peter Ind and Al Levitt at Manhatten Studios, August 15, 1953

Part III

A Reconsideration of Lennie's Legacy

11 mythmaking about lennie

When I began this book I was concerned to talk about the Lennie I knew. So many people have written about Lennie already. To look at his legacy you need to reflect carefully on these assessments, otherwise this book becomes just another view pasted on top of the others. I think we need an overall shift in thinking about this legacy.

Lennie certainly raised some strong reactions – both good and bad. In fact, sometimes the reviewers seem to be talking about very different people. But whether the reviews are positive (to the point of being gushing) or negative (almost to the point of discrediting him), they have not necessarily gotten their facts right or have been influenced by previous comments. A web of myths has therefore been spun about him. Some of the myths that I think need to be reconsidered are:

- Lennie's contribution to jazz was early on overplayed and then reassessed and found wanting
- Lennie had a school
- Lennie had disciples
- Lennie led a whites-only, cool school of jazz
- His music was cold and unemotional
- Lennie cheated to get the effects he wanted
- Lennie could not keep time (this one kills me!)
- He used the rhythm section just as a metronome, so he could shine
- Lennie gave up playing to teach
- Lennie was a recluse

So let's look at these myths in relation to what reviewers have actually said.

> Lennie Tristano (who died in 1978) is the head of the previously mentioned Tristano school, which had such great importance at the time of the crystallization of cool jazz. He played long, sweeping, sensitive melodic lines (often almost in the sense of Bach's linearity) over complex harmonic structures. As Lynn Anderson put it: "He was the first

piano player to spontaneously improvise extended chord stretches... He was the first to improvise counterpoint... Another of his innovations was his conception of bypassed resolution, so that harmony does not always move in the way you think it should..." Tristano anticipated the harmonic freedom of free jazz by as much as ten years. (Berendt 1983: 279–80)

In 1951 Tristano founded a school of jazz in New York; the first significant institution of its kind. For his teaching staff he used his most important pupils, including Konitz, Marsh, Bauer, and Sal Mosca. From this point he increasingly withdrew from public life, appearing rarely and issuing only a few experimental recordings as an adjunct to his teaching. He gradually lost his staff as his pupil-disciples embarked on their own careers. (Kernfeld 1988: II, 50)

Very clear, isn't it, from two recognized reference sources on jazz? Lennie founded a school, no less? I wish I knew where that school was. It certainly wasn't in his studio, as far as I know. I am sure that those musicians who played and studied with Lennie will be interested to know that they were teaching staff in an institution. As I discussed in Chapter 3, the reality was that in 1951 Lennie leased a small loft above a sheet-metal workshop on E 32nd Street in Manhattan. Several of us helped ready the place for use as a music studio/teaching facility. At the rear was a toilet and some minimal kitchen facilities. A sound insulating partition separated off the front part of the loft, which was used sometimes for teaching and also functioned as the control room, housing Lennie's tape and playback equipment. That was it.

As we saw in Chapter 10, although Lennie had composed some incredible music – "Wow," "Crosscurrent," "317 East 32nd St" – his main endeavors lay in developing his ability for jazz improvisation, and this was also his focus as a teacher. And his respect for the great jazz innovators – Lester Young, Charlie Christian, Charlie Parker, and the early Louis Armstrong – was grounded in their improvisational abilities. In this he showed that he was not fixated in any one idiom, but in the principle of improvisation itself. It was that insight, plus his dedication to the spirit of the music, that more than anything fascinated those of us who studied with him and helped to inculcate in us the value of staying pure to the music, not to a particular style, but to the spirit of improvisation. We were not disciples under the influence of a guru. This idea of disciples implies that we had no voice of our own, that we were merely jazz clones. Personally, I have found myself being regarded as though in all those years in New York the circle of musicians associated with Lennie were the only people that I ever played with. The reality is somewhat different.

What the critics have arbitrarily compartmentalized as styles hides the fact that during those years, especially the fifties, there was great interaction between young and old jazz musicians of all styles. Not only was it exciting for us younger musicians, but the older musicians also welcomed the experience of bringing younger musicians into the fold. For me it meant playing with people like Red Allen, Buster Bailey, Pee Wee Russell, Vic Dickenson, Red Norvo, Jo Jones, Teddy Wilson, and Billy Strayhorn, who had been involved in the earlier jazz, as well as those who had a strong established personal following: Buddy Rich, Coleman Hawkins, Roy Eldridge, Duke Ellington, Dave Brubeck, Gerry Mulligan, Chris Connor, Duke Ellington, Red Norvo, Sam Donahue, and Benny Goodman. In addition it meant playing with some who were moving the boundaries and some of the then younger generation who have since gained a significant reputation: Stan Getz, Herbie Mann, Carmen McCrae, Bill Evans, Tal Farlow, Jimmy Raney, Bobby Scott, Zoot Sims, Tommy Flanagan, and Toshiko Akiyoshi – not forgetting, of course, Jackie McLean and Donald Byrd. There were literally hundreds in the New York jazz scene; some of them are well known to jazz aficionados, such as Duke Jordan, Nat Pierce, Art Taylor, Dave Amram, Eddie Bert, Kenny Clarke, Hank d'Amico, Buzzy Drootin, Ben Webster, Dick Hyman, Marian McPartland, Flip Phillips, Joe Puma, Billy Strayhorn, Tony Scott, Elvin Jones, Jo Jones, and Philly Joe Jones, but not always so well known to the jazz public. There were many others who were very much a part of the scene but for some reason received little recognition. Where, in the "authoritative" books on jazz, do we find musicians like guitarist Al Schackman, drummers Ronnie Free and Ronnie Bedford, tenor saxophonist Carmen Leggio, pianist Patti Bown, and alto sax player Vinnie Dean? All of them were prominent on the jazz scene at that time.

A prime example of how reality becomes distorted and a false history develops can be found in Francis Newton's book *The Jazz Scene*. Written in 1959 (a mere ten years after those classic recordings made by the Lennie Tristano Sextet) and published in 1961 by Penguin Books, it describes the so-called "cool school" thus:

> Leading "progressive" players like the pianist Lennie Tristano, the saxophonist Lee Konitz, even took to theorizing, founding academies, and teaching, a thing hitherto unheard of in jazz, where musicians said what they had to say in notes and not words, and learned what they had to learn by apprenticeship, like Renaissance painters. These are the players and composers who claim to be inspired by Johann Sebastian Bach and eighteenth-century classicism – an admirable model, but a very surprising one. Intellectualized and formalized jazz such as this, drained of much of its old-fashioned red blood, naturally

appealed particularly strongly to young white players, who are much better able to compete with colored ones on territory which is, after all, close to the one in which all white musicians have been brought up. Cool jazz therefore attracted an abnormally large number of young white recruits, especially in California, where Los Angeles became the headquarters of a "West Coast School." (Newton 1959: 106)

Obviously, this passage contains the familiar assertion that Lennie and Lee founded academies. I don't know whether or not Newton actually created this myth, but certainly one could not find a better example of jazz mythmaking.

Next comes the myth of "intellectualized and formalized jazz" – again, Newton may or may not have been the originator of this erroneous concept, but his comments could certainly be seen as a second myth. The irony is that Lennie, being as he was a very perceptive person, was then parodied as intellectualizing jazz. Newton's comments turned the reality of what Lennie was and what he stood for on its head. The additional comment describing the music of Lennie Tristano being "drained of much of its old-fashioned red blood" seems simply an attempt to deny the strength and intensity of Lennie's playing. Fortunately, recordings, once made, are there for all time. The musical integrity and intensity of those great recordings – even if missed or glossed over – can always be revisited. The third and most politically damaging myth concerns his comments about race, white musicians "competing" with colored ones – it is sad that Newton could not have enjoyed the camaraderie, the jam sessions, the excitement shared by all jazz musicians, especially in New York during that fertile creative period in jazz from the late forties through the mid-fifties. Gone are the days when Bird would help Lennie from the stage at the Three Deuces, gone are the days when they would play together as the leading jazzmen of their time. Gone are the days when achievement in jazz could be acknowledged for its own sake. And who now knows what happened? Nowadays, with political correctness uppermost, honesty takes a back seat. There are no winners in such a situation. The loser is the music itself.

Again, in the *Illustrated Encyclopedia of Jazz*, there is the same myth:

...blind pianist and teacher Lennie Tristano attracted a small dedicated group of disciples in the '40s and '50s for what was popularly called "the Cool School."

Running counter to the prevailing passion of bebop, Tristano experimented in linear improvisation, long, undulating Bach-like lines, counterpoint, atonality, a low decibel count and intense and subtle rhythmic complexity... In 1949, the Lennie Tristano Sextet with altoist Lee Konitz, tenorist Warne Marsh, Billy Bauer, recorded a classic (*Crosscurrents*). Over a steady rhythm, the players wove in and out of each other's lines lightly and precisely. "Intuition" from this session dispensed with an harmonic base and is arguably the starting point of the New Thing – certainly free collective improvisation has never sounded so seamlessly beautiful ...

Though his detractors have accused Tristano of sounding bloodless and academic, Charlie Parker respected his music and the two men played together on the All Star Metronome broadcast ("Anthropology"). Tristano's moving blues for Bird ("Requiem – Lines") proves that the cerebral approach need not preclude feeling. Multi-tracking on "Turkish Mambo" so that the three lines move in different times, "East 32nd Street" and "Line Up" caused a storm of controversy at the time, 1955, but would pass unnoticed in the technological '70s. In this case, the music justifies the means. (Case et al. 1986: 179)

The author is almost surprised about the feeling, but you have to ask, even in the seventies, could anyone have conceived and played an improvisation of that quality and complexity? Critic Ira Gitler, who seemed most sympathetic to Lennie's achievements, was still unclear about some aspects of Lennie's playing. He described the overdubbed lines in "Turkish Mambo" (already discussed in Chapter 9) as "one moves from 7/8 to 7/4, another from 5/8 to 5/4 and the third from 3/8 to 4/4." He doesn't mention the sound of the metronome in the background, which in fact provides the link to the multiple rhythmic patterns. Gitler unnecessarily complicates matters. This unique track has the metronome beating a quarter-note rhythm. What is most intriguing is that it has no orthodox time signature at all. The metronome is merely a co-ordinator. You can choose according to what rhythm you hear as predominant and what kind of time signature you accept. If you regard the metronome as beating quarter notes, the other superimposed rhythms are all based on eighth notes. The rhythms are introduced one at a time, the first being a continuous phrase of seven eighth notes. Because these repeated phrases are set over the steady metronome beat of quarter notes, they do not convey a primary time signature of seven, but only a subsidiary time rolling over the quarter-note metronome beat. Then after a few of these 7/8 phrases a new rhythm is introduced, that of a 5/8 phrase. This is a combination of three eighth notes and an eighth-note triplet. Once this in turn is established, a third rhythm is added – this is of a twelve eighth-note phrase. As jazzmen relate easiest to 4/4 rhythm, it is usually heard by them as though the metronome was beating a 4/4 time. But hearing it this way is arbitrary.

What is not arbitrary are the eighth-note phrases set against or over a steady quarter-note metronome. But this still does not mandate a time signature, as we know it. The final addition of a bluesy-type right-hand improvisation does give a final indication of 4/4 time, but this is just implied by the kind of phrases played by Lennie. As far as I am aware, this is the first and perhaps the only recording (with the exception of free-form jazz) without a specific time signature. If we take the arbitrary 4/4 as a basic time signature, exact repetition of the interlocking phrases occurs only after 105 bars. Without understanding this, it may not be easy listening but it is incredible musical conception!

The *Illustrated Encyclopedia* review concludes: "Always a recluse, the great pianist did not choose to record again until 1962 (*The New Tristano*), which in terms of melodic invention, facility with complex time signatures and sheer technical mastery remains unsurpassed." During the time between the release of the first and second Atlantic albums (1955 and 1962) Lennie continued to record while supposedly reclusive – though little has subsequently been released. What this account does not seem to take into account is the lack of opportunity to perform publicly, as during those years, jazz was losing ground to more commercial forms of music.

The idea of Lennie as a recluse continues:

> That same month [in 1959], a musician arrived in New York who seemed to challenge the basic premises upon which all these masters had built their music. It was the signal that the transformation of jazz into an art music, which had been underway at the beginning of the decade, was nearing completion at its end. His music would be given a variety of labels, including Free Jazz and New Thing, but it was clear that jazz now had an avant-garde in the modernist European sense for which accessibility would take a back seat to individual expression.
>
> Armstrong and Ellington, Parker and Gillespie, Monk and Davis, Mulligan and John Lewis and Brubeck, had all been content to make their individual statements while working upon agreed-upon rhythm, harmony, and chord sequences. Ornette Coleman rejected all that. Jazz, he said must be "free."
>
> He was not the first to declare his independence. Ten years earlier, the pianist and theorist Lennie Tristano and the alto and tenor saxophonists Lee Konitz and Warne Marsh had recorded with a sextet several free-form, collectively improvised sides – including one piece aptly called "Intuition"... (Ward and Burns 2001: 413)

After a brief mention of the pianist Cecil Taylor, the reviewer goes on to state: "but Tristano was a recluse who disliked playing in public..." The same book also states: "Lennie Tristano's 'Intuition' and 'Digression,' a 'free' group improvisation (without pre-stated melody, harmonic structure, or tempo) were considered so avant-garde in 1949 that Capitol Records refused to release them. Yet, again, these were isolated performances, and though they heralded jazz schools (third stream, the Tristano cult), they were not the stuff of a movement" (ibid.: 362). Such is the brief coverage given in Geoffrey C. Ward and Ken Burns's monumental book on jazz to one of the great contributors to the evolution of jazz, and possibly the most significant white jazz musician in the development of the music.

The question looms: does music lose in significance if it is not considered to have commercial potential (or perceived lack of commercial potential) and so fails to reach a sizable audience? Does Lennie's challenge not count because it was too avant-garde?

The red herring of Tristano being classified as a recluse in both the *Illustrated Encyclopedia* and in the Ward/Burns history virtually infers that it was his fault that the first free-form music was ignored in favor of that of Ornette Coleman ten years later. Why was Ornette Coleman seen to "challenge the basic premises upon which all the masters had built their music" when Tristano had already done that ten years previously? I have already talked about free-form music in detail in Chapter 10. I think that the fanfare around free-form music, ten years after Lennie, has more to do with rebellion, provocative action, and packaging than with musical achievement

The majority of jazz publications (when they mention Lennie at all) admit his greatness, yet somehow find reason to minimize this in some way. Often this has been by claiming that his music never appealed to the black music fraternity, or that he never employed black musicians. This is the saddest of all the comments to me: that his music was "white jazz." Or, as saxophonist Lew Tabackin commented: "Tristano took the blackness out of the music." What a misguided comment! Such views have unfortunately led to the belief that Lennie was racist. But drummer Max Roach had described it like it was: "Lennie was in New York City and he was downtown, and Charlie Parker and Monk and all of us were uptown. Lennie had a school and of course what Dizzy and Bird and Monk had that was the other school. And of course we intermingled. I played a lot, jammed a lot with Lennie during that time, a lot of us did." Max recognized, as did Bird and other African American jazz musicians, that Lennie had something valuable – as, of course, did Bird and Dizzy and the others with great creative value – and each respected the others and learned from them. It was never a question of racism, but of mutual appreciation and learning. All this seems to have been forgotten in the intervening fifty years.

Lennie both played and recorded with black musicians. Mingus studied with him. When I played with Lennie's quartet in 1952, Roy Haynes was the drummer. Also Roy was the drummer on those two tracks, "Passtime" and "JuJu," recorded in November 1951. When I was interviewed on Phil Schaap's radio show in New York in 2000 and was asked did Lennie ever play with Bird, for the moment I was surprised (not realizing at the time the emotiveness of the question). It seemed an odd query to me. There were the occasions on which Bird visited Lennie and played with him at his E 32nd Street studio. Apart from the Metronome All Stars tracks ("Overtures" and "Victory Ball"), there was a recording in the early days of Birdland with Bird, Dizzy, and Lennie playing "Tiger Rag" together. However, since they were two of the leading jazz musicians in the late forties, they would often be working with their own groups, but that didn't stop them playing together, as Lennie described:

> Before we were to go on together to do a couple of Mutual Network shows ("Battle of Styles"), I was sitting at the piano, playing something. He [Bird] started playing with me, and he played his ass off. He wasn't used to the chords I played. I play sort of my own chords ... I don't remember the tune, but whatever I did, he was right on top of the chord, like we had rehearsed. (Reisner 1974: 224)

And it was not only a musical appreciation. Lennie again:

> I knew Bird since the time he came back to New York from Camarillo. I can say that he has been nicer to me than anybody in the business. My group was opposite his at the Three Deuces. He sat through my entire first set listening intently. When it was over, the two fellows I was playing with left the stand, leaving me alone. They knew I could get around all right, but Bird didn't know that; he thought I was hung up for the moment. He rushed up to the stand, told me how much he liked my playing, and subtly escorted me off the bandstand. (ibid. 223)

His reverence for Parker is well exemplified by his now classic, oft-repeated remark: "If Charlie Parker wanted to invoke plagiarism laws, he could sue almost everybody who's made a record in the last ten years" (Gitler 1966: 246).

There are a number of recordings where Lennie and Bird played together. In Billy Bauer's book, he has a photo of himself, Lennie and Bird playing together (taken at the Metronome All Stars date) that was used as a postcard. According to Billy this is now sold in museums as a poster.

Beyond a solid understanding of the facts, the focus has to be on a good technical understanding of music to really appreciate what Lennie is doing. For example, let's look at two comments on one of his most innovative works, "Requiem," his tribute to Bird: "Tristano aspired to a pure dispassionate piano sound (even recording one of his most down-to-earth improvisations, 'Requiem,' at half speed so that, when played back, it would have an other-worldly ring to it)" (Brian Priestley, in Carr et al. 1988: 506). "'Requiem,' the blues for Charlie Parker, makes use of overdubbing in that Tristano accompanies himself in places, but there is no speeding up of the tape" (Gitler 1966: 239).

So who is right? The first is wrong (there was no slowing up of the tape) and the second is only partially right, since he overdubbed only that last tremolo chorus at the end. Let's look at another example: "The two November 1951 recordings, 'Passtime' and 'JuJu', Tristano had Ind and Haynes back him in the unadorned style he prefers and then, listening to the playbacks, added additional piano tracks, *some of which were speeded up by engineer Rudy Van Gelder in the mastering*" (ibid.: 237, my emphasis).

Now I played on this one so, I *know* it is not true, but how many times must such statements be made and where do the writers get their information from? The critics' opinions are believed to be reality when even careful listening will reveal the truth. Many times people made comments about Lennie's rhythm sections, as if he needed them to be no more than a metronome so his own playing could be premier. It is true that he always wanted good strong swinging time, but no fireworks. The pyrotechnics exhibited by many bebop drummers were anathema to him. But let me tell you, to play in an accompanying rhythm section with Lennie was not easy. It required tremendous skill, understanding, and conviction. It often felt like being buffeted, always having to be completely on top of the music and ready for any surprise directions and still holding the rhythm firm, no matter what. It has stood me in good stead ever since to play strongly and consistently no matter what was going on. Sometimes everything would be going along fine – and just when you felt the band was swinging along comfortably Lennie would suddenly go *womp*, with an unexpected, sudden and whimsical interjection, and rhythm sections would often panic. One needed to be very strong not to cop out in such situations. But if you kept your feeling of strength and were able to maintain a real pulse, the music could be very exciting. As for the criticism that came my way – on account of my being a dull workaday bass player "merely" playing a strong uninterrupted 4/4 with Lennie – I just wished the critics could have realized how difficult it was to swing a steady beat against (or with) such unusual and creative improvisation as Lennie's.

I have to mention something that Lennie allegedly said that puzzled me. In Safford Chamberlain's book about Warne Marsh, *An Unsung Cat*, Lennie described the multi-taping of "LineUp" and "East 32nd Street" to an anonymous interviewer. Explaining that he always had a problem with rhythm sections, he said, "I recorded the rhythm section first, so the rhythm won't mess up." Now Jeff Morton and I made those and some additional tracks for Lennie at the time we were going on the road with Lee's band. We had played regularly at the Wednesday and Saturday sessions at Lennie's studio from 1951–54 and he asked us to record these so that he could have something to play along with while we were away. Perhaps my memory tricks me, but in all the time we played together, both at his sessions and in clubs or recording, I was unaware that either Jeff or I were messing up. (I wish Jeff were here to confirm or deny this.) Lennie's comment to me not long after these tracks were released was simply that with hindsight he wished he had recorded the rhythm section a little louder – at the time limited recording facilities did not allow for remixing. Someone who wants his rhythm section tame would not say that! He also said that in his opinion Jeff and I were *the* rhythm section at that time, and that he felt we had not been given our due as far as the critics were concerned. So was the comment about not messing up an off-the-cuff comment or could he have been fed up because we were moving on, or was this just an interpretation of the reviewer? That was virtually the last time I played at the sessions – for I then went touring with Lee and following that there was a year's residency for me at the Hickory House. It was during that time – in 1955 – that Lennie lost his studio. Who knows why or even if he did say that? Lennie was anyway somewhat less than forthcoming about technique, wanting people to work it out for themselves, so maybe that was it.

Many musicians, in failing to understand what Lennie was doing, accused him of not swinging. Though Lennie was very dominant in his playing, I didn't regard it as dominating for the sake of power, but just incredible skill. It was just great, unbelievable improvisation. I remember those exhilarating experiences as though they were happening today. Writing about it brings it all back so clearly. I have been the target of criticism that maintains I am merely a disappointed and disillusioned bass player who has lost out as jazz has moved on. Who cares if I have lost out? I still have ears, I still play and it is still clear to me that those years were very special musically. But don't take my word for it:

> One longstanding fallacy, for example, is that Tristano demanded his drummer serve as a metronome, quietly, subordinately presenting the "regular" passage of time against which he and his saxophonist(s) could set contrasting metrical patterns. Art Taylor was no shrinking violet [and neither were Jeff Morton or Al Levitt] and his presence – not just suggesting a pulse, but creating his own variations and

interruptions of the beat – is strongly apparent throughout these performances. Doubters should listen once more to "All the Things You Are," which frees up his bop chops, lets him slide in and out of mambo rhythm, at times hammering his point across, or where he wallops a backbeat worthy of an R&B band ... he provides a propulsive undercurrent that allows Tristano and Konitz the choice of digging into rigorous swing or gliding across the beat effortlessly as if floating weightless above the chords... (Lange 1999)

So why is there such dispute about Lennie's contribution? And why has someone, who at one time was regarded as one of the foremost jazz creators, in recent years been overlooked, almost to the point of obscurity? This is a question addressed by others. I recently saw two items on the Internet about Lennie – both consider the same thing:

Unfortunately the jazz critic's tendency to inflate the major figures' status often comes at the expense of other musicians' reputations – men and women who have made significant, even essential, contributions of their own, are, for whatever reason, overlooked in the mad rush to canonize a select few. Lennie Tristano is one of those who have not yet received their critical due. (All Music Guide website)

The largest, most lingering – and highly unfair – criticism of Tristano (and collaborators such as Lee and Warne) ... is that their music is over-intellectualized ... At least a portion of this controversy, emerging back in the late 1940s and 1950s, may have been due to non-musical reasons, having to do with personality cliques, racism, snobbism, musicians afraid of losing jobs or their audience to something different, critics unable to understand something outside of their (limited) area of experience. (Lange 1999)

It was Lennie's choice that there are few recordings. He was a perfectionist. Now, long after he has gone, we are left with little evidence of his wealth of playing. My personal opinion is that though some of the recordings reach beyond anything anyone else has achieved, not all of his recordings evidence such greatness. I feel that locked up within him, perhaps, in his later years, was a great sense of disappointment. Being blind and having the same challenge as the rest of us and having to earn a living in this financially unforgiving culture only compounded the difficulties that Lennie was faced with. Alas, it is reminiscent of what happens to so many great artists who, because of their achievements, fail to realize the success commensurate with their abilities.

Though I had little contact with him during the final years of his life, my impression is that Lennie surrounded himself or was surrounded by aficionados who may have been very protective and

– albeit inadvertently – fostered the concept of him being a recluse. But wouldn't it be a natural reaction to be protective when there was so much negativity? My understanding is that in his last years he finally lost his house – a tragedy. However, during a telephone conversation with his son-in-law Lennie Popkin recently, I raised that point and Lennie Popkin, who was around in those later years, said that during his final years Lennie Tristano promoted concerts for Liz Gorrill, Connie Crothers and Sal Mosca, and that he held twice-weekly sessions at his house, hardly the activities of a recluse.

Was it a simple matter of one who took the fancy of the jazz world way back in the forties, but that later appraisal of his music showed him to be far less influential and revolutionary than was originally believed? Certainly, that is the impression created by much of what has been written about him in the intervening years. Despite this, there are those, as illustrated above, who believe that such negative criticism hides an uneasiness that perhaps here was someone of great influence whose music and ideas have for some reason fallen outside the popular image of jazz. And this is the aspect I would like to explore here.

12 lennie tristano and the enigma of non-recognition

It is an uncaring world. We enter this world helpless, but full of curiosity. For many, curiosity is killed by bad experiences. Some are strong enough to overcome the difficulties they are faced with and, despite this, achieve great things. Some are born with handicaps. Others may experience handicaps later in life, and then face the challenge of how to overcome what has befallen them. Most live their lives experiencing their hopes, their love, their achievements, and their disappointments unremarked by the majority. Others seem to shine like stars, gaining fame or notoriety. Some exert tremendous influence, even changing the course of civilization. Some become icons as though by their very lives they mirror the hopes and longing of the majority.

But what about those achievers who gained very little recognition for their efforts? History has taught us that some individuals, despite having a profound influence on the course of history, have hardly been recognized during their lifetimes: Roger Bacon, an English monk who lived a reclusive life, whose work was recognized only a century after his death; Lamarck, who, with simple experiments, founded the science of genetics and also worked unrecognized until after his death. Arguably Alfred Wallace was the first to recognize evolution; but this is remembered as Darwin's achievement, not Wallace's. Nikola Tesla gave us AC electricity (and many other discoveries – some not yet commercially developed), yet his achievement goes largely unrecognized. The world of art has also had so many great artists living and dying in poverty, unrecognized. It is very salutary to go and see Van Gogh's last accommodation in the Auberge at Auvers-sur-Oise – a tiny attic room, without even a view from the small skylight. What a way to end! Maybe we would not have ever known about Van Gogh had his brother not supported him virtually throughout his creative life.

The unanswered question is how many individuals have achieved significant works, and yet have remained unknown to this day? Maybe few or none at all, but perhaps we will never know for sure. Also, we appear far readier to recognize the geniuses of evil than of good (look at Hitler, for example). One thing that is becoming clear in recent years is that history, real history, is far more complex than it is frequently presented as being.

I have already commented that all through the history of jazz we find numerous instances of musicians whose contribution to the music far surpasses their public image. Why is this? Sometimes they do gain recognition for a brief period, only to be bypassed a short time afterwards. The majority of such musicians seem to have one thing in common: they lack the ability or willingness to publicize themselves. This is only one part of the story. For there are also numerous instances of musicians who, while not necessarily being publicity-shy, do not seem to make any effort in that direction, yet the jazz public takes to them anyway. Jazzmen that come to mind are Bix Beiderbecke, Chet Baker, and Kenny Wheeler. In the case of Bix and Chet, a tragic lifestyle seemed to play a part in their popularity. Kenny Wheeler, the soft-spoken Canadian trumpeter, is a regular guy who plays beautifully. All three deserve the recognition that has come their way, but it has not come about through self-seeking publicity. But these are the exceptions. Why are some publicized and others not? I think timing is one reason; a marketable quality (even one that the musician may not be aware of) is another, but also not being too challenging is an important explanation.

In the 1980s, Thomas Kuhn wrote a book about new paradigms in thought. The traditional concepts, which themselves had been stepping stones to new insight, eventually prove to be a hindrance and no matter how revolutionary they once appeared must inevitably be relinquished so that conceptual progress can occur. Such progress is seldom straightforward. At times an older paradigm may be retained, but with the proviso that its application is limited. Newtonian concepts of space are an example. For most practical purposes the Newtonian concepts suffice, yet in cosmology, Newtonian concepts are seen as a limitation. Similar paradigm shifts occur in art and music, though at the time of their introduction they are seldom recognized as such.

More often than not, the emergence of new facts that counter the prevailing world views meet with stiff resistance. This can lead to the academic persecution of those who first make such discoveries. Sometimes this may amount to no more than severe frustration, but in other circumstances careers can be ruined. Semmelweiss, who realized the supreme importance of aseptic measures to counteract puerperal fever (childbed fever), in suicidal rage at the rejection of his insight, plunged his hands into infected tissue and died as a result.

Sigmund Freud worked alone for ten years, developing his insight, which eventually became known to the world as psychoanalysis – while continually being shunned by colleagues. As a result of his preoccupation with the sexual etiology of neurosis, promotion passed him by. Freud wrote how people would cross the street to avoid meeting him. Only when he was called upon in desperation to treat a member of royalty suffering from hysterical paralysis, and with the success of this treatment, did fame and acclaim eventually come his way. At least as far as science is concerned, there can be an eventual confirmation, and with it the concomitant paradigm shift, though history has shown that this can sometimes take so much time that the original creator may be long dead, as in the case of Roger Bacon or Lamarck. Or maybe it takes the suicidal desperation of a Semmelweiss to prove the point.

In art and music, though deeply rooted in reality and in our psyche, a new paradigm may be quickly accepted, or conversely meet with criticism that effectively sidelines it. It is terribly ironic that Vincent Van Gogh, who apparently sold only one painting during his lifetime (and reputedly was never even paid for that) should, a century after his death, command the highest prices ever paid for any artist's work. Here, obviously, is a supreme example of an artistic paradigm beyond that of his contemporaries and, in Van Gogh's case, my view is that the true merit of his artistic work still awaits a deeper understanding.

In the case of jazz, with its multiple creative streams, there have emerged grades of acceptance that have been exploited commercially. This of course greatly affects the livelihood of the creators of the music. It is necessary to realize, as with the other arts and as with science in general, that current levels of acceptance (or rejection) of jazz are not necessarily objective. Much time can be needed before we are able to appraise creative efforts clearly. However, after such a long passage of time, most of the witnesses to events have since left this earth. Inevitably there are always those who come along afterwards and weave their web according to their own beliefs and prejudices. So genuine appraisal may never take place.

We can see why paradigm shifts inevitably begin with a first wave of pioneers who are generally rejected and even likely to be subject to persecution and ridicule, and many years may pass before due recognition is given to great creativity. As an example, when I was at school during the thirties, Bach was considered a minor composer, his music being regarded as mostly for the church and not worthy of major consideration. These days, Bach is rightly regarded as one of the major composers of all time.

Lennie was one of those pioneers, but many have used his ideas as their own and so perhaps need to undervalue his contribution. Having benefited so much from Lennie's teaching and having passed on at least some of those aspects, what is it that is so special and what is it that differentiates it from classical musical training? Fundamentally, Lennie's contribution is that of playing everything, including exercises, as *music*. Much of this emphasis is lost in today's jazz education. Though there is much precociousness in students of this generation, the lack of that fundamental emphasis of always playing everything (including exercises) melodically leads to a kind of empty skill. Though the concepts now firmly embedded in today's jazz education originated in Lennie's teaching, it is regrettable that much of the core of his teaching has been overlooked. His influence has permeated the world of jazz education.

I recognize a psychological pattern here – not merely with regard to the influence of Lennie's teaching, but as a common human failing. It concerns the usurping of knowledge from others without acknowledging its source. Concomitantly there is a social silence, as happens when people recognize the usurper but fail to stand up and point out the truth. It is the same pattern of social silence or acquiescence which, in its extreme form, allowed the Catholic Inquisition to take place, and allows the rise of a dictator like Hitler. When the insight given to us by certain innovative figures appears to be revolutionary for the time, the originators are ignored or sometimes actively persecuted for their insight. When, later, such insight is thought safe or acceptable, others usurp that knowledge and present it as their own. Inevitably, when that occurs, something is lost. In the case of Lennie's teaching some of the essence of what he taught has been lost as the focus has shifted to method rather than insight.

Lennie Tristano's contribution to jazz is of major significance. This is apparent in some at least of the few recordings he made during his lifetime and also in the influence he left upon those who studied or played with him, some who were major contributors in their own right, such as Charles Mingus and Bud Freeman. As others confirm: "Tristano's influence reaches across many styles. Among those pianists who have paid allegiance to him are Don Friedman, Clare Fischer and, above all, Bill Evans; among the younger ones are Alan Broadbent [who also studied with Lennie], Connie Crothers and Kenny Werner..." (Berendt 1983: 280).

There were many other well-known musicians who were reputed to have studied with him, but I have no first-hand knowledge about this and Lennie always kept in confidence the names of those who studied with him. He was, as ever, a discreet man.

During my lifetime it has been my fortune to come across a few remarkable individuals who have given much but who certainly have not received due recognition. I see numerous reasons for this.

First, part of the explanation has to lie in Lennie's own personality. The more I explored the idea, the more it became clear to me that one of the reasons Lennie's music did not receive the promotion it deserved is because Lennie refused to play the "game." Way back in the forties, the music critic Leonard Feather had a series of programs on a New York radio station, to which many famous jazz musicians of the time (of which Lennie was one) were invited. The concept behind the program was that Leonard Feather would play selections from the latest jazz releases and then ask for comments on the merits or demerits of the music. The obvious problem was that here were jazz musicians being asked publicly to voice their criticisms about their professional colleagues' music. Predictably, everyone avoided incisive comment. Lennie remained silent until halfway through the program when, not entirely off-mike, his voice could be heard saying, "I think I'll split." He did not want anything to do with this. Lennie was too direct to become the darling of jazz.

Bird, in contrast, was very aware of the foibles of media people. Not long before he died, Bird, together with Lee Konitz, was invited as a guest of Father Norman O'Connor's jazz radio program in Boston, Massachusetts. At one point Lee was asked his opinion of a well-known musician who had been hailed as an innovator. Lee, who had strict views on who was a contributor to jazz and who was not, exclaimed, "I don't think [X] has contributed anything of great significance to jazz," whereupon Bird leaned towards the microphone and, giving Lee a big wink and a smile, said, "I *like* him." Bird would not compromise his music, however. But for the media and for the social bullshit he would mischievously say what was required of him.

Lennie's music was before its time and people found it controversial. Even today his music sounds challenging. And he would not compromise. One of the things that Wilhelm Reich stressed is that we should ignore irrational comments about our work and just get on with the work itself. Lennie certainly took a similar view and maybe Reich influenced him. But what Reich did not realize was how this negativity toward his work would eventually destroy him. Lennie's focus on the work alone also cost him something.

In a world where ideals and aspirations are constantly being compromised, Lennie's refusal to do so was not only rare, but also raised subconscious guilt and resulted in antagonism. In my opinion it is that more than anything else that lies behind the negativity towards Lennie's music. Just as I was finishing this last editing, I came across an analogous situation in Michael Moore's book *Stupid White Men*, which really struck a chord. He was talking about Ralph Nader, the Green

Party politician who ran for president during the controversial Bush/ Gore election in 2000.

"Nader represents who they used to be but no longer are. He never changed. He never lost the faith, never compromised, never gave up. That's why they hate him. He didn't change his tune, didn't move to the suburbs, didn't start structuring his life around 'Let's see how I can make the most money for me, me, ME' " (Moore 2002: 212).

Regarding Lennie, it was far easier to parrot the old line about his music being cerebral and cold or simply to retreat into the excuse that he was a recluse, rather than accept that lack of compromise. Admittedly, Lennie, always very principled, would not perform unless conditions were suitable. He wanted playing conditions to be right for him to perform – a good piano and good sound – which they seldom were. He disliked the average jazz club for being noisy and full of inattentive people. (But can you imagine what it would be like, being blind, to go and play somewhere full of vast amounts of noise and no idea whether anyone was even aware of your playing?) The Cantorino brothers who ran the Half Note (originally located at Hudson and Spring Streets) in Greenwich Village, really admired his music and in the later years (late fifties through to the early sixties) his most frequent appearances were at their club. I see it as part of Lennie's wisdom that he did not succumb to the temptation to take any gig regardless of the conditions. I have had many experiences where the opportunity to play proved a veritable nightmare. Even recently, I was invited to sit in at a jam session at a local club in a small town in France (at Pierrelaye) just north of Paris, a club, incidentally, in existence because of an enlightened mayor's support. I discovered to my cost that the bass was poorly set up and was directly in front of the bank of amplification used by the previous bass guitarist. During that first tune I had to move the bass around constantly, trying to stop feedback. The only immediate solution meant that my bass was right in the direction of the piano player's ear. It took three tunes to finally find a more appropriate position and to coax the instrument into some sort of musicality. Friends who were with us and did not realize what was going on thought I was out of practice; those who didn't know me wondered what I was doing and the piano player just thought I was a complete egotist! Bassist Rufus Reid has obviously had similar experiences and he said he would play only his own bass and then only after having done a soundcheck.

Jazz criticism seldom pauses to consider the reality of playing live, or the jazz musician's struggle to survive – and that what is written about a jazz musician can have deleterious effects upon his/her career. This repackaging of Lennie as cold, cool or no longer hip really seems to me to be trying to find a way to continue to rationalize false criticism (as Lange suggested), with everyone competing for commercial success.

The marginalization of Lennie and his music always perplexed me and still does concern me personally. The comparative obscurity that now surrounds Lennie and his work was beginning to be apparent during the latter years of his life, though I was back in the UK by then. From comments that others who knew him made, I am surmising that professional loneliness did affect him in his latter years, but I was not around then. But in a way, what else would you expect? He gave so much as a player and a teacher, and saw his efforts bypassed or usurped by others.

So a third explanation for why Lennie has not received due recognition also relates to commercial factors that influence who is or is not heard.

Even in the jazz world of the late forties, commercial exploitation was taking place. I have already mentioned that Joe Glaser had long exploited Louis Armstrong's talents (albeit to Louis's advantage) and there had been many commercial bands – those of Artie Shaw and Duke Ellington for example – that were a part of the jazz scene, yet had proved to be money spinners. Lennie himself at one time had a manager. In the early fifties, Nesuhi Ertegun, co-founder with his brother Ahmet of Atlantic Records, was an ardent fan of Lennie and his music. Though I always liked Nesuhi, by 1959, I found him more the impresario and less of a jazz fan than in the early years. In the late fifties, he was still recording Lee Konitz and also recorded the Armenian group Norikes (New Dawn) led by the late Chick Ganimian, who played a very jazzy oud. The album *Come with Me to the Casbah* also included Armenian clarinettist/saxophonist Souren Baronian, who had also studied extensively with Lennie (and Lennie's influence on Souren, known as "Sudan," is still evident in his playing today). But Nesuhi was concerned with commercial success. By the late fifties Nesuhi's enthusiasm for Lennie's music had waned, and he was then involved with more commercial aspects of jazz, such as the music of Ray Charles, Chris Connors, and Charles Mingus.

It has become even more apparent in recent years that promotion has taken an increasingly important role in achieving success. The last generation of the twentieth century has witnessed unparalleled egocentricity. Success in these times appears synonymous with self-publicizing. Born in the twenties, the belief was instilled in me that success came merely with achievement – the idea that one had to have a publicity agent just would not have occurred to anyone, so those who relied solely on their achievements were doomed to disappointment if they expected that achievement alone would bring the world's attention to their work after the fifties. This, I think, happened to Lennie at a time when there was increasing need to compete for jazz work, more jazz musicians were on the scene and commercial interests prevailed.

Recently I came across a rare instance of critical honesty in a London *Times* review (June 29, 2004) by jazz critic Clive Davis, admitting that, although he appreciated Charlie Parker as an innovative jazz musician, he disliked his music. Clive Davis has every right to express his likes and dislikes, especially having had a lifetime of studying and listening to jazz. Leaving aside whether his criticism is objectively valid or not, it does raise an important point. That is to encourage people to be honest about their likes and dislikes, rather than telling them such and such is great, implying that if you don't agree there's something wrong with you. But much jazz criticism has erred by building a monolithic picture of what is great and what isn't, without giving credit to the reality of a multidimensional creative world. Interestingly, readers were asked to email the newspaper on the subject: "Are Some Arts Legends Overrated?" Readers were not asked, however, whether or not there were others who have been underrated.

Lately there is a dawning recognition of what has been described as the "dumbing down" of culture, and much of what has been achieved in music and the arts has fallen prey to this process. For what is of particular importance is the effect this commercial/political context has (and has had) upon jazz musicians themselves. In many ways jazz had achieved its greatest success in the mid- to late forties; it was then the popular music of America. The spirit of the music encouraged enthusiasm in the face of adversity. Much of this has been written about – especially in regard to the hardships faced by black musicians during those early years. Critics have seldom paused to realize that there was never enough work to go around to support the number of creative jazz musicians trying to earn their living from the music. Those who did succeed and became well known in their field were not the only ones with valid contributions to make to the music.

Much damage was done to the spirit of the music, and the sense of camaraderie from the fifties was lost. How far have commercial interests since pushed jazz only as entertainment? There are those – perhaps more worldly-wise – who nevertheless saw their role primarily as entertainers, like for example Louis Prima. This does not necessarily mean that they are not creative, but it does mean that their priority was to entertain and only secondly to be creative.

But what of those who have contributed greatly, though as far as the jazz public is concerned, remain comparatively unrecognized? Let us look at the matter from a different viewpoint, that of the musicians themselves. More than in most professions, jazz musicians' earning abilities are directly related to their public profile. When your livelihood is dependent upon your public persona then, no matter what, you have to take care of that. Consciously or unconsciously this sets musicians against one another. This causes a split in their energies, between their musical creativity on the one hand and, on the other, ensuring that they are seen as "Mr. Big." For example, it was well known that clarinettist Benny Goodman would always insist that in any publicity his name would appear at the top of the bill.

From an agent or manager's point of view, the reality is seen very differently. Those who promote jazz acts or stars are primarily concerned with the potential earning power of those they promote. A musician's creativity is not a prime factor for a promoter. "Will he/she draw the crowds?" is their paramount concern. As the musician gains experience, as long as the work holds out, confidence in his or her abilities grows. Should a musician encounter a rough patch, an extended period without employment, this means not only tightening what is probably already a slender purse, but also being denied one of the supreme pleasures of creating music. Having perhaps spent a decade or more as a professional musician, there is no ready alternative for earning a living.

Furthermore, taking a "day gig" tends to make a musician feel a failure. Additionally, day gigs for the otherwise unskilled usually pay poorly, and the musician generally discovers that after leading a life as a professional musician, the day gig can seem like a never-ending purgatory. Many musicians – even some well-known ones – have gone through such a patch. It takes a particular strength of character to come through those experiences unscathed. Unfortunately, a more usual route can be taking to the bottle.

Many jazz musicians in the sixties suddenly found themselves without jazz employment, and as a compromise (considered better than settling for a day job) obtained positions in theater pit orchestras. The boredom of repetition of the same music night after night, and the long breaks between acts where music was required, in New York, led to sojourns at Charlie's Bar or the Brass Rail, where gin or scotch was sold at very affordable prices. The inevitable result: the need to dry out and the enforced lack of any employment during this drying out. It is a hard road to climb, both emotionally and financially. The alcoholic failures in music are legendary (Pee Wee Russell, for example), but not all of these come about through over-imbibing while working.

There is also the unspoken but implied pressure from society in general. Jazz musicians in particular are often envied for their ability to survive without the pressure of everyday work drudgery. Such comments as, "Yes, but what do you do for a living?" when informing others that you are a musician, or (worse) a jazz musician, carry the implication that, somehow, you have evaded the responsibility of real work. The fact that you might have put in more study than is necessary to obtain a medical doctor's degree remains outside the public's concept of "jazz musician." In mid-life, to have to face the prospect of menial, low-paid work after all the study to become a jazz musician is extremely demoralizing. You tend to remember the times when, after playing a good solo, you had received appreciative applause. How the mighty have fallen! Each is a human tragedy, seen by outsiders merely as an indication that jazz is an unhealthy occupation. The loss of your livelihood or failure to be able to provide sufficiently for your family has to be one of the main causes of depression. Seldom are such failures taken into account when assessing or reviewing musicians' recordings or gigs, unless, as in the case of Billie Holiday, the tragedy almost becomes the prime motive for writing about them.

As I see it, the changes in social and commercial attitudes toward the music forced the musicians themselves to compromise in various ways. Some tried to boost their reputations by exaggerating their abilities; many turned to teaching, either in universities or privately. Others, such as Ronnie Ball, turned increasingly to arranging or simply joined the commercial world of the "music business." Then some, like tenor saxophonist Ted Brown for example, took up a secondary profession out of necessity due to family commitments. The stress this can cause often has a marked effect upon jazz performance. Overall the music tended to be more strident, more ego-oriented. Music that was simply beautiful hardly found a place in the evolving new world of hard-nosed practice and fierce competition epitomized in Reaganite and Thatcherite politics. The reign of jazz politics, I call it.

There were some unexpected opportunities: for example in 1975/6 I teamed up with Lee and Warne and drummer Al Levitt touring several European countries, and a number of LP records were produced. However, what actually happened is, to me, just an example of the pressure and demands then facing jazz. I can look back on it with a wry smile now – but only now! The first concert at the Bimhaus in Amsterdam was possibly the best. Augmented by UK guitarist Dave Cliff, there was an excitement and desire to play together – without ego battles. Alas, this did not last. The group came together as a co-operative seemingly fortuitously. In December of 1975 Warne had been invited by a Danish jazz society to give some concerts in Denmark. At the same time a last-minute cancellation at Ronnie Scott's Club in London resulted in a hurried call to Lee from the Scott management. American expatriate Al Levitt was living in Paris – a plethora of phone calls and the tour was organized. What followed was a classic example of how jazz politics intrude upon the music. Though there were high spots throughout the tour, there were times when we worked as a quartet and Dave Cliff – relatively unknown at that time to European audiences – was omitted. Always the question of money gave rise to frictions within the group. Lee and Warne were hailed as jazz stars, while the remainder of the band – Al, Dave, and I – were seen as merely the rhythm section.

By the time we played in Denmark, both Al Levitt and myself were replaced for some of the recording sessions in favour of Alex Riel (drums) and Niels-Henning Ørsted Pedersen (bass). So much for the co-operative band. It took an effort of will on the part of Al and myself not to regard ourselves as second-rate, dispensable components. The attitudes of the audiences and the promoters were similar: Lee and Warne were the stars and their attitudes (and how they were treated) began to reflect this. At the beginning of the tour we were musical compatriots, producing group music of a high quality. A noticeable rivalry also began to manifest itself between Lee and Warne. Lee had a higher reputation, having been more outwardly successful. On the other hand Warne, though having a lesser profile, was such an incredible player, and this began to be obvious during the tour and affected relations between them. The fact that tenor saxophonist Warne had a range both below and above Lee also had its effect. The original co-operative arrangement was that money would be divided in shares, with allowances made for expenses and an additional allowance given to whoever had arranged the particular concerts. For those arranged by Al – mainly the work in France – he would receive what in effect was commission. I would receive a commission for work in England, Warne in Denmark and Lee in Holland and Belgium. Perhaps inevitably, this arrangement broke down – as many gigs came directly through Lee or Warne, due to the publicity they had received. Front-line instrumentalists are almost inevitably regarded as leaders, and rhythm sections as workhorses. Much of the touring continued with Al and I driving the equipment in my car, while on a number of occasions Lee and Warne traveled first class by air. This put additional strain on band relations, especially as Al and I would frequently arrive at the gig dog tired, while Lee and Warne arrived fresh for the concerts.

The tour then proceeded with Lee and Warne receiving higher fees, in addition to the cost of their airfares, while Al and I were effectively demoted to living as roadies cum rhythm section. There were even arguments as to payment for the use of my car. I reached the point where I vowed to myself just to save whatever money I could from the tour – and never again to undertake such an arrangement. Such an example shows how commercial pressures and the focus on reputations rather than the music can interfere with and sometimes destroy jazz creativity.

There were, of course, many examples of this changed concept of "rhythm sections." Such distinctions had not been clear in the late forties and early fifties. For example, when I toured with Lee in the early fifties, Jeff Morton and I were not just the "rhythm section" but regarded as an integral part of the band. But as the commercialization of jazz proceeded apace, the concept of rhythm sections as workhorses accompanying "jazz stars" began to take over. When the first ever jazz festival was held at Newport in 1954, bands were booked as bands. Later, festivals began hiring rhythm sections to accompany various "stars." Similar situations arose regarding rhythm sections for recording dates. Milt Hinton and Osie Johnson (bass and drums respectively) became one of the stable combinations called upon for innumerable dates. These were good players, as was the rhythm section of Wendell Marshall and Kenny Clarke. Later, other similar sections were formed, for example Paul Chambers and Philly Joe Jones. There seemed to be no requirement or consideration of musical compatibility between these standard rhythm sections and those "stars" they were to accompany.

There were those, however, who found a way out of this dilemma. Drummer Max Roach teamed up with trumpeter Clifford Brown and this became a working group. Also notably, Charles Mingus formed his own group and led from the bass chair. He called the shots, and being such a character, became a success and subsequently recognized as a jazz star in his own right. That seemed to be the only route open. One wonders how jazz would have developed had there not been the intrusion of jazz politics and music policy often dictated by record producers, the jazz press, and accountants. But not all rhythm section players coped well with the demeaning position they found themselves in. As a member of a rhythm section in those days, you needed to be an all-round player, not a great soloist. (I believe that the great bassist Oscar Pettiford lost out on what could have been a very lucrative few years – simply because he was such a great soloist.) For many there was a solace (if only temporary) in narcotics or alcohol – not for me, I hasten to add. These were attempts to relieve the frustration of having your self-belief unfairly eroded. Listen to the development of jazz from, say, the greats of the thirties – Lester Young, Charlie Christian, Roy Eldridge – to the boppers of the forties – Charlie Parker, Bud Powell, the 1949 recordings of the Lennie Tristano

Sextet – and, in the early fifties, to Clifford Brown. Then listen to the later music of John Coltrane, Archie Shepp, and Pharoah Sanders. True, there has been an evolution in jazz – but what, precisely, is this evolution? Today we have numerous jazz stars or would-be stars playing "in yer face" music. What happened to the beauty in the music, so evident in the earlier years?

Commercial interests have ensured that certain musicians have retained their reputation while others have received little recognition. Re-evaluation is needed, first to reinstate those, like Lennie, whose contribution to the development of jazz has been overlooked and, second, to bring to light how this could have happened.

So, fourthly, considering the reasons for Lennie's non-recognition, we need to look at his contribution in a very specific way.

Commercialism was anathema to Lennie. He remained unshaken in his view that, as a creative jazz musician, you had a clear duty to be faithful to the spirit of the music alone. In one interview, when he was questioned about being an entertainer, he said that his responsibility was to the music. He did not claim to be an entertainer, but added that he could be very entertaining among friends. Remembering this anecdote led me to thinking that no one would expect a classical piano player to be able to tell amusing anecdotes, but they do expect it from jazz musicians. Somehow they expect them to be "racy," as if they should not be taken seriously.

Understandably, Lennie's outlook was shared by many who studied with him. Outsiders have often been critical of what they considered a rather high-handed attitude. There is little doubt that the commercially non-compromising views of Lennie and those of many of his associates have contributed to their relative obscurity in the world of jazz. Lennie's belief meant that earning a living by playing jazz and being true to the music was a precarious scenario, or at least would provide a livelihood that would last only as long as a fickle public would listen; it meant finding an alternate or supplementary source of income. The jam sessions that many of us participated in, in the early days, helped enormously to keep our musical enthusiasm alive. Increasingly the world outside, even the commercial jazz world, seemed alien to the true spirit of the music.

Lennie took his teaching as seriously as his playing, and both were essential to his creative life. For Lennie both stretching creativity beyond the expectations of his potential audience and jazz enthusiasts moving on to other aspects of jazz left him with a smaller following than the mainstream of the music.

To reappraise Lennie's music you also have to consider what it is that people are looking for from jazz. What is the attraction of jazz? And what do jazz fans really understand about the music they are attracted to? Come to that, how many critics really understand the music upon which they make judgments? What, even, do the musicians understand of each other's music?

I think that in order to develop a clearer understanding of this, it is perhaps wise to consider three separate aspects: jazz as musical development; jazz as entertainment; and jazz as musical education. A good live performance is, of course, all three. Unfortunately we have become so used to having recorded music as a background to other activities, that seldom is the necessary attention given to really appreciate jazz. It is probably for this reason that jazz with more obvious entertainment value gains a higher profile and thus becomes commercialized.

We need to look more at this entertainment aspect. Jazz is sometimes expressed and/or viewed as music of protest. Sometimes it is regarded as music to dance to. It can be viewed as a streetwise expression of ethnic minorities. It can also be regarded as the new music of the twentieth century. The musicians who create it have their own concepts of the how and why of the music. The listeners and the critics may also have an entirely different way of comprehending the music. There are some advantages of merely being a listener, as against being a performing musician. For example, the listener does not have to concern him/herself with harmonic structure or instrumental technique. The listener need not be aware of how musicians may have influenced each other, or who first developed a particular creative concept.

However, for those concerned with the technical aspects of jazz, it is not just the musical idea or idiom but the actual quality of the performance that matters. Whereas with classical music there are large areas of agreement as to how a work should be performed, jazz is not subject to such constraints. If a musician is highly influenced by another, he/she may express to some degree the sound and approach to playing developed by the original influence. This can be very confusing to the listener, who may attribute a style or influence, not to the originator but to the musician who is, in turn, influenced by the originator. As we discussed, if a musician reaches greater commercial success than the originator of his/her particular style or approach, the awareness of the thread of musical development can become obliterated. There have been other such misunderstandings in the history of art and science, notably Shakespeare/Marlowe, Darwin/Wallace, or Newton/Leibniz, where there is still debate about who was the creator and who was the one credited with the work.

For those who just want to be entertained by jazz, much of this debate does not matter. But Lennie's legacy is not about entertainment. The real benefit came to me much later, when jazz improvisation really became such a fulfilling part of my life: the pleasure in letting go – letting the music take over. At such times, it matters not whether people understand what you're doing. It is just the sheer joy of creating something new. The music just unfolds. The challenge remains to be technically able to handle what comes streaming through you.

Such experiences make me critical of those who develop their jazz vocabulary and string together a series of licks that passes for jazz. When I hear that I know that those who do such things have never experienced what I know to be the real creative drive. Playing jazz means surrendering to the spirit of the music, not in being able to control it so as to produce what has now become known as "smooth jazz." Jazz has nothing smooth about it – neither is it rough – it's just about creating a living musical line.

This is not to deny that natural talent plays a big part. Obviously, some are more talented than others, but I know from my own experience as a teacher that some of the most talented can be lazy, while others with less obvious talent but who also possess an intense desire to learn can, like the tortoise, overtake the hare.

Few realize that the great jazzmen have worked very hard to develop their abilities. Lester Young admitted that he had learned from the recordings of Frankie Trumbauer and Bird in his turn had expressed his gratitude to Lester, from whose recorded solos he had learned and benefited. Billie Holiday would work and rehearse intensively. The current portrayal of jazz musicians doesn't help – little emphasis is given to the amount of hard work that has gone into their playing. Their skill and tremendous expertise was a result of continuous study and practice, not just hanging loose in seedy clubs. We need to look more closely at what the jazz scene was *really* like. It is peculiar to me that hard work and discipline are undervalued. People want to view music as a miracle of creativity that just happens, without work or effort. In fact effort is seen somehow as inauthentic.

I remember the time when *Tristano* was released by Atlantic Records (discussed in detail in Chapter 10); it drew so much reaction. Some were extremely enthusiastic, but to my surprise many in the jazz community expressed resentment. There was criticism that multi-tracking was unethical and smacked of trickery – how strange such comments appear today, given all the manipulation that underlies the majority of contemporary recordings. When, several years later, pianist Bill Evans recorded an LP that used multi-tracking no such criticism was voiced. It was as though Lennie's music was some kind of unethical wizardry. It is as if the critics somehow resented the development of jazz improvisation beyond what had been considered acceptable limits. Bird himself had in earlier years been the victim of a number of unjustified negative reviews. Critics eventually backtracked when it was no longer possible to maintain previous stances. But with Lennie it seems that we have had to wait fifty years for such an overdue reappraisal. Perhaps no one could have foreseen at that time the future development of jazz.

That henceforth jazz would take different and more commercial directions in the future was not then apparent. In many ways Bird had been the spiritual leader of jazz, but with his death, it became a free-for-all for anyone who could claim the crown. Looking back on those times, it appears now as though Lennie's music was the only music not to be commercializing. Despite its creative merit it became an anachronism as far as the rest of the jazz world was concerned.

I knew Lennie as a charming but proud man, fully aware of his contribution to jazz. My guess is that in the last years, he felt the chill of the outside world of commercial jazz and that probably contributed to his early death. Author Louis-Ferdinand Céline's words in *Journey to the End of the Night* about the World War I carnage seem ironically appropriate: "Are we merely blades of grass to fall under the cosmic mower?"

But maybe times are really changing (despite the awful dumbing down of our culture). It is to be hoped that we are reaching a stage where material goods alone are not the panacea to mollify dissatisfaction, and that people will begin to become more aware of what is great in jazz – and in the arts generally – not to accept a cow in formaldehyde as a work of art, nor random sounds as great music but, rather, for what they are: as challenge and rebellion. The distinction between creativity and challenge needs to be recognized in the art world.

A recent review by Budd Kopman in the December 2001 issue of the jazz magazine *Cadence* suggests such a change, in discussing a reissue of *Lennie Tristano Classics 1946–1947*:

> Lennie Tristano is just so damned interesting. He had a clear vision of what he thought jazz was about and stuck to it. He wanted his rhythm sections to be pure timekeepers, and abhorred any kind of emotive playing, focusing instead on subtle melodic lines and rhythmic patterns. In response to the accusation that he is cold I quote Charlie Parker (from the liner notes): "As for Lennie Tristano, I'd like to go on record as saying that I endorse his work in every particular. They say he's cold. They're wrong. He has a big heart and it's in his music." (Kopman 2001)

13 mythmaking and prejudices in jazz

I have tried to focus on the positive and constructive issues around jazz. But no appraisal would be complete without some discussion about the various prejudices concerning jazz. A consideration of Lennie and his legacy has to be put in this wider context and, in fact, the issue of his non-recognition is to me part of the debate about jazz and the directions it has taken and why.

But let's start with the effect jazz has generally. Does any other artform evoke such strong reactions? Opinions about jazz are often provocative. There is the widely held view that jazz is a chaotic form of music played by drug-crazed mavericks. There is the view that it is somehow musically inferior to classical or other forms of music. Some see it as merely self-indulgent. There are those who view it as protest music created by the socially disadvantaged or a major cultural or ethnic form of music. Then there is prejudice within the ranks of jazz musicians themselves – some see only certain forms of jazz as being "pure." Then there is the prejudice displayed by those who market jazz, which tends to limit the music to what is expected to sell.

We discussed some of these issues in the last chapter, but perhaps the most difficult issue is of race and ethnicity, which plagues all of the world's cultures today but has always cut across the world of jazz. I want to focus on this in this chapter. A prevalent view is that jazz is black music, appropriated by whites, with whites making the money out of it and blacks providing the inspiration. What I have written in this book will, I hope, tend to bring a more balanced perspective, particularly about those creative years in jazz from the late forties through the fifties. It came as a shock to me to be faced with questions about this on a radio show, to realize that Lennie Tristano's music was considered by some to be "white jazz" (see Chapter 10) and by inference that he played only with white musicians. For this reason I have to unravel this issue and set the record straight. The emergence of rock has played a large part in marginalizing jazz, but factions from within the jazz fraternity have also had a negative effect. Clearly, racial problems have plagued American jazz in one way or another since its inception. We discussed previously the position of black writers such as LeRoi Jones who, especially in the early sixties, saw jazz as black music usurped and exploited by whites. An anonymous musician, interviewed by Berendt, shows what this means in its extreme form:

> You see we need music ... our own. We have nothing else. Our writers write like whites, our philosophers think like them. Only our musicians don't play like the whites. So we created a music for ourselves. When we had it – the old type of jazz – the whites came and they liked it and imitated it. Pretty soon it was no longer our own music ... No Negro can play New Orleans jazz today with a clear conscience ... You see as soon as we have a music the white man comes and imitates it. We've now had jazz for fifty years and in all those fifty years there has not been a single man, perhaps leaving aside Bix, who has had an idea. Only the colored men have ideas. But if you see who has got the famous names; they're all white ... We must go on inventing something new all the time. When we have, the whites will take it from us and we have to start all over again. It is as though we are being hunted. (Berendt, quoted in Newton 1959: 205)

Rather than being an accurate appraisal of jazz it is more of a reflection of the insecurity of some black musicians. Though that insecurity is understandable given the position of many black people in America, it doesn't validate the argument. To cite Bix as the exception that proves the rule is again false. To point to others such as Django Reinhardt (a French-speaking Gypsy) or Jack Teagarden (an American Indian) as acceptable because of their race is demeaning to them as players. To be objective about the music it is essential to go beyond considerations of race, social standing and even considerations of success. Author and cornettist Richard Sudhalter has tackled this argument from an academic perspective in his book *Lost Chords*, and received a mixture of criticism and praise for his efforts. His view is that both black and white peoples have contributed but that white contributions have also been underplayed.

It is unfortunate that such detailed and in-depth scholarship can easily be interpreted as racist, simply because it is described as the "white" contribution to jazz. In fact it researches the evidence, for all races, black, Creole, Italian, Jewish, East European even British influence and contributions, a mammoth task, spoiled in my opinion by its subsidiary title. Richard has tried to counter the present-day viewpoint that tends to underplay or dismiss as derivative the jazz contributions of musicians from "other" cultures, and he does much to redress the balance of today's misconceptions. In contrast, the recent American PBS series on jazz, by Ken Burns, presents a different viewpoint, focused mainly on African American musicians. But, in fact, both positions continue the posturing about who is right and who is wrong that has bedeviled and undermined jazz.

To me the debate is far broader than a simple black–white division as promoted, particularly from the sixties onward, by many players and critics. Of course great credit has to be given to black musicians. There are certain crucial aspects of jazz created originally by the great black jazz musicians – which in turn influenced jazz created by others, and helped other races to shed their own cultural rigidities, especially the obvious rhythmic aspects of jazz. It was aspects of rhythmic looseness and freedom of phrasing that captivated Lennie Tristano's ear, plus the freedom of melodic improvisation, as the creative talents of Lester Young and Charlie Parker manifested so clearly. All races have recognized rhythm, but there is a world of difference between, say, militaristic rhythm and the looseness of jazz rhythms, which allow the music to flow wavelike over the fundamental pulse, and allow phrasing to start and finish in unusual places. Developing this ability gives additional freedom for jazz soloists to "tell a story."

Due respect needs to be given to the fact that jazz was born in America, while taking into account the fact that jazz is now a worldwide phenomenon. It originated in the USA as a folk music. The earliest roots of the music go back to the Negro spirituals and to the marching bands of New Orleans, which we discussed in Chapter 8. This was before our time. Very few are left who actually experienced those early days. We should be grateful to the chroniclers of the music, not just the recording artists but also to those who interviewed those early participators, for information about those times. Historians will, however, verify that though it may have its roots from black people singing gospel and blues, it has also relied on contributions from other races. Recognizing these innumerable influences in jazz must not detract from the incredible contributions from such black musicians as Louis Armstrong, Lester Young, and Bird. But in turn they were influenced, also, by the European musical tradition. It is regrettable that a music derived from so many rich creative sources should be riven by racial arguments.

Within half a century jazz has developed into an American multiracial musical culture. As jazz has developed during the course of a century it has given rise to many differing styles. It has also become noticeably more complex. I see jazz now as a complex music, relying on contributions from many different sources. Its development has to be seen as multiethnic.

Take, for example, the issue of rhythm. From its beginnings jazz has always been associated with rhythm. To be able to play rhythmically with a "jazz" feel has also become an essential aspect of the music. But there have been developments and changes. In the twenties the music was seen as "hot," reflecting the "Roaring Twenties" and giving rise to the dance styles that sprang from the rhythm of the music, starting with the cakewalk and developing as variations of the charleston, which involved wild movement of legs and arms so completely out of keeping with the sedate, stiff-bodied ballroom dancing of the time. The thirties are identified as the swing era, which reflected the new age of the sleek automobile and the pulse of its idling engine. Lester Young was proud of the fact that on the track "Taxi War Dance," with Count Basie's band, he was able to imitate the New York taxi horn as part of his solo. The focus of the dance was as much on beginning to swing and move the whole body rhythmically as it was on freeing the limbs. The forties reflected the tensions of World War II and its aftermath with jazz and the movement of the bebop era as expressions of rebelliousness against the established order. People were beginning to be more openly rebellious and anarchic in their sense of rhythm and style of dancing, much more overtly sexual – using the whole body and movement from the hips – than had been dared before. These were changes and shifts that involved different people and different cultural influences.

Then there are the Latin American influences on jazz, ranging from Bird working with Machito, a famous Latin musician in New York in the late forties and fifties, to the later recordings of Stan Getz with Carlos Jobim and Astrid Gilberto. Even musicians as commercial as George Shearing used Latin rhythms.

Another major influence has been Middle Eastern music. Dave Brubeck and Lennie Tristano were influenced by Middle Eastern rhythms (Dave Brubeck's "Take Five" and "Blue Rondo à la Turk" for example). Their approach extends the rhythmic rather than the melodic aspects of Middle Eastern music. I was personally influenced by working with an Armenian band – on the track "Arak" (released on my *Looking Out* album) the improvisation included quartertones that were a direct influence of playing with these musicians. Though in the late fifties one of their recordings made it to the charts in the USA, maybe this peaked too early, as only recently have Near Eastern influences on jazz been widely recognized. Jazz "standards" (mainly originating as popular songs) became a cornerstone for jazz and the composers were of all races, many immigrants from Europe and Russia, part of the musical melting pot that became Tin Pan Alley and the jazz fraternity, from which emerged the greater jazz culture. It is clear that people of all races have been contributors to jazz – though the seed came from those early days – apparently in New Orleans and mainly from black or Creole bands.

We need also to acknowledge why some black jazz musicians take a particular perspective. It is unbelievable that legislation against segregation was not ratified in the USA until the sixties and the new laws designed to prevent segregation had to be fairly heavily imposed, even at that late date. Many pockets of such prejudice still existed, especially in the southern states, and black musicians in bands would have to use the service entrance at venues or be unable to stay in the places where they provided entertainment.

For example, on the road in the fifties with a jazz group that consisted of both black and white musicians, we would send in the white guy to book the motel and at the end the black guy would pay the bill. We all knew that sending in the black musician at the beginning might mean that mysteriously the hotel had suddenly become full. Once ensconced in the accommodation we felt relatively safe and of course the motel proprietor wanted his money! And with the new anti-racial laws, he did not have legislation to uphold such redneck attitudes. It was our small way of making a point. Roy Eldridge worked out a similar strategy that overcame such restrictions: "When the bus pulled up I would take the bags out, like I was a porter, I'd go to the desk clerk and say, 'Keys for Mr. Eldridge – where's his room?' They'd give me the keys and that was that! Never paid any attention to me until I came to pay the bill."

In some cities there were still separate unions for black and for white musicians. Mercifully, there has been progress in that this no longer exists, but still the reality is that black musicians often live in one part of town and white musicians in another.

There were significant changes in the late fifties and sixties. However the southern states of the USA were still actively resisting racial equality. As the Federal Government acted to legislate against racism, much of what had been overt racist activity went underground. Even in states such as Pennsylvania (well north of the Mason–Dixon Line), racial prejudice was still very much in evidence in the sixties. Once, when working with Roy Eldridge and Coleman Hawkins, where I was the sole white member of the group, we were stopped by a Pennsylvania patrolman for no other apparent reason than the fact that I was a white guy traveling with blacks. The attitude of the cop was very different from the big brother protector of freedom that officialdom liked to portray. Never mind that these were some of the world's most treasured jazz greats – all the cop saw was black trash and, by association, white trash.

During the early fifties in New York there was less evidence of racial prejudice and tension – at least within the jazz fraternity. And there were strong indications (and hopes) – with the new Federal laws against racial discrimination – that some of the evils of racial prejudice were finally being tackled. As I have discussed, those jam sessions in New York were seldom all-white or all-black (see Chapter 3). The greatest musicians were respected, not on account of their financial status, their culture, or their background but because of their creative abilities. I found the majority of black musicians were much more open with me. Being European and coming from a different culture was a decided advantage and I found that there was a natural and mutual respect. When I emigrated to the USA I left a United Kingdom whose population was almost exclusively white. I had never been exposed to racial tension (partly because there were so few non-whites living in the UK in those days and partly because I was born in a suburban fringe of London that until the twenties had been rural. Its residents were either of rural English stock or of people who worked in London proper and commuted to the outlying suburbs.) Racial tension therefore came as something as a shock to me. There had been no black people at all in my upbringing; the arrival of immigrants to the UK from the Caribbean occurred several years after I had emigrated to the USA. If there had been any racial tensions in the UK in those years of the late forties, I certainly never became aware of them. This was to my advantage when emigrating to the USA. What made it easier for me in New York was that I just shared a common interest in jazz with all musicians.

It appears to me that one of the underlying reasons jazz was so demeaned by everyday America was because it brought black and white together. That very factor, which ideally should have been welcomed as a democratic ideal, was maybe secretly disliked, from various directions. The whites would be viewed by redneck America as "lowering" themselves to the social standards of the blacks, and the blacks would be secretly accused by other blacks of selling out to "whitey," this being the current slang at that time. The Western world, at least, pays lip service to racial equality on the one hand and on the other hand seldom demonstrates conviction about racial equality by its actions. Blacks on the whole are instinctively aware of such attitudes and the derisory term "whitey" sums up the two-faced attitude of the white Western establishment. The white man is seen as the former slave owner, the oppressor, the one who controls, who wields power over the less fortunate.

Occasionally I found myself accused (because of my British nationality) of being the oppressor, of being of the nation that was the chief slave trader. "Absolutely not guilty" was my reply. "My father was a respectable artisan and came from artisan stock. My forebears on my mother's side were country people who worked on the land and had little control over their own lives – let alone other people's lives." The problem is that such race-based definitions undermine the great contribution of people from a variety of backgrounds – Mediterranean, Eastern European, Latin American, Middle Eastern and even Celtic. All are lumped together as the "white" contribution, when their influences can be quite different.

But whatever rumblings or accusations went on away from the band-stand, the one thing that pulled us together was the music. When it was really "happening" we were all involved. And it was through the music itself that I made real contact not only with white Americans – who after all were also of a different culture than mine (for example, Warne was Russian/Dutch, Lee's family were originally from Germany, Lennie's from Italy), but especially with African American musicians. We had in common our love of jazz, which set us apart from ordinary Americans.

Also, playing alongside the older generation of black musicians, play-ers such as Coleman Hawkins, Roy Eldridge, and Red Allen for example, I discovered that, though they still quite rightly felt angry over many of their experiences of racial prejudice, they were very open with me and we became good friends.

Looking back on it, what stands out strongly to me was the ability of the older musicians to relate to me as a person, not merely seeing me as a white person. In Roy Eldridge, for example, I found a real friend, and I treasure his memory – not only as a player – but also as a friend. I had long been aware of Roy's playing; it was Lennie who pointed me in that particular direction. No other trumpet player, before or since, ever reached the intensity of Roy's sound. And it was not only his sound but also his melodic concept. When Roy, in the early forties, was working with the Gene Krupa band, Anita O'Day the featured vocalist, some of the greatest melodic trumpet playing is to be heard on Roy's soloing, for example, Gene Krupa's "Green Eyes" and "Let Me Off Uptown," where Roy sings duos with Anita. Above all, the track on which he was featured with Gene, "Rocking Chair," for me remains one of the greatest jazz trum-pet solos ever. It is this combination of the intensity of his sound and the clever but simple way in which he handled the solo: truly a work of art. I later found out that, in the early days, Roy's music had similarly had a strong influence on Lennie. Most people know Roy's music from the "Jazz at the Philharmonic" recordings, but these were more in the nature of riffing and whipping up audience excitement rather than just the pure beauty of those earlier solos.

In the years that I worked with Roy, from the late fifties to 1961 (in fact only a few years but it seemed more!), we were good friends; he was such a good man. Perhaps a story can best illustrate the man himself. In those days, for most of the out-of-town dates, even some distance from New York, you were literally on the road driving through the night. On returning from a gig in Detroit, we had reached the vicinity of Pittsburgh by early Sunday morning, having driven all night. Roy said, "Do you mind if we stop and I visit my old man?" I said of course not. Pittsburgh was his hometown. On the way in he showed me the hall where he played his first gig. And then we called on his father, who was just coming out of church – it was mid-morning Sunday. His father was at least six feet tall, silver-haired, a very charming man. Roy, as is well known, was short in stature, hence his nickname "Little Jazz." Roy introduced me and we chatted briefly and then his father said to him, "When are you going to settle down? I got a good job going for you, it pays a bill fifty a week [which was OK in those days – $150]. It's just nine to five checking trucks." Roy said, "Thanks, Pop, but I have some wild oats to sow first." This was 1960; Roy was born in 1911!

On one of these long trips, traveling on the Pennsylvania turnpike, on a stormy night with heavy rain, on our way back to New York, Roy was driving and the others were sleeping in the back. I was staying awake to keep him company (lots of energy in those days!). The windshield wipers stopped working. With no possibility of immediate repairs and wanting to get home as soon as possible, we found some twine, tied it around the wipers and with the side flap window open we turned on the gospel music and alternately pushed and pulled in time with the music and eventually arrived in New York! Every time I saw him after that he always reminded me of that incident. He was Aquarius, and always interested in space and flying saucers. I would bring a telescope with me and sometimes we would pull off the turnpike, miles from any city, and just look up at the stars and wonder.

Paradoxically, relations were not always so open with the younger generations of black musicians. Frequently I would come full tilt against an attitude that claimed that jazz was black music – and being white I had no right or even the appropriate instinct to be able to play it. We have talked about this. I mention it here because their attitude was so different. It seemed part of that hard, driving, rather mean attitude that came increasingly into jazz music in the late fifties and early sixties. The need to compete, to be at the front no matter what – all seemed symptomatic to me of changing attitudes generally, linked mainly to the greater competition for a chance to play. Miles's comment about Lennie seems particularly typical of that attitude, even though at other times he recognized how unique Lennie's contribution was. Still he could say:

A lot of white critics kept talking about all these white jazz musicians, imitators of us, like they was some great motherfuckers and everything. Talking about Stan Getz, Dave Brubeck, Kai Winding, Lee Konitz, Lennie Tristano, and Gerry Mulligan like they was gods or something ... Now, I'm not saying that these guys weren't good musicians ... But they didn't start nothing, and they knew it, and they weren't the best at what was being done...

[...]

People were still talking about Chet Baker and Lennie Tristano and George Shearing, all that stuff came out of *Birth of the Cool*. (Davis 1989: 146, 165)

Miles must have known that this was not true. *The Birth of the Cool* was recorded in 1949, as were Lennie's sextet records, and it was from his association with Lennie Tristano and coming to notice from that that Lee was invited to be part of the *Birth of the Cool* group. Lennie was doing something far more creative than *Birth of the Cool* and he had been doing this since 1946, first with the trio with Billy Bauer and then later with Lee and Warne, even if his recording did come a few months after the *Birth of the Cool* album. It seems more a question of using race as a convenient put-down. I played with Miles Davis when he was young, in 1952 at a club called the DownBeat on W 48th Street with Lee Konitz, Max Roach, and George Wallington on piano. He wasn't like that then. He had had success with the *Birth of the Cool* album and he was playing some of these arrangements. The gig was Oscar Pettiford's and I substituted for him three or four times. Miles then was in one sense just one of the guys, but you could see the prestige of that album had given him confidence and an edge. This position hardened so much later. What stood out in Miles's playing, at that time, was that in contrast to bebop musicians, he never tried to play fast or furious. His improvisation seemed thoughtful, almost tentative by comparison, and that became his style.

But not all African American musicians took this stance. Later, in London and running the Bass Clef, despite by this time being a club owner and therefore "the boss," I experienced a kindliness from other musicians. The American musicians in particular seemed to have an innate appreciation of my role as a club owner and what that meant in terms of work, money and commitment, not as an exploiter of musicians but as someone trying to create the opportunities for jazz musicians to play. Maybe Americans are more aware of how hard it can all be and how much it takes. It was such a different attitude from the sniping that would often come my way from some (but not all) of the UK jazz musicians. It is instructive to look at all those who have put clubs together and tried to make them work. Ronnie Scott and Pete King and their struggles with Ronnie Scott's are exhaustively described in John Fordham's book *Jazzman*; Steve Rubie has managed all this time to keep the 606 club in Chelsea playing jazz, but at great personal (and financial) cost; and more recently there has been Terri Quaye and then Salena Jones, who both invested in trying to make sure that there were more venues for jazz musicians. It is a difficult path to take, and you really appreciate people with understanding and concern who show support.

Three musicians I remember with particular fondness for their kindness and support are John Stubblefield, Eddie Henderson, and Kenny Barron. In my view, they are some of the most talented of what I regard as "the younger generation" of American jazz musicians (I'm sure they would laugh at my description of them as the younger generation, but that is how I see it). They were very supportive of my club and we played some good music together and kept in contact after that. One of Kenny's always superb performances has resulted in a beautiful recording of his music, recently released (Wave 34) as *The Artistry of Kenny Barron*. The first track on this CD is just incredible playing to me, again not really given due recognition. He builds his solo chorus after chorus, and for the listener it looks as if he has reached an ultimate peak, but then he builds even further with another and another chorus. This is an incredible *tour de force* on a beautiful Brazilian tune: "Morning of the Carnival." It has been gratifying to meet such wonderful people and to not have to feel that racial differences intervened or that our meetings were merely on a professional level. Where some musicians played the racist card when I ran the club, I found it was usually because they wanted lots of their friends to come in free to listen to them or they wanted to argue for more money when there simply wasn't any available. I personally think it is much more a question of personality rather than race: Dudu Pukwana, Abdul Teejay and Mwana Musa are just great guys – it shows in how they play and how they view life. Even though she, again, does not have the recognition she has deserved, when Carmen Lundy, whom I accompanied, sang at the club the audience just knew it was special. Good music is good music.

Another person who has become very special to me since he first played at the Bass Clef in 1986 with Jamey Aebersold's Jazz Faculty is Rufus Reid. During that first concert, on a whim we played a bass duo together and this became a regular feature of those annual concerts, continuing until 1997, after which Rufus resigned from the team due to other commitments. Our friendship and mutual regard for each other's bass playing led finally to putting into action a suggestion by Jamey Aebersold that we should make a video together. This we subsequently did, in November 1998 at the Manchester Crafts Guild, in Pittsburgh (an incredible project to check out if you haven't heard of it already). This has yet to be released as a DVD (although it is scheduled for late 2005), but we have now released the music as a CD, *Alone Together*. What we have is the pleasure of creativity, our love for jazz improvisation. As Rufus said on the liner notes, "Every time Peter and I play together, we have lots of fun. We are never trying to outdo the other. The song is the priority, always." This is what jazz is all about. I would like to comment here that this CD was dedicated to "the Judge," Milt Hinton, that legend of the double bass and a key instrumentalist during the jazz era right through from the forties to the sixties who has been an inspiration not only because of his playing and beautiful photos but also because of who he was. Sadly he is no longer with us, but we were pleased that he and his wife Mona heard the CD and supported it.

What is so heart-warming to me, having been immensely enriched by the jazz culture, is that the majority of African American jazz musicians whom I know and have played with are open. Understandably, they are greatly dissatisfied with a society that is still white-dominated, but are open enough to know that there are many white people who do not have negative attitudes.

We travel around the world and meet people of incredibly different backgrounds and cultures. I would no more lump together the good jazz musicians that I have worked with in the Caribbean, such as Adrian Clarke the pianist in Barbados, or those jazz musicians from South Africa, with African Americans, than I would lump together Tomasz Stanko and Humphrey Lyttelton as white musicians. I really want to stress the multiracial, multicultural aspect of jazz.

I feel that we need to do this anyway to stress that jazz is alive and developing, rather than a dying music form. Recently a jazz critic said to me: "Jazz is dead, now it is the turn of world music." Isn't it weird to you – it is to me – that what went before always has to be killed off in order to give new developments legitimacy?

I believe that defining Lennie's music and teaching as the cool school was a way of demeaning it, of trying to kill it off (another prejudice). The description was used originally as a kind of epithet – being cool meant that musicians associated with that group had reached their level of ability by "studying" – as though this circumvented a need for real talent – with the implication that only those with natural talent would reach the genuine sophistication that distinguished the great jazz players. Peculiarly enough, the appellation "cool" was seldom applied to black musicians, so it had a secondary innuendo to it that it was OK to be a white jazz musician as long as you were a rough diamond (so to speak). But if you were a white musician and had studied with Lennie Tristano you lacked a real gutsy feel for the music and had obtained your expertise intellectually – kind of through the back door.

Gradually the concept of the "cool school" became viewed as a style. It then began to embrace a wider group of musicians – those identified as West Coast musicians – either because they were born on the West Coast (primarily Los Angeles) or because they had moved there to become part of the music scene. This also had racial overtones: for some reason, those musicians such as Charles Mingus, who were black and who grew up on the West Coast, were never thought of as belonging to the cool school. My own sense of equality sees the need to unpick this underlying racial aspect of the appellation "cool school." (Even though it is so difficult to make such an analysis without being subject to misunderstandings.) Lennie, unable to distinguish the color of a person's skin, from his musical insight alone lauded the great innovators – who until that time had been predominantly black.

What a terrible irony that in these latter days, Lennie is seen by some as a protagonist of "white" jazz. But Lennie himself, though white, suffered the tragedy of being blind. To be a blind person, one not only faces the handicap of blindness, but often being treated (in common with those bound to a wheelchair existence) as somehow not quite human. No wonder that he empathized with the social struggle of the black community. I have related some of the anecdotes told to me by Lennie – yes, they can be viewed as humorous, but visualize being faced daily with such dumb comments as "Mr. Tristano, how do you manage to convey the food to your mouth?" (Lennie's reply was, by the way, "I tie a piece of string to my teeth and to my fork.") But with his acute musical and social perception he soon became a champion, not merely of the black jazz musician as such, but of those who really were the great creators of the idiom. And yet the Tristano cool school is often portrayed as a white musicians' group. How terribly ironic. How forgetful, how historically inaccurate, and how demeaning to the memory of Lennie and how demeaning to his sense of fairness and his readiness to give recognition where it was due. Perhaps it is appropriate to point out yet again that Lennie was held in great respect by the black jazz fraternity of that time and that he played and recorded with many of them (including Bird and Dizzy). Lennie told the following anecdote: "One evening after he [Bird] had consumed a fifth of Scotch, he chased everyone out of the room except me. He told me he wanted to start a record company with me. It never happened, but it was a flattering thought; and though he never said anything further about it, I think he meant it at the time" (Reisner 1974: 225). Lennie was also a pallbearer at Bird's funeral. Need I say more?

You have to ask why is jazz so much a debate about classifications and who is in or who is passé? I find it intriguing. I remember when I was running the Bass Clef, I was completely surprised one year when the club was voted as "In" by *Wire* magazine and I received an award for services to jazz. The very next year I was equally surprised when we were voted as "Out." I had been doing exactly the same thing, going about my business in exactly the same way, both years!

If you read the various books about jazz there are huge debates about what it is and is not. (And I suppose in a sense this book is adding to them!) I feel that jazz musicians themselves are so fixed on exclusion, exclusivity and defining themselves as the "in" elite and sticking the knife into others. Jazz is a fraternity that is its own worst enemy. Why not give due recognition to the various previous contributions to jazz and build up a positive perspective on all the music and its variety? No wonder young people are turned off jazz. Marginalization from without is bad enough – but marginalization from within? What are we talking about?

As to marginalization of jazz by those outside of it – this is a particular way, I think, of dealing with jazz. If jazz is seen as somehow fringe then it is a way of demeaning it and not having to give it due recognition as well. And there are wider implications here. Jazz is so often dismissed. Stigmatizing jazz as the "Cinderella of the arts" means that it is given a low profile but also, more importantly, that it does not have to be taken seriously for funding purposes. In the UK, there is a tendency to look at jazz as though the agency is funding "urban poverty," as though jazz musicians were mendicants subject to charitable handouts.

However, although jazz is often denigrated, seen as marginal or "too way-out," it is ironically always drawn upon when substantive music is needed. For example, how many commercials/films etc. rely on jazz music good, solid, original jazz classics – to provide mood, atmosphere, and a sense of gravitas?

Low on the list of grant availability, it is expected to thrive anyway, little thought being given to just how a jazz musician does survive. The popular view is that jazz is merely the product of an underworld, of a disenfranchised group who lack the training of classical musicians, and whose music is of inferior quality to that of opera or symphonic music. But for those of us who have become hooked on it, it's a different matter. As Scottish jazz guitarist Jim Mullen put it: "You grow from childhood to adolescence in the belief that like your parents you will eventually meet a woman who will become your wife, you will have 2.4 children and embark on a regular career. But one day you happen to hear jazz, and from that day on you are fucked."

You then descend into the realms of second-class citizenship, with only the beauty and excitement of the music to sustain you (very poignantly portrayed in the play *Sideman*). Then comes the uphill struggle, to strive to reach the potential of other players whose music has charmed you, while facing the equally uphill struggle of how to pay the bills. For the jazz musician faces the same taxes and state-imposed charges and penalties of living as do other mortals, the big difference being that the authorities are always suspicious, that you are either on drugs or earning a fortune, maybe because a sound recording of yours gets occasional air play. But if you are an architect or an accountant you must be a regular guy and therefore totally above suspicion.

Although it is seen as OK for ethnic minorities to be considered worthy of support, under the umbrella of jazz this is part of the patronizing approach that serves to marginalize the music. It is an effective way of never having to recognize its creative contribution to the mainstream of music. Since jazz is considered to be of low worth, then one can have a clear conscience giving it only minimal support, since it is not like opera or classical music — it is only jazz, after all. I would be happy to claim this assessment as my own, but sadly it is one that others have made to me too about the activity of UK funding bodies. Considerable amounts of money are allocated to jazz quangos — those bodies set up to discuss the situation in regard to jazz or to advise musicians on how to apply for funding — but very little goes to the vast majority of musicians trying actually to develop their creativity.

It can of course be argued that jazz is not very popular anyway and that this fact excuses jazz receiving very little grant or state support. But to me it is interesting that, in the UK, funding (whether state or private) for opera is at the rate of over £6 ($10) per seat, while funding for jazz is only about six pence (10c) per head. Jazz is hardly catered for at all, either on radio or television, in the UK. Compare this to France, for example. When we first went there, we asked about the frequency of the jazz radio station and were given five to choose from! As I was finalizing this chapter, I heard the news that in the UK they are debating legislation to prevent any form of live music being played without a government license. Notwithstanding this, anyone can set up a disco virtually without restriction or licencing. I think this puts the knackers on live music generally in the UK. Does this spell a final death knell for jazz musicians in the UK?

I think that part of the problem of jazz not being given due recognition is that in some respects the battleground is between commercialism and musical integrity. The essence of jazz, from its earliest stages, was that it challenged musicians. Too great a challenge is not a commercially sound proposition.

As occurs in the other arts, there has been a progression from extreme simplicity to the greater complexity we find today. All the while there is interest and fascination in jazz – such development is inevitable. However, as development takes place, complexity unfortunately often leads to a diminution of popularity. This can often reach a point whereby few can fully appreciate the subtleties of the music. This should not be confused with those who egotistically proclaim that their meanderings are evidence of supreme creativity.

The fifties jazz democracy of the outsider, the underdog, focused on creativity, began to give way to what, in retrospect, I would call a proto-yuppie culture. In the fifties and sixties, when America woke up to the fact that in jazz it had its own unique artform, a new attitude emerged. Most wanted to get on the bandwagon and become counted among the "jazz greats." As the fifties progressed, different attitudes manifested themselves. The change was not so apparent at the time. Those who clung to the simple concept of merely becoming better players were often disillusioned, as work did not automatically come their way. Though mild compared to the culture of market adoration of the nineties, previously unnoticed divisiveness began to be apparent. It was in the mid-fifties that jazz festivals came into existence. Then US State Department tours commenced, featuring jazz as a unique form of American music. The commercialization process had begun. It is only upon reflection that those changes we discussed in Chapter 12 now seem so obvious.

From the mid-sixties onward rock groups began to dominate the music scene, earning more than even the best-known jazz groups could demand. From that vantage point, the fifties now seems like a rare space in the music industry, a time when small jazz groups could survive, when small clubs survived, and the big music bosses often overlooked the emerging jazz talent. In the late forties and early fifties, a number of independents recorded some of the most creative jazz, companies such as New Jazz, Savoy, and Prestige. A host of independent record companies sprang up, some (such as Atlantic) becoming big; others (Blue Note and Riverside) being greatly successful without reaching for the skies.

From the sixties pop music, first rhythm and blues, then the twist, plus the enormous commercial potential of Elvis Presley, Bill Haley, and a host of other performers, had eclipsed much of the interest in jazz. Jazz musicians, desperate to retain some kind of following, began to market themselves or find agents who would market them. The jazz scene itself had changed. Racial issues regarding jazz had once more increased divisions within the music. By this time many players, white and black alike, were becoming marginalized (with some notable exceptions – Miles Davis, John Coltrane, Stan Getz, Dave Brubeck, and Gerry Mulligan – whose commercial potential was still seen to be strong). To its disadvantage, jazz began to be closely identified with Black Power, and although Lennie retained a following, he was criticized as producing "white jazz" – emotionally cold and intellectual – a tragic misunderstanding of his music and of him personally.

For the last forty years we have been living in a commercially exploited pop era. This has artificially exaggerated the gap between creativity and general acceptance. Consider a well-known example. Johann Sebastian Bach – arguably the greatest and most prolific composer of all time – wrote a piece called "Air on a G String." In the UK at least – because this music was selected as the sound accompaniment to a cigar commercial – virtually everyone is familiar with it. Because it is so well known, does it necessarily imply that it is his greatest composition? Supposing in another country a well-known soap powder had for its musical accompaniment Handel's *Messiah* and that became the favorite there. Does this mean, therefore, that great creativity depends only upon popularity? If this were so, creative judgment then would depend upon the amount of exposure a particular composition received. Some time ago, my partner Sue was given a tape of popular classical pieces, which identified them primarily via the Hamlet ad, the Hovis ad etc!

From such an argument one can see that jazz in particular – and in fact all creativity – is seldom seen objectively. When a creative art, say music, painting or any other, reaches a point of development where the majority no longer follow, a dangerous situation sets in. When this happens, the artist may be viewed as unworthy of serious attention. In such a situation the artist's work is then at the mercy of those who dictate what should be seen or heard. Commercial interests (or apathy) play a part in such decisions, and so does the appointed hierarchy – who may feel that what they are seeing or hearing is a threat to their own position as arbiters of excellence – and, dare we say it, might actually be at a level of skill or expertise that they don't understand!

Other aspects of creativity have long passed through such developments, for example in classical music and painting. It is averred that composers such as Mozart and Beethoven were at times jeered at performances of their music, music that today sounds not only acceptable but also easy on the ear. In a similar way, the French impressionists were condemned by the art establishment of the time and this necessitated their forming their own groups to exhibit their work. A hundred years later, an impressionist painting is universally viewed as great art (and commands great prices). A cultural lag between creativity and widespread appreciation seems almost inevitable.

People need really to relate and understand what is happening, rather than relying on critics/vogue/fashion and what is in or out. Perhaps the most universal appeal that jazz holds is its apparent freedom and the seeming abandon with which it is played. We have talked already about how impressions of such freedom can disguise the amount of study and discipline needed to reach that level of expression. But if someone is attracted to jazz on a comparatively superficial level – maybe just because it sounds "free" – it is likely that the more subtle aspects of the music will escape their notice. Thus one musician's creativity may be profound, and another's may be superficial. Our tyro may have no awareness of any qualitative difference between the two but respond only to the impression of freedom and abandonment.

The problem is particularly acute in the UK. Contrast this with America, where jazz still has considerable popularity, there is more openness to it, it is recognized as part of the country's history and receives wider radio coverage. It may not reach the popularity of rock or pop – but jazz at least gets into the charts in the USA. This begs questions re the UK. Would jazz be more popular if it were given a chance on radio or TV? Many people dislike the jazz they have heard; why is this (is it merely because what they have been exposed to grates on their ears?) In other countries – France or Brazil, for example – jazz is played alongside other popular music so it is heard as part of people's lives.

My experience in running the Bass Clef is that many people who visited the club – sometimes merely out of curiosity or because it was trendy – expressed their pleasure at what they heard there. The most frequent comment was, "I hadn't realized that jazz was so enjoyable." But their previous exposure to what they thought was jazz had often been through listening to the music of self-indulgent musicians imbued with their belief in their own creativity to the exclusion of the listener. That is a particular kind of ego trip that treats improvisation as a kind of musical snobbery. Peculiarly enough, this "no-holds-barred" kind of free-form has found an audience.

My own personal view is that music of that kind symbolizes the frustration of many who feel themselves to be, to a greater or lesser degree, alienated from the culture that spawned them. Also that it appeals to a kind of intellectual snobbery that regards the older standard jazz creativity as being passé. In other words it is liked because it is a challenge and "where it's at." I think that time will sort out the wheat from the chaff.

And indeed this is the state of current civilization generally. The effect is that of downgrading culture. In the realm of the arts (including music), someone who is "in" can be someone who elects just to be clever, rather than working really hard to develop their skills. Lacking the insight of the original creative artist s/he is clever enough to see "trademarks" – habits perhaps unconsciously developed by the original artist – which are then consciously used to fool the critics and the gullible, those who profess to love art but do not really make contact with it. Others who similarly recognize certain "trademarks" will then use these as a "style." Such a person will not be an innovator, but at best a craftsperson. Though the development of a craft is an essential first step toward becoming an artist, it is only a first step. This is the lesson that Lennie Tristano learned after playing in the "style" of Art Tatum (as discussed in Chapter 6).

It should be noted that what characterized many of the great black jazz musicians in the early days was their ability to be themselves in their music. No matter who influenced them, they invariably emerged with something of their own individualistic quality. It's not merely a matter of education in the academic sense, but the ability to be "moved" in the sense of experiencing in themselves the creativity of their peer influences. No matter how sincere the intent, the academic approach inevitably tends to intellectualize. It is testimony to Lennie's understanding that he helped us to find that creative level within ourselves.

Today's jazz students seem precocious in their ability to absorb and develop as jazz musicians far more rapidly than, say, those of us learning during the forties and fifties. Today's teaching rightly embraces many aspects necessary for learning how to be a jazz player. The jazz music vocabulary that was in the process of development during the forties and fifties has now been analyzed and is part of the standard curriculum for jazz students. But in the UK, at least, there seems little emphasis on making the music your own, becoming a genuine creative person in your own right. This, I feel, has much to do with the British emphasis on intellect and the fear of emotionality. But I also notice similar tendencies nowadays in the USA. As I have said elsewhere: in America, too, jazz musicians are becoming journeymen rather than creators.

Having spent a lifetime in jazz, it is on the one hand gratifying to see so many young players so fluent in their music. On the other hand, few carry the conviction and sense of presence that the earlier jazz musicians had. One naturally wants the best of both worlds, the modern-day fluency and also the strength of feeling that was expressed by the pioneers of the music.

When I first became aware of jazz, I was too young to appreciate who created what. It did not even cross my mind that I owed respect to anyone who had created the music. For me it was just there, analogous, I suppose, to the way people today just turn on their television sets, without a thought of the research and development over the past sixty-five years that has given us such a marvel of technology. And at twenty-one years of age and arriving in New York, my enthusiasm for what I heard was uncluttered by such considerations. Do today's teenagers stop to ponder how pop music emerged? They go for what excites them – regardless of how it all came about. Looking back to those days, I can now see clearly that my contact with the world of jazz came about at a time of maturity in jazz and was an incredible piece of luck for me. The sophistication of musicians such as Charlie Parker or Lennie Tristano did not come out of thin air, but only after thirty years of constant evolution from those who came before them.

And the challenge of jazz was essentially the freedom of improvisation. The vocabulary of the jazz idiom, even if it were a copy of original improvisations, enabled composers and arrangers to write music that by its essence conveyed musical freedom. Each development had to overcome conservative attitudes, as though the new freedom appeared outrageous and threatening to established society. When, as a young teenager, I heard Glenn Miller's AEF band broadcast from London a version of "Little Brown Jug," it sounded preposterously daring – just from the fact that a folk tune was being played at an unrestrainedly swinging tempo.

I suspect that Lennie, having grown up with the music, had concerned himself less with the origins of jazz and more with those whose talent and insight had taken improvisation to new heights. Lennie's unique ability to evaluate what was needed to develop such abilities led to his breakthrough in teaching methods. It was not enough to reach his students on the ego level, but to open up the instinctual level of what Freud had termed the "id."

So the question is whether or not a jazz musician is primarily derivative or creative. Both are matters of degree. But to achieve genuine creativity, one has to shed preconceptions of style, fashion, and tradition and jump into the deep end, as it were. This is not merely a matter of anything goes; it's not that simple. It is a matter of intellectual honesty, of allowing creativity full rein, without being anarchic. The point can be reached whereby something takes over; you *allow* your self to play. But unless you have absorbed the knowledge and understanding of the music, to let go in such a way leads only to poor results.

It needs both discipline and freedom combined. Musicians reach that creative aspect of themselves at different levels of musical understanding. Often self-absorbed, they are seldom objective in appraising the creativity of others. The struggle to maintain position in the world of jazz, with frequent failure to do so in later life, often leads to bitterness and alcoholism. It is common to associate jazz with sex, drugs, and alcohol. Thus jazz comes to be viewed as decadence, or at best a form of creativity expressed by mavericks. Society seldom stops to realize the financial and social struggle that confronts jazz musicians. Many view jazz as the product of licentiousness. More accurately, jazz is an attempt in music to transcend the limitations and restrictions of the culture.

Narcotics can appear an easy way out. In the world of jazz there *was* the reality of narcotics, which further complicated matters. For most people it was smoking a little pot (now no longer a criminal offense for personal use in the UK). But many went further, and there were obvious tragedies of people getting hooked on hard drugs. Such tragedies knew no racial or gender barriers: Bird, Miles Davis, Chet Baker, Gerry Mulligan, Fats Navarro, Stan Getz, Billie Holiday, Anita O'Day are all such sad tales of beautiful music interspersed with drug problems. Read Anita O'Day's account for a perceptive view of how this can happen. Many were deceived by the apparent freedom that came from the use of narcotics. The police relentlessly targeted some, such as Billie Holiday and the comedian Lennie Bruce, making their creative struggle even more difficult. I knew Lennie Bruce very well; he was a good friend, and I think his perceptiveness as a social and political critic has been seriously undervalued because of his association with drugs. It made no difference that Lennie Bruce had prescriptions for any narcotics he might have possessed – he was targeted. Despite his increasing popularity, it became harder for him to get work in clubs as the police would intimidate the club owners. It was also hard being around drug users – playing alongside one that had a habit, you could also be at risk from the authorities by association. Many have talked about the transcendence that can be reached through narcotics and the opening up this gave to the music – but this usually came at a very high price, emotionally and in terms of health. If you read the superb diary of Bird compiled by Ken Vail, it is almost too painful to chart his life during those last years, 1945 to 1955. Admittedly, he was the worst one for making his own life difficult, but his life is a continuous round of traveling, living in hotels, trying to send money home to Chan and keep their family going, as well as battling over the right to be paid decently for what he did.

"When Babs Gonzales ... tried to persuade Parker to get off drugs, Bird's answer was, 'Wait until everybody gets rich off your style and you don't have any bread, then lecture me about drugs' " (Hentoff 1976: 194).

Or Lennie ruminating on Bird and drink:

> He had good manners. He always made sure to introduce a person all around if he came into a room. I have never heard Bird put on his fans. He was always kind and sweet to them, accepting their praise gracefully.
>
> I have found great degrees of hostility in the music business. It is a grueling profession. The world is seen as a bar after a while. The hours, the dulling, deadening surroundings, the competition, hassles, the drinking which either produces maudlin moods or aggressiveness of an ugly sort. It is no wonder that no one can sustain a high level of creativity without stimulants of some sort. (Reisner 1974: 225)

This was at a time when new commercial directions in jazz were becoming all too evident. How hard it was for those who wanted to focus on creative musical development. Many jazz musicians wanted to be taken seriously – it wasn't just Lennie. Fats Waller was classically trained and wanted all his life to record classical music. Bud Powell studied classically and I mentioned hearing him playing C. P. E. Bach's Solfigetto in Birdland. Bird himself had talked about contemplating studying with the classical composer, Edgard Varèse, to help him develop a further direction of his playing, but he never managed it.

Lennie trod a different path and as lone pioneers he, Warne, and others who are associated with his music appear (with the exception of Lee Konitz) to have been overlooked by the mainstream of jazz. Jazz is the poorer – for clearly the music that developed out of Lennie's influence is of great artistic merit. Though not a professional optimist, I remain convinced that eventually it will find a rightful place in the scheme of things.

This brings to the fore an aspect of jazz that has frequently been a bone of contention: how far should it be entertainment? Many people appear only to respond to jazz as entertainment; they may not lock into its musical complexity. The image of jazz as an exotic, free, rebellious reality can be appealing to someone who spends their week in a dull, debilitating office context, an easy release at the weekend. Popularity versus creativity is a particularly difficult area for many jazz musicians.

This is amply discussed in Sudhalter's *Lost Chords*: "At its beginnings, hot jazz was functionally a form of entertainment. Louis Armstrong and others never tired of reminding all and sundry that a musician took a bandstand or stage to play to an audience which had paid to see and hear him" (Sudhalter 1999: 131).

There is no dichotomy if the musician's creative urge develops in line with what people have come to hear. Difficulties become apparent, however, if the musician's creativity goes beyond the expectation of the audience; or the musician plays in a similar vein as before, but his audience moves on to other aspects of the music; or the musician loses his grip and his audience dwindles through disappointment. In this last case it is unfortunate for the musician(s) concerned, but creativity is notoriously fickle and not all musicians are able to sustain their creativity throughout their working lives.

But just as some turn on to jazz because it gives a sense of freedom, it can also be this sense of freedom that is intensely disliked by others. To survive in some of the awful and personally debilitating jobs that people have to do to make a living, they have to armor themselves so they may not want to be reminded of the compromises they make and the implications of the jobs that make them significant amounts of money. To live your life that way involves compromise. It requires being very controlled and staying in power. Jazz, by its very nature, seeks to open people to the intensity of the music. Any sort of tugging at the layers of armoring that many people surround themselves with raises anxiety and discomfort, if not open hostility. If you think that the vast number of people who might be able to approve financial support for jazz are often the very people who will find it anathema, it is hardly surprising that there is such prejudice against it and such a sense of rejection.

But in discussing jazz we have to focus on the creativity and cut through all the various prejudices, attitudes, and egos that hide this very crucial and singular fact. Regardless of how I am seen, what I know is that I was there – and can describe it, irrespective of my own contribution. Funnily enough, this whole business of having been there in New York at that time can seem challenging to some people, but maybe that's because comments about that reality might sit uncomfortably with their own preconceptions, the perspectives they have adopted or used, or the myth of jazz that they have built up for their own purposes (whatever those are).

Perhaps it is fitting for another jazz musician to have the final word here. Tenor saxophonist Joe Henderson, born in 1937, was around fourteen when he first heard Warne Marsh with Lee Konitz and Lennie Tristano on their earliest records.

> Those records just opened my ears... That was a very magical kind of sound they had... I had heard Flip Phillips and Lester Young, Coleman Hawkins, and a lot of people that were associated with Jazz at the Philharmonic – and then somewhere in there Warne Marsh and Lee Konitz

showed on the scene...there is a vital part of whatever it is I am today, I am sure came from that zone. From hearing players like Marsh and Konitz, who has some technical mastery over the instrument, as well as great feeling, I mean in terms of what they came up with as creative people... (Chamberlain 2000: 277)

And, as a last comment, let's let one of the recognized jazz greats say it for us. Miles Davis, talking about the avant-garde of the sixties, said, "What's so avant-garde? Lennie Tristano and Lee Konitz were creating ideas fifteen years ago that were stranger than any of these new things. But when they did it, it made sense" (Berendt 1983: 105).

14 reappraisal

I would like to conclude this book by drawing the threads together from all the previous chapters and restating what I think the real legacy of Lennie Tristano is. (And for those who only read the conclusion they will have a good idea of what the book is about!)

Looking back on it, undoubtedly, the period from the mid-forties for about a decade was a high point in jazz development. Jazz at that time actually retained a public following that sustained it. I came to New York smack in the middle of this high point. It was many years later, well after the following for jazz had dwindled, that I could look back and realize how fortunate I had been to arrive in New York during that wonderful time. It was not that jazz musicians were becoming wealthy; very few reached that peak of affluence. Rather, it was a time when there was enough work and appreciation of jazz by a wider audience to convince us that jazz improvisation and its ongoing development really did count.

But this did not happen. Jazz went in another direction, where improvisation became used much more as a fill-in or decoration rather than the core of the music, and the focus concentrated more on commercially popular (and maybe less complicated) jazz. Lennie, however, maintained his commitment to exploring improvisational possibilities, as did many other musicians.

To understand why that meant Lennie losing favor, you have to ask why improvisation, which had been so central to jazz development, ceased to be at the forefront of jazz music after the mid-fifties. This is particularly puzzling, since there had been a long history of improvisational development up till the mid-fifties by some key jazz figures. Louis Armstrong in the twenties was a leading improviser. By the middle of the thirties Pres – Lester Young – moved the whole improvisation agenda in new directions. By the late thirties, guitarist Charlie Christian paved the way for development on that instrument. And by the mid- to late forties Bird was rapidly taking improvisation to new levels. A wide range of musicians had felt the new vibe of bebop and were focused on extending improvisation to new levels: Bud Powell, Dizzy Gillespie, and Fats Navarro for example. A younger generation of improvisers were also emerging, such as Miles Davis and Thelonious Monk, whose fame would come later in the fifties.

In the early fifties and until his death in 1955, Bird was really the king. And Lennie was up there too, referred to as the "high priest of jazz" in live coast-to-coast radio broadcasts. At the end of the forties he had been a poll winner, as best piano player, best small-band leader and best composer. I am sure Lennie did not relish being referred to as the high priest, but I mention this to indicate that at least some of the public appreciated his innovative appeal.

What Lennie had was a deep understanding of improvisation and the need to continually stretch the boundaries. He also played with a wide range of musicians and played also with his own group focused on exploring improvisation, especially with Lee Konitz and Warne Marsh. What was also unique about Lennie was that he was able to help many other jazz musicians to develop beyond their current levels.

He was not a guru, manipulating impressionable musicians. In 1952, during the time that Lee joined Stan Kenton, Lennie pointed out to me that Lee had taken his (Lennie's) concepts further than he had yet been able to do himself. He expressed this rather ironically, in that Lennie himself had been slower in developing his concepts to his own advantage, while paradoxically Lee had already mastered them. That admission by Lennie gives us some insight into his grasp of what was needed to develop further mastery in jazz improvisation. It shows that he knew it was not a matter of conscious knowledge alone, but of deepening that knowledge to instinctive levels, which is what jazz is really about.

By 1955, some three years later, with the release of the first Atlantic album, *Tristano*, Lennie clearly showed the range of innovation that was possible, with his use of overdubbing on "Lineup" and "East 32nd Street"; using multiple rhythms on "Turkish Mambo" as well as indicating what could be achieved in live piano playing and his studio recording in the hauntingly beautiful tribute to Bird, "Requiem for Bird."

Lennie stayed in New York and increasingly focused on teaching, only occasionally going out on the road. But it was not just that he was a lone voice. Other musicians associated with him went off in different directions and found their individual voice – but all committed to the spirit of improvisation – myself included.

The irony that I see is that although a number of his associates, Lee Konitz and Warne Marsh in particular, also went on to develop their highly individualistic styles, it seemed to me that the cohesiveness of Lennie's group improvising, so outstanding in the sextet sides made in 1949, was already on the wane.

The concert recorded in Toronto in 1952 with Lennie as leader and Warne Marsh and Lee Konitz on saxes, Al Levitt on drums and myself on bass, contains some of the best improvisation by Lennie, Lee, and Warne but despite this lacks, in my opinion, some of the cohesiveness that was so noticeable on the 1949 sextet records. As I see it, the focus that Lennie gave to his students concerning individual development sometimes had an unfortunate side effect: a focus on individual rather than group playing.

There were some later exceptions to this, namely the group led by Warne Marsh with Ted Brown, Ronnie Ball, Ben Tucker, and Jeff Morton in Los Angeles in 1956. Here again was some remarkable group playing. Also the tapes made by Ronnie Ball from The Haig and from Maynard Sloate's Modern Jazz Room in Hollywood during that same period are superb in their improvisation and cohesiveness.

Similarly, a group emerged during 1957 and 1958 with Lee Konitz, particularly evident when accompanied by guitarist Billy Bauer. In his chordal accompaniment Billy gave a special contribution to jazz, and was a perfect ally to Lee's very lyrical playing at that time. That period of Lee's leadership can be heard clearly on *The Real Lee Konitz* (Atlantic, 1957) and on the recently released companion CD to that album *Lee Konitz – Jazz of the Nineteen Fifties* (Wave 39).

But what became increasingly apparent was that with the focus on jazz as a marketable product, a more commercial view regarded jazz as entertainment, and with increasing numbers of jazz musicians on the scene and the advent of the pop scene and less work for jazz musicians, all this had its effect. As a direct result, jazz became more hard-edged and more strident (and even more competitive and ego-driven). Improvisation, as it had previously been developing, lost its focus.

In spite of this Lennie never deviated from what he believed in. He stuck with his convictions and would not commercialize. His dedication, plus the lack of general appreciation by many jazz critics, led inevitably to his being sidelined. Despite this his playing and improvisational skills developed to monumental proportions, the 1962 album *The New Tristano* being the creation of a lone giant of jazz.

In memory of Lennie I would like to summarize what his legacy is for me.

Prior to Lennie it was believed that jazz could not be taught. The general opinion was that jazz was "instinctive" – one either possessed that rather special ability or one didn't. True, there were studies, mostly on an individual basis. There existed no methodology of teaching in those early days (prior to the late forties). But Lennie's teaching – though it varied with each individual student – was underlined by a clear methodology. This methodology differed from customary academic studies in that Lennie laid great emphasis on the manner in which the student was encouraged to absorb the learning. As I described earlier, in Chapter 10, Lennie placed particular emphasis on the value of scales as the basis for understanding harmony. All too often scales are regarded, by tutor and student alike, as some kind of necessary penance that must be exacted before one is allowed to tackle the more interesting harmonic studies.

Lennie required that students had technical mastery of all the keys. In those early days most jazz musicians were familiar with only about half of the twelve key centers. Lennie would not move his students forward until the scales became totally familiar, familiar in the true sense: like family. In the eagerness to learn, the student might easily push him/herself to a point of technical mastery, which might obscure psychic tensions, and result in intellectual brilliance but lack musical conviction. The late Ronnie Scott expressed this: after listening to a precocious young wizard who had fallen into that trap, he exclaimed, "I am impressed but not moved."

Lennie focused on familiarity with great jazz solos. That scales themselves are music is amply demonstrated by the song from *The Sound of Music* "Do-Re-Me." The secret is in absorbing one's musical studies as music, not as an exercise. It was Lennie's analytic ability that led him to such considerations. These were simple aspects that had been overlooked prior to his teaching. Lennie would also encourage his students to learn other musicians' recorded solos. Specific emphasis would be laid on how this should be tackled. Lennie always insisted that the student learn to sing the solo first and only after becoming completely familiar with the solo should the student then learn to play it. So often the student will prefer to transcribe the solo (i.e. to write it down in musical notation) and then learn to play it from the transcription. But doing it that way bypasses the essential aspects of absorption of the solo. Indeed, that is one essential way in which jazz has been transmitted over the years. But Lennie was the first to conceptualize the importance of such an approach. Again this differed markedly from the classical approach.

Though both Pres and Bird used such learning approaches to develop their ability, it was a step forward consciously to advocate this as a teaching method. Now, fifty years later, this learning of solos is par for the course, although even today the emphasis is not always on the value of first learning to sing the solos. Many of these have now been transcribed, so it is often simple for the student to bypass this most essential of learning tools – to first learn to sing the solos.

Lennie was a consummate jazz soloist – one only has to listen to the "Requiem for Bird," for example to realize that in Lennie there was a monumental talent, unsurpassed even today. That this was recorded almost half a century ago and is hardly known except to the cognoscenti is yet another part of the puzzle. How can such a major jazz talent continue to be so marginalized?

Lennie is, sadly, known only to a group of aficionados. Ask a jazz musician about Lennie Tristano and immediately he will know of his music. Ask an ordinary member of the public and they will shake their head, completely unaware of his existence. It is a poor reflection upon our culture, in this time, that with all our communication facilities, someone of such influence in jazz should remain unknown outside a small circle of aficionados, although it could be said that at least some of this is due to Lennie himself, certainly not because of his contribution to jazz, but possibly because he was not so much in the public arena. In later years it appeared he had a coterie of followers, who were, perhaps understandably, protective of him and his work. I was not around then. What I have written about him comes from first-hand knowledge. For me it is enough to bring to the attention of a wider public the power and majesty of his jazz.

Lennie is still highly regarded by those who have been influenced by his music. It would be a mistake to believe that, although marginalized, Lennie's music is completely ignored by today's jazz musicians. There are groups springing up in various parts of the world who have rediscovered this music for themselves. In England, when I first returned in 1966, I found a number of musicians who not only followed the music of Lennie, Lee, Warne, etc., but also were themselves developing similarly.

The late tenor saxophonist Chas Burchell, altoist Bruce Turner (who had taken lessons from Lee while working as a ship's musician on board the *Queen Mary*) and guitarist Dave Cliff have been significantly influenced by Lennie and Lee. In the USA the prominent black tenor saxophonist Mark Turner (formerly with the Akira Tana/Rufus Reid group Tanareid) has been highly influenced by Warne Marsh. (It was Rufus Reid, by the way, who chose one of Lennie's lines as part of our recent video and CD together – possibly a bow in my direction on account of my association with Lennie, but more significantly because of the challenge and musicality of the line itself.)

Lennie was a charming man of unshakable conviction and a great influence, so difficult to reconcile with his relative obscurity. This book has described Lennie the man, as I knew him. Like many men of exceptional ability, he had great charm. It would be unfair to describe him as a womanizer, though women were charmed by him. A man of unshakable conviction, he expressed his beliefs with such sincerity that it was impossible to disagree with him. Now half a century has elapsed since the time of his greatest influence; it is hard to reconcile this with the relative obscurity of his jazz reputation in recent years.

Increasingly, jazz was multiracial but Lennie was frequently marginalized as "white cool." As Richard Sudhalter frequently pointed out, throughout jazz history (until 1945) there had been many bands and influences springing from racial mixing, and in my experience this was very much the case until the mid-fifties. During the time that I worked with Roy Eldridge and Coleman Hawkins (1960–61) I was frequently the only white member of the group, and race did not come into the musical or social equation, but it frequently became apparent that some of the younger black musicians saw things from a different perspective, and they began to be protective about what they believed was their own music. It was not a very prominent backlash, but it did happen and caused grumbling among some of the white jazz fraternity, enough for them to coin the phrase "Crow Jim" in describing the attitudes of some of the younger blacks.

So perhaps the mainstream has increasingly marginalized Lennie's music, because few black musicians were, in the popular view, associated with Lennie and his associates. It drew further opinions that it was not only "cool" but also "white cool." However, this was not the reality. Lennie's associations with Bird, Mingus, Roy Haynes, Max Roach, and many other musicians of the time were close. It seems to have been conveniently forgotten that they frequently played or worked together. Those musicians had respect for Lennie – on both intellectual and emotional levels. One has only to listen to Lennie's exceedingly moving improvisation "Requiem," in memory of Bird, to realize the love and respect Lennie held for that great jazz artist. Also the fact that Lennie was a pallbearer at Bird's funeral exemplifies the respect and regard that the black jazz fraternity had for him.

Rewriting of jazz history has influenced why Lennie is overlooked. Jazz, still the Cinderella of the arts, has so often become the domain of those who impose their preconceptions on what really took place. Such falsification of events – a rewriting of history – has been a major factor in overlooking the influence of Lennie Tristano, the influence through his recordings and the personal influence of the man himself. As the years go by there are fewer of us who were around at that time to tell it like it was.

Unfortunately, as frequently happens in other disciplines, the "experts" take over, and what really happened becomes lost. I am, of course, aware that, having played with him for those years, from 1949 through the fifties, I am professionally motivated. It could be claimed that for this reason I would tend to exaggerate the importance of his influence. I will leave this for the reader to decide.

Jazz musicians are frequently misrepresented as drug-crazed mavericks. The history of art and music contains many myths, but the myth of jazz being created by wayward drug-crazed mavericks is not only wide of the truth, but also serves as fodder for those who instinctively feel threatened by true artistic greatness. Lest this seem far-fetched, you only have to listen to so-called jazz radio, with its classic phoney accents promoting what they refer to as "smooth jazz." There is, of course, a larger proportion of the public who will tune in to such soporific and artistically narrow efforts and on our commercially-oriented planet it all makes a crazy kind of sense. It is, perhaps, a vain hope that jazz critics will stick their necks out and really listen to what went on during those fertile jazz years of the late forties through to the fifties. Perhaps an even more vain hope is that jazz criticism will become more objective and redress the entire issue of jazz development. However, the commercialization and trivialization of the music has adversely affected later jazz development.

Jazz is marginalized by the pop music business. Recently I spoke with veteran jazz critic Ira Gitler in New York, and he was bitterly disappointed over the way in which jazz has been sidelined in favor of music of lesser quality. Such dumbing down is not a new phenomenon, as critic Charles Edward Smith put this very poignantly, talking about the downturn in Chicago jazz at the end of the twenties: "The musical spirit ... was swallowed up in the maw of something bigger and considerably less great than itself, the popular music business" (Sudhalter 1999: 215).

This aptly describes jazz generally, when the so-called rock and pop revolution took over. But even prior to that, the various splits in directions of what was in the fifties and sixties referred to as "modern jazz" marginalized the so-called Tristano "cool school" almost as though this was an embarrassment to the mainstream of jazz.

Marginalization has also taken place at the hands of commercialism. Seldom is it realized that many of the musicians themselves suffer from such marginalization of their efforts. Commercialization accounts for much of this. Though there are various funding organizations that ostensibly have grant money for the furtherance of jazz, the greatest proportion of this usually goes to the administrators, with little left for the creators of the music. In Lennie's time such grants were virtually unheard of. Many of those associated with him were great musicians in their own right, but faced great frustration and little recognition that had adverse effects upon their health and creative spirit. It is difficult to avoid bitterness in such situations, for the jazz musician does not live in isolation: he or she has bills to pay just like those citizens who receive greater rewards for their efforts. How frequently have I heard the opinion voiced by jazz musicians that they instinctively distrust anyone in the music business that does not actually play? Can you wonder why?

Just as I was completing a re-edit of this book, I came across the following review — so I am not alone in thinking that it is time for a reappraisal. From *Jazz Journal*, March 2002, reviewing *Lennie Tristano – The Lost Tapes* (Jazz Factory): "It can be argued that Tristano has been over-praised in some circles or at certain times, but my impression these days is that he's neither lauded enough nor sufficiently recognized as a seminal influence, which makes this release as important as it is welcome."

We recently went up to the Wirral in Cheshire and visited Sue's parents' grave, and one of the inscriptions has stayed in my mind – a very simple stone with just the name and the inscription: "Love's final gift – remembrance." It equally applies to the legacy of Lennie. It should be remembered because the music came out of the love for it, not out of competition.

One of the ironies of our culture is that as soon as someone becomes a public figure, they cease to be seen as human but as some kind of icon to be regarded almost as though they are a commodity. I knew Lennie as a warm, larger-than-life person, with a mischievous sense of humor – always a friend. How could someone like that be described as the creator of intellectual, formalized jazz, drained of much of its old-fashioned red blood, as Frances Newton did?

This is not the person I knew. Lennie, Warne, and I were once staying at a self-catering apartment hotel while on an out-of-town gig in Boston, taking turns to cook. When it was my turn to cook I went to the supermarket (the Great Atlantic and Pacific Tea Company) and purchased a frozen turkey, together with vegetables. Bear in mind there were no microwaves in those days, and this was even before the era of plastic bags. It was a race against time to defrost it and cook it in time so that we could eat before going to the gig. It seemed the meal was a success, so much so, that after eating a first plateful, Lennie said, "I think I'll have some more of that bird," plunged his hand into the carcass and pulled out a paper bag with the gizzard and liver neatly wrapped up inside. Despite being blind he realized what had happened and ribbed me, saying, "What is this?" – holding the bag up in mid-air. It took me some time to live that one down.

During the times we spent at his Manhattan studio, he was often up to some psychological prank or other. On one particular occasion he related an anecdote, the point of which was to make everyone itch. Most of us quite subconsciously reacted to the story – scratching ourselves – without thinking about it. Pianist Lloyd Lifton, perhaps more wary of such pranks, resisted the temptation to scratch for maybe a couple of hours. Finally he exclaimed, "All right, motherfucker" and started scratching – long after we had all forgotten about it. Lennie just smiled in that knowing way he had.

There was an occasion during one of these sessions when the doorbell rang. Lennie answered it and it was Mingus – obviously upset. "Where's Ronnie Ball?" said Mingus. It was clear to Lennie that Mingus felt he had a score to settle with Ronnie. "Ronnie's not here – won't I do?" said Lennie. "No," said Mingus – "that's not fair – you're blind!" Then as an afterthought: "Well, let's turn the lights out – to make it even." "I don't need the lights out," said Lennie, "I'll take you on." And Lennie (who was at least a head shorter than Mingus) faced him, put his hands on Mingus's shoulders, and slowly brought his knee up into Mingus's groin. Of course there was no fight, and for the rest of the conversation Mingus could no longer face Lennie, just staying sideways on to him. This was astute of Lennie – it did not break their friendship – but made the issue quite clear: no messing. That's the man I knew.

So let's have a reappraisal. Long live jazz! And long live jazz improvisation!

Peter Ind,
London, Annan,
Auvers-sur-Oise,
June 2005

bibliography

Bauer, Billy (1997) *Sideman* (as told to Thea Luba) (New York: Bauer).

Berendt, Joachim (1983) *The Jazz Book* (St Albans: Granada).

Carr, Ian, Digby Fairweather, and Brian Priestley (1988) *Jazz: The Essential Companion* (London: Paladin).

Case, Brian, Stan Britt, and Chrissie Murray (1986) *The Illustrated Encyclopedia of Jazz* (London: Salamander).

Chamberlain, Safford (2000) *An Unsung Cat: Warne Marsh* (New York: Scarecrow Press).

Davis, Miles, with Quincy Troupe (1989) *Miles: The Autobiography* (London: Macmillan; New York: Simon and Schuster).

Feather, Leonard (1986) *The Jazz Years* (London: Quartet Books).

Fordham, John (1986) *Jazzman: The Amazing Story of Ronnie Scott and His Club* (London: Kyle Cathie).

Gitler, Ira (1966) *Jazz Masters of the Forties* (New York: Da Capo Press).

Hentoff, Nat (1976) *Jazz Is* (New York: Random House).

Jones, LeRoi (1963) *Blues People: Negro Music in White America* (New York: Morrow).

Kernfeld, Barry (ed.) (1988) *The New Grove Dictionary of Jazz* (London: Macmillan).

Kopman, Budd (2001) reviews section, *Cadence*, December.

Lange, Art (1999) "Changing the Shape of Music: Another View of Lennie Tristano, Lee Konitz and Warne Marsh," *Coda*, January/February.

McKinney, J. F. (1978) *The Pedagogy of Lennie Tristano* (PhD Dissertation).

Moore, Michael (2002) *Stupid White Men* (London: Penguin).

O'Day, Anita, with George Eels (1983) *High Times, Hard Times* (London: Corgi).

Newton, Francis (1959) *The Jazz Scene* (London: Penguin).

Reisner, Robert (ed.) (1974) *Bird: The Legend of Charlie Parker* (London: Quartet Books).

Russell, Ross (1972) *Bird Lives* (London: Quartet Books).

Shipton, Alyn (2001) *A New History of Jazz* (London and New York: Continuum).

Sudhalter, Richard (1999) *Lost Chords: White Musicians and Their Contributions to Jazz 1915–1945* (New York: Oxford University Press).

Vail, Ken (1996) *Bird's Diary 1945–1955: The Life of Charlie Parker* (New York and London: Sanctuary Books).

Ward, Geoffrey C., and Ken Burns (2001) *Jazz: A History of America's Music* (London: Pimlico).

select discography

Lennie Tristano

Sax of a Kind / Marionette (Capitol 57 60013)
Intuition / Yesterdays (Capitol 7 1224)
Wow / Crosscurrent (Capitol 57-60003)
Lennie Tristano (Atlantic 1224)

I have especially recommended these as an introduction to his music. All of his recordings are fascinating, but these are probably the easiest introduction to his music. Also recommended is the six-CD box set (Mosaic MD6-174)

Lee Konitz

Lee Konitz Meets Gerry Mulligan (Pacific Jazz 609)
Jazz at Storyville (Black Lion BLCD 760901)
Lee Konitz and Warne Marsh (WEA K50298)
The Real Lee Konitz (Atlantic 1273)
Peter Ind Presents Lee Konitz in Music of the Nineteen Fifties (Wave CD39)
The London Concert (with Warne Marsh, Wave CD16)

Warne Marsh

Lee Konitz with Warne Marsh (Atlantic 1217)
Warne Marsh Quintet – Jazz of Two Cities (Imperial 9027)
Ted Brown Sextet – Free Wheeling (Vanguard VRS 1956)
Release Record – Send Tape (Wave LP/6 and Wave CD6)
Jazz from the East Village (Wave LP10 and Wave CD10)

Ronnie Ball

All About Ronnie (Savoy MG 12075)
Lee Konitz (Black Lion BLCD 760922)
Storyville Presents – Lee Konitz in Harvard Square – Storyville LP
(Ted Brown Sextet) *Free Wheeling* (Vanguard VRS 8515)
Buddy Rich in Miami (Verve MGV 8285)
Release Record – Send Tape (Wave CD6)

More Jazz from the East Village (WAVE CD10)
Peter Ind/Looking Out (WAVE CD111)

Contact address re information on Ronnie Ball: R. K. Pipkin, 125 Little Aston Lane, Sutton Coldfield, West Midlands, B74 3UA (UK); email: leepipkin@aol.com

Willie Dennis

All About Ronnie (Savoy MG 12075)
Jazz Workshop – Trombone Rapport (Debut 5-14)
(Charles Mingus) *Blues and Roots* (Atlantic 1305)
(Gerry Mulligan) *At the Village Vanguard* (Verve 68396)

Tox Drohar

(Lee Konitz) *Inside Hi Fi* (Atlantic 1258)
The Real Lee Konitz (Atlantic 1273)
Peter Ind Presents Lee Konitz – Jazz from the Nineteen Fifties (Wave CD39)
No Kidding (Wave LP9)

Sal Mosca

Sal Mosca and Peter Ind at the Den (Wave LP2)
(Lee Konitz) *The Very Cool Lee Konitz* (Verve 8209)
(Peter Ind) *Looking Out* (Wave LP1) and (Wave CD111)

Ted Brown

(Ted Brown Sextet) *Free Wheeling* (Vanguard VRS 8515)
(Warne Marsh) *Jazz of Two Cities* (Imperial 9027)

Peter Ind

Looking Out/Jazz Bass Baroque (Wave CD111)
Triple Libra – Peter Ind and Martin Taylor (Wave CD24)
Alone Together (Rufus Reid and Peter Ind) (Wave CD36)

Billy Bauer

Duet for Saxophone and Guitar (Prestige) No catalog No.

index